THE
UNOPENED
LETTER

THE UNOPENED LETTER

a dose of reality changes a young man's life forever

RW HERMAN

This Book is provided courtesy of the Amelia Island Book Festival's Authors in Schools Literacy program, made possible through the generosity of the donors and sponsors listed below.

William L. Amos Sr. Foundation, Jack & Charlotte Roberts, Pat & Bob Stichweh, Rayonier, inc., First Federal Bank of Florida, Rod & Betsy Odom, WestRock, Debonair-Steve & Jerrie Sell, Giro di Mondo Publishing- Mark & Marie Fenn, Howard & Judith Pines, Jim & Suzie Hocker, Rosemary & Gordon Hart, Bruce & Barb Heggenstaller, Brant Kelch, Nassau Arts & Culture, The Giffin Family Foundation, Mary Elwell, Jennie & Kim Blue, Eileen & Stewart Ira, Amie Brunelle, Kathryn Otter, Barbara Blank-Karpowski, Cynthia Holler, Sandra Mann, Susan Rudov, Jane Chittick, Susan Kearney, Jacqueline Kennard, and Victoria Doughtery

Giro di Mondo

The Unopened Letter: A Dose of Reality Changes a Young Man's Life Forever

This is a work of creative nonfiction. The events are portrayed to the best of the author's memory. While all the stories in this book are true, some names and identifying details have been changed to protect the privacy of the people involved.

Published by Giro di Mondo Publishing,
a subsidiary of The Ottima Group, LLC
Fernandina Beach, Florida
https://www.girodimondo.com

Printed in the United States of America.

Cover and interior by Roseanna White Designs
Cover images from www.Shutterstock.com
Editing by Emily Carmain, Noteworthy Editing

Author photo by Boston Photography of Fernandina Beach, FL

FIRST EDITION (Hardcover print)
ISBNs: 978-0-9990514-6-7 (Hardcover)
        978-0-9990514-7-4 (Paperback)
        978-0-9990514-9-8 (Digital)

Library of Congress Control Number: 2020923256

*To all the shipmates and officers who helped
shape a teenager into a man.*

Of special recognition:

Rick Baker
Jeff Blom
Carl Bullick
David Elmen
Charlie Farenga
W.H. Goforth
John A. Harkins
Paul Harper Jr.
Gene Hattaway
Leroy A. Heath
Terry Holsomback

Ralph Jones
Tom Kite
Jessie Lee Jr.
Dan Miller
James P. Norton
Thomas J. Reese
John Sears
David E. Selby
Frederick Smith
James T. Vagenas
Burr C. Wilcox

This book is written in loving memory of my mother,
Angeline Herman, who saved all the letters I wrote to her
so that this story could be told.

CHAPTER 1

December 7, 1965, Minneapolis

IT WAS COLD, EVEN BY MINNESOTA STANDARDS. THE weatherman said zero degrees. Yet I felt compelled to get in the car and drive to Mom and Dad's house to check the mail. Although I now was living with my uncle, Dr. Sherman Nelson, I had not changed my mailing address.

My thoughts had kept me awake most of the night, wondering if I'd made a big mistake by withdrawing from classes at the university a few months ago. I was nineteen, unmarried, and at the time, the decision seemed to make sense. I had reached a breaking point trying to handle my family responsibilities, carrying a full class schedule while working forty hours a week, and watching our country in turmoil over a conflict somewhere in Southeast Asia. I wanted to sort out my priorities and do what was best for me.

The day I turned eighteen, I had become eligible to be drafted into the military. As a student, I'd had a college deferral, and when I withdrew from school, I'd lost that—but I'd been confident that I'd be okay for a while.

Stepping into the house, I was relieved that nobody was home—I didn't want to get involved in any family issues. I picked up the mail on the floor, and one envelope immediately stood out. My hand shook as I removed it from the stack. The return address couldn't have been more revealing: U.S. Selective Service System. I didn't need to open it. I knew exactly what it would say. *Uncle Sam needs you. Richard William Herman, you've been drafted.* I had gotten "The Letter."

I threw it, still sealed, onto the coffee table. My knees gave way, and I sat heavily onto the sofa. I felt light-headed, as though I needed more oxygen and my lungs weren't cooperating.

When I'd dropped my classes, I thought I would have at least six months, if not a year, to figure out what to do next. Then I could decide if I wanted to reregister for my sophomore year here at the University of Minnesota, or maybe move away and enroll elsewhere. Perhaps I would even join the Peace Corps. I had no idea what I might decide, given a chance. But I'd had only two months to think about anything.

During normal times, my decision to quit school for a while would not have been an issue. But the news was full of stories about escalating hostilities in Vietnam, and President Johnson was ordering a steady increase in troops. Like most kids my age, I knew that if drafted, I had a ninety-nine percent chance of serving in the Army, and it was highly likely I'd get acquainted with the jungles of Vietnam.

I sat there for nearly an hour, sometimes closing my eyes, trying to breathe deep and make sense of my chaotic thoughts. I was not opposed to serving my country and had never given serious thought to the idea of fleeing to Canada or becoming a draft dodger, as some others were doing. Still, I knew my family would probably pressure me to avoid active duty if there was any way out of it. But to me, that wasn't an option. I'd better not give them the chance to get involved. If necessary, I'd go—but I wanted it to be on my terms.

Finally, I left the house, carrying the letter that I would never open. I knew what I had to do next.

CHAPTER 2

"YOU DID WHAT?" MY UNCLE ASKED CALMLY.

It was late afternoon that same day, and Uncle Sherm had arrived home accompanied by Denise, his fiancée, a graduate student in psychology. I'd asked them to get a drink and take a seat, as I had something to tell them. There was no ignoring the subject. Besides, both Sherm and Denise could read me like a book.

"I received my draft notice today," I said, "and rather than open it, I went down to the Federal Building and found the Navy recruiter. I handed him the unopened letter and told him if I'm going to go into the service, I'd rather go to war on a ship than on foot. The recruiter took my letter, smiled, and told me, welcome, let's see what the Navy can do for you."

Denise, not so calmly, said, "Richie, Richie, Richie, have you lost your mind? You didn't have to do that. Your family could have gotten you out of it somehow. Tell him, Shermie. No one in this family needs to go into the service and go off to who knows where—to fight in who knows what stupid war that we shouldn't be involved with anyway. Tell him, Shermie."

Uncle Sherm, a renowned clinical psychologist, stared ahead and took a long drink. "Rich," he said, "that was a big decision you made today, and although I may disagree with it, I do support it. I have to think that you have thought this through and are doing what you believe is best for you.

"The question I have for you now is, have you figured out how you plan to tell your parents? You know they are not going to be happy to hear that you enlisted. After all, not only will you be going away, but they'll have to deal with Louie—with no chance you will be returning home soon."

Denise was beside herself but remained quiet, knowing any

further discussion was futile. She also knew I was Uncle Sherm's personal project, trying to allow his nephew a chance at a life of his choice, not forced into a world burdened by the responsibility of being a caregiver while still a teen. And now, this kid had to make a decision that would probably decide his future and shape his life forever.

We sat in silence for a few minutes. How would I tell my parents? I could hardly sort out the turbulent memories of the events that had led me to leave home this fall and move to my uncle's house.

A year ago, I'd been a teenager like many others, trying to figure out where my life was headed. One thing made my situation unusual: although the youngest of three children, I had the responsibility of caring for my twenty-year-old brother, an insulin-dependent diabetic. Louie's diabetes contributed to numerous health problems, including addiction to painkillers, requiring constant attention. My parents, Angeline and Clayton, had been worn out physically and emotionally taking care of Louie since his birth. They gradually grew dependent and used to my assuming the role of parent. My older sister, Marlys, was fortunate to have gone away to college; now married, she had moved to the Michigan Upper Peninsula.

Unlike her, I'd remained at home after high school. My parents allowed me free room and board as long as I was going to college; I worked to pay for tuition, books, car insurance, and other expenses, an arrangement I thought was fair. When I entered the U, things were going pretty well. I had a decent job, a '57 Chevy Bel Air two-door sedan, the envy of many, and my brother seemed to be getting his life to a point that he was less reliant on support from me.

As the 1965 spring semester progressed, Louie had started having little episodes; he would forget to take his insulin shot or forget to eat properly, leading to insulin reactions, minor at first and quickly resolved with a shot or burst of sugar. Little did I know they were affecting me. Although maintaining a B-minus average, I struggled to concentrate and always seemed tired. More and more, I was having to look after Louie, making sure he took care of himself. I didn't complain. No one listened to me as Louie was the one to whom everyone paid attention. Besides, whenever I tried to tell my parents about his antics throughout the years, they would never believe me.

When I was seven, Louie had talked me into climbing out his

second-story bedroom window using bedsheets. He then pulled the sheets away, and I fell, luckily only spraining my ankle. I told my story, but everyone laughed and said how cute I was trying to be Superman, the version my brother told them.

Now, Louie was back to his old tricks of missing an insulin shot or whatever it took to force me to give him attention. This went on for months until I was running late one day, and he offered to drive me to my calculus final exam. As we approached campus, Louie made a left turn in front of an oncoming semi-truck. We were hit on the passenger side, just behind my door, and the force spun us around several times. Fortunately, there were no serious injuries. Louie told the police he thought he had time to make the turn, but I knew otherwise. Finally getting to class, I explained what happened and, although the proctor was sympathetic, was told I had to take the test and do the best I could. I had a big headache, managed a C on the exam, and, of course, everyone felt sorry for Louie.

I grew more tired and constantly felt worse until I was finally taken to our family doctor and diagnosed with mononucleosis. Part of my recovery required complete bed rest, and my sister said it would be best if I came to stay with her and her husband, Jim, in South Range, Michigan. At her house, I didn't have to do anything except get well. Once recovered, I remained there for the summer. To this date, I probably owe my life to my sister and brother-in-law for taking me in and allowing me to recover fully.

Returning home for the fall semester, I fell right back into the routine of being Louie's caregiver. Then one afternoon, instead of going straight home after classes, I decided to join several other students in a study group. I called to check on Louie, and when he didn't answer, I immediately headed for home. I found him on the living room couch, foaming at the mouth and getting stiff. I loaded him into his convertible with the top down, the only way his rigid body would fit, and rushed him to the emergency room. When I arrived, blowing the horn repeatedly, I told the emergency personnel that Louie was in diabetic shock and going into a coma. Getting little reaction, I screamed that he needed 150 cc's pure glucose *now*, or he would die. They looked at me like I was nuts, until finally, one attending resident said, "Do as he says." As soon as he received the shot, Louie began responding immediately and would live to see another day.

I asked to use the phone and called my dad. He said he was tied up but would be there when he could. Then I called my mother and was told the same thing. That was it. *I can't do this anymore!*

I called Uncle Sherm. I don't remember much about the call, but later, I learned that once his secretary answered and realized it was me, I collapsed. Sherm canceled all his patients' appointments and was there for me immediately.

My uncle had me move in with him and my cousins that very day. For the next several weeks, I tried to concentrate on my studies. Although the responsibility of taking care of Louie was gone, I still found myself distracted and always worried about not only my grades but my life in general. I'd decided to withdraw from school—it was still September, and there was no penalty to do so—and take an incomplete for my classes. Then I could relax and figure out what to do next. Of course, this decision didn't exactly pan out. That unopened letter meant my future was settled—at least for the next four years.

CHAPTER 3

December 8, 1965, Minneapolis

I KNEW I COULD NO LONGER AVOID THE DREADED conversation with Mom and Dad. Even though it was already a done deal, I wasn't sure how they would react. I also knew there was no such thing as the right time.

My parents are wonderful people and as patriotic as the next. My father, at age eighteen, had joined the Minnesota National Guard and served two years. Honorably discharged, he joined the Civilian Conservation Corps (CCC), a work relief program that was part of President Roosevelt's New Deal during the Great Depression. My father talked fondly of his experiences there and said it prepared him well for returning to find employment in the public sector before World War II. In 1945, Dad was drafted, found fit for, and called to duty. He never thought about not going, but the war ended before he was required to report, so he never saw active duty.

Of course, that war had the support of all America, and the mindset was different then. When the war ended, everyone was proud to be American, and service members returned to open arms and cheers of all the country's citizens. Today, although it might be a perception and possibly the minority opinion, it seemed those who fled the country or burned their draft cards and refused to enter the service were honored and received favorable press. In contrast, those who served their country were chastised, booed, spit on, and frowned upon. The American public's mixed emotional environment weighed heavily on all the young men facing the draft, and I was no exception.

My whole life, Mom and Dad both worked, getting home

between five and six p.m.; family meals during the week were rare. I needed to wait until I knew they would both be home and made sure it was after seven p.m. Every day, like clockwork, Mom lit a cigarette at seven, saying it relaxed her. Also, Dad would have a few drinks in him and would be mellow, as usual.

On Wednesday evening, I sat down in their living room and informed my parents about receiving my draft notice and that I had enlisted in the Navy for four years. Mom just looked at me, while Dad slowly nodded his head with, I think, a little smile. As always, he waited for my mom's reaction before he ventured an opinion. As long as it didn't go against something the Teamsters Union supported, he always sided with Mom. And, as if on cue, Mom spoke first.

"My first reaction is we've let you down. Are you going into the service because the pressures with your brother got to be too much? I know we're responsible for you moving in with your Uncle Sherm. I thought things were better now. Why do you have to join?"

"It's an accumulation of a lot of things, Mom. I was hoping to take a little time off to think and sort through things, but Uncle Sam seems to need me now. Getting the draft notice just forced my hand." I noticed her frowning as she took a long drag on her cigarette.

"But on the positive side," I said, trying to sound upbeat, "by volunteering for the Navy, they were able to put a stop on the draft process, and the recruiter is working with me to get the best deal possible. He said my college credits will guarantee me some school choices before I have to go anywhere, and I could even advance faster than the others. So I think I've at least made the most out of the situation. And you know I support the military and will be proud to serve. I would never even think of trying to shirk my duties. Denise has already read me the riot act about how 'The Family' could have gotten me out of it."

Mom smiled at that. She liked Denise with her ability to take a stand and make her opinions known. Mom had always been regarded as the smartest in the family and the most outspoken and capable defender of her beliefs. "When do you have to go?" she asked.

"I don't have a date yet. First, I'll have an enlistment physical, and then if I pass, I'll be assigned a date to report. My physical is next week, and I will take it at the same time all other volunteers and drafted men do. But because I'm going into the Navy, I will be given head-of-the-line preference throughout, and it should be relatively quick."

"You'll pass," Mom said. "Except for that little bout with mono, you've always been healthy. So then where will you go, and how long will you be gone? Why did you pick the Navy? Do you get vacations? Can you pick where you go and what you do?"

"Take a breath, Ang," Dad finally chimed in. "He's just made a big decision, and he doesn't know it yet, but he hasn't a clue what's going to happen. Well, son, it's obvious it makes no difference what I say, as usual. What's done is done, no matter what Denise, your mother, or anyone in the family says. Frankly, I hoped this day would never come, but now that it has, I'm proud of you."

"Clayton, of course we're proud of him, but he didn't have to do it, and that's the point Denise was trying to make. I agree, it's done, so we will support you. It's just going to take some time to take it all in. My baby, going off to war, for God's sake!"

"Mom, Dad, I'm not going anywhere yet, so let's not think too far ahead."

"Obviously, you didn't," Mom said sarcastically. "But enough … what can we do to help you now?"

"I'm just glad telling you is over. The recruiter said I would hear from him after my physical, and we'll go from there. He did say it would be after the holidays before I go anywhere, so I should enjoy them while I could. Let's concentrate on that for now, okay?"

With that, Mom lit another cigarette, Dad went to get a beer, and we all settled in to watch that new game show, *Jeopardy.*

CHAPTER 4

December 15, 1965, Minneapolis Courthouse

THE WEEK FLEW BY AFTER MY CHAT WITH MY parents. When I'd met with the recruiter, I signed a Letter of Intent to enlist, which they used to stop the process of my being drafted. Before I could be sworn into the Navy, I had to pass a physical examination and a local background check. I was quickly learning that the government could move fast when it was to their benefit and that they led, you followed.

My physical took place eight days after meeting the recruiter. I reported early so I could check in and let them know I was here because I was joining the Navy. Chief Anders said this would help me get through the process a lot easier. When I arrived, at least fifty others were there, most smoking cigarettes and milling around. Spotting a man in uniform, I introduced myself.

"Excuse me, sir."

"What you want, kid?"

"My name is Rich Herman, and I'm here for my physical."

"So is everyone else."

"I was told by my recruiter, Chief Anders, to let you know I was volunteering for the Navy, and he said I would be going ahead of the others."

"Navy, huh? What, you don't like the Army? You afraid to be a Marine? You not pretty enough for the Air Force."

"No, nothing like that." I didn't like where this was going. "I was just doing what my recruiter said."

"Look, kid, I could care less who you are; I never heard of a Chief Anders and could care less what you were told. This is a physical for the military, so go to that table over there, find the paper with your name and number, and take a seat. And keep your mouth shut."

"Yes, sir," was all I could think of saying. I guessed Chief Anders had me coming the wrong day. Why else would he have told me to mention I was going into the Navy? I found my paperwork, assigned with today's date, and now I was even more confused about what my recruiter had said. I waited with everyone else as more and more guys filled the room.

"Listen up," another man in uniform said. "If you have an even number, fall in on the left, and if you have an odd number, that's me, fall in on the right. March into that room, find a locker, and strip down to your skivvies. Take off all your jewelry and anything that's not a skivvy, and stow it in the locker. Then stand tall and keep quiet."

It seemed like that was easy enough to do, but I couldn't believe the confusion. There had to be 200 of us now, and over half couldn't figure out what line to get in. I helped a couple of guys, and eventually, we moved forward into a vast locker room where the confusion got worse. One guy said he wasn't taking off his jewelry for nobody. Another said he promised his wife he would never take off his wedding ring. And these guys were anything but quiet.

The whistle that blew was the loudest I had ever heard. The man blowing that whistle was one of the biggest I had ever seen. And being in a pressed green uniform with high, shiny black boots, a hat like a state trooper, and a chest of medals made him a very impressive figure. To my surprise, the room got quiet. He walked around, looking at us all before stopping.

"I'm Sgt. Dunn," he said, "and for the next few hours, I am your new best friend or your new worst enemy. Your choice, gentlemen. Stay quiet and follow my orders, and you'll be out of here in a couple hours. If you decide you can't follow my orders, we may be here for a very long time. Your choice. For those of you who have already decided not to follow orders by leaving your religious crosses or wedding bands on, I will be coming to see you soon. I'll step out for a minute, and I hope it has disappeared before I return. Your choice, of course." He flashed a brilliant smile and left. I didn't have any jewelry on, but I checked just to make sure.

"Now," he said when he returned, "look your paperwork over,

and make sure the information is correct. If anything is wrong, let me know now; otherwise, it's on you if you go through the next couple years as a screwup who has never had it right from the start." I noticed Sgt. Dunn going to check on the jewelry holdouts, and I gathered no one decided to challenge him.

"Okay. For you gentlemen on the left, go through the door straight ahead at the end of the room on your side. For you gentlemen on the right, go through the door straight ahead at the end of the room on your side. You're all going to give blood, get weighed, have your height taken, and have an eye test. When you're finished, stand fast and wait for further instructions."

My line made it through the door and started this phase pretty well. I had grown quite a bit since high school, when I graduated at five-foot even, 103 pounds, looking thirteen years old. Today I was five-foot-six and tipped the scales at 120 pounds, but still looked thirteen years old. As I approached the eye exam, I was a little concerned. Now that I had decided to enter the Navy, I wanted to go. I didn't want to be found unfit because of my eyesight and then have everyone say that my family got me out of it after all. I had to pass.

I noticed the examiner wasn't paying much attention to those taking the exam and asked each one to read line eight if they could. I figured this was the 20/20 line. Moving forward, I looked at that line as soon as I could. If I tilted my glasses and squinted, I could make it out. I started memorizing. By the time it was my turn and he told me to read line eight, I confidently said, "D, E, F, P, O, T, E, C." He signed my paper, and I moved on. This was too easy.

Next, I got in the line where two guys in white coats sat at a desk drawing our blood. Someone told us to have our sticker labels with our names ready to give them and to make a fist when we were two men away from being next. I had given blood hundreds of times because of Louie's diabetes and the need to check me regularly. However, I never had to give standing up, while freezing in only my skivvies, to someone I didn't think knew what a vein was. I was lucky; he only stabbed me three times before he was able to get his sample. Finally, Sgt. Dunn returned.

"Okay, children, you've made it this far, and only seven of you have decided that they didn't want to be my friend. Maybe they will when they return next week to start all over again. You're about to go into the next room and make a lot of new friends. When you enter, find your number on the floor, stand on it, and wait for instructions. Doors are opening, go."

In that room, I saw a gigantic cement table filled with what looked like paper cups. After what seemed like hours, Dunn reappeared with six men in white lab coats carrying boxes. "Ladies, don't be bashful, drop your skivvies, and do what the doctors tell you." We then found out what was in those boxes—plastic gloves. The doctor stepped in front of me, listened to my heart, looked at my throat, had me say *ah*, then look left and right and cough as he checked who knows what.

Once everyone was examined, Dunn called out, "Turn facing the wall, bend over, and spread those cheeks." There was a lot of moaning, but I did what he said; I did not want to return next week. Finally, we were told to stand and pull up our skivvies.

"Just about done," the sergeant yelled. "Go to the table, find a cup, and pee. Make sure it's at least half full. Put the last sticker with your name on the cup, place it on the table, and go back to the locker room. You can get dressed and go home. You will be contacted with the results of your exams."

After using a cup, providing the correct amount, and putting my label on it, I headed for the locker room, happy that this day was over.

"Hello," I answered the phone a week later.

"Herman, this is Chief Anders. Congratulations, you passed your physical, and apparently, you haven't done anything serious enough to disqualify you from the service—your background check came back clean. You're good to go."

"That's great, Mister Anders."

"No, Herman, it's Chief Anders, and you better get used to it. Come down tomorrow at 0800, and we'll go over all your paperwork and get you a date to report for duty."

"Yes, sir, Mister, ah, Chief Anders. See you in the morning."

I arrived at the recruiting office fifteen minutes early, to find the door locked and the office looking empty. Then, out of nowhere, precisely at 8 a.m., the doors opened, and Anders said, "You going to stand out there all day, Herman? Get in here and take a seat. We have a lot to go over to get you ready for the big day. I'm going to give you some paperwork to sign after I tell you what it is. You can trust me, Herman, I've done right by you, and you're getting a fine deal. I think you may be getting one of the best enlisting deals ever made. So sign as we go along, and ask any questions you have. However, it looks outstanding, so don't worry." The next thing I knew I had signed about two dozen forms, and it was over.

Another chief came over, and I heard him say, "Hey, Anders, did he sign? He did? You dog, you." Then he turned to me. "Welcome to the Navy, kid. And thanks for helping Chief Anders out. It's getting close to the end of the month, and he was in trouble meeting his quota. You may have just saved his butt. A Christmas gift, I'd say."

"Don't pay any attention to him," Anders chimed in. "He's just jealous because I out-recruited him this month." I had no idea what they were talking about.

"Now, Herman, go home and enjoy the holidays. I'll be calling you soon and give you a date to report to the courthouse downtown. There you will be officially sworn into the Navy and receive your orders to the Navy Recruit Training Center, Great Lakes, Illinois. Say your goodbyes before you show up because you'll immediately get your orders and go to the airport to catch your flight. Any questions? Good. And once again, congratulations."

My head was spinning as I headed home. What had I gotten into? Little did I know it would be awhile before I found out.

The holidays came and went, and I heard nothing. Finally, I called Chief Anders to ask if he had any information for me, and he said my time would come, be patient.

I called again in February and again in March. The same story. It takes time to process, I was told. Everything is fine. Funny, everything went fast after that first day, December 7, when I handed Chief Anders my draft notice. Until I passed all the tests and was accepted.

Then, April 13, the phone rang and it was Chief Anders.

"Report to the Minneapolis Courthouse, Room One, tomorrow morning at 0700," he said. "Do *not* be late. You're going to be sworn in, get your orders, and be taken to the airport. Tomorrow night you will be in Great Lakes Naval Recruit Training Center and officially a member of the U.S. Navy. Good luck, Herman, and look me up sometime."

"Yes, Chief. Thank you, Chief. Is it okay—" I realized he had hung up.

I called Mom and Dad, telling them I was finally going and would write when I could. They wished me luck, but we'd been preparing for months already and left it at that. I checked my small suitcase and then asked Uncle Sherm if he'd take me to the courthouse in the morning.

I was at Room One right on time, along with about thirty others. It turned out I was the only one being sworn into the Navy. Two were going into the Air Force, two into the Marines, and everyone else had been drafted into the Army. An officer, I assumed because of all the medals on his chest and shiny things on his shoulder, came in and said, "All enlistees, stand at attention." We did.

"I am about to administer the Oath of Enlistment. Raise your right hand. and repeat after me. 'I, state your name, do solemnly swear that I will support and defend the Constitution of the United States of America …. so help me, God.'" Everyone did so, or appeared to do so. "Congratulations. You are now officially in the U.S. Military branch that you chose." And he was gone.

Someone else in uniform said, "As I call your name, come forward and get your orders and plane tickets. Then go out front, and get on the bus that says Military – Airport." I heard my name and received my first orders.

At the airport, a guy took our luggage, and I looked for my flight. Then, I heard my name being called. "Richard Herman, please report to the USO desk. Richard Herman, please report to the USO desk." I saw a sign, followed it, and found a guy about my age sitting behind a desk marked Information.

"I'm Richard Herman," I said.

"Let me see your orders." I handed them over. "Here," he said, "are your new orders and plane tickets. You're going to boot camp in beautiful San Diego instead of Great Lakes. Lucky you."

"What, why?" I blurted. "I don't know anything about this. Does Chief Anders know?"

"You don't have to know anything about it, and I never heard of Chief Anders. Obviously, the Navy needs you in San Diego. And you better hurry—your flight is already boarding."

"My suitcase. What about my suitcase?"

"I'll call down and have it changed to your new flight." *He can do that?* I guessed I didn't have much choice.

"But everyone thinks I'm going to Great Lakes. I have to call them."

"Not enough time. You can call when you land in San Diego."

I heard "Last call for boarding Western Air Lines Flight 223 to San Diego." And I headed to California, and no one in my family knew. I was beginning to realize Chief Anders may have forgotten who I was. Welcome to the military, Rich.

CHAPTER 5

April 1966, San Diego, California

AS I WALKED OFF THE PLANE—MY FIRST FLIGHT ON an airliner—the hot air hit me. The flight attendant had said it was sixty-eight degrees, but it felt like a hundred. Wearing a winter coat probably didn't help. I was supposed to be near Chicago, not in southern California. Okay, the coat would have to go. I wanted to call Mom and Dad right away and let them know where I was but decided to wait until I knew a little more. I headed for the baggage area to look for my suitcase; I'd been told to pack only essentials for a day or two. I was concerned after my orders change, but there the bag was. The guy at the USO came through after all. I felt like I had found an old friend and wasn't alone.

I saw a man with a sign reading New Navy Recruits. When I approached, he nodded, motioned for me to get behind him, and kept waving the sign. Several other guys came up, and he kept nodding. When the baggage claim area cleared, he finally spoke.

"Okay, all you wannabe Navy guys, head outside. Put out your cigarettes, and get on the bus that says USNTC. Do not light up again until you are told to do so." This brought a lot of rumbling among the guys. Although both my parents smoked, I didn't start until I went to college, and then I only did so, like drinking coffee, to fit in. As I wasn't a heavy smoker, being told not to light up was no big deal.

The eleven of us went out, boarded the bus, and remained silent. Everyone seemed nervous about what was coming next. The airport was located across the street from the naval base. On the fifteen-minute trip, I took in my new surroundings and saw my first palm tree—and my first mountains. I wondered if we were close to the ocean. I'd never seen the ocean.

We stopped at the entrance to the base, and a sailor with a rifle got on board. *No, that isn't a sailor. Is that a Marine uniform? Why would a Marine, with a gun, be at a naval base?*

"Listen up," he shouted. "You are about to enter the United States Naval Training Center. If you have anything with you that may be considered dangerous or unauthorized on a naval installation, you better tell me now. No questions asked. If I find any item on you, or in your possession, that I think shouldn't be here after the next ten seconds, you may be spending your first day here in the brig. Ten, nine, eight—"

That was as far as he got. A guy in the front shot up and held out a knife. Another recruit, with long blond hair, stood and pulled out what looked like some colored candy in a small plastic bag.

"And why did you think you needed to bring a knife to boot camp?" the guard asked the first guy. "You think us Marines can't protect you little Navy boys? Well, answer up!" The guy with the knife, shaking now, said something about where he was from, everyone had one and knew how to use it. The Marine laughed, opened the knife, and broke the blade off, right in front of his face. "You don't know jack, you idiot. Now sit down and be glad I don't have the time to teach you what a Marine does to fools like you."

The guard proceeded to the guy with the bag of candy. "And you. Is this a bag of LSD?" Wow, I'd never seen LSD. "I should shove this whole bag of pills down your throat, and we all could watch you take a trip to Never-Never-Land. How dare you insult us by bringing your hippie crap to our base? If I hadn't said no questions asked, I'd be dragging your butt to the duty officer right now and making sure you never wear a Navy uniform. Do I make myself clear?"

I thought the guy was going to cry; he quickly nodded that he understood. The Marine looked at each of us as he went up and down the aisle, then returned to the front of the bus. "Okay, Earl, I think we're done here. Take these guys to receiving, and enjoy the rest of your day. Say hi to Helen and the kids for me." He departed and waved us through.

"A little advice, boys," Earl said. "When you get off this bus, you will be entering a whole new world, unlike anything you ever thought possible. You signed up for this, so don't complain now. Do what you're told, and you'll be okay. Your lives are about to change forever."

I certainly had no reason not to believe him. This morning I was at the Minneapolis Courthouse getting sworn into the Navy and getting tickets for Great Lakes, Illinois. Two hours later at the airport, I was handed new orders to a boot camp thousands of miles away. This afternoon, I was on Earl's bus on the West Coast. Had this really happened?

We pulled up in front of several wooden buildings with benches out front. The doors opened, and Earl stood and smiled. "This is it. Your new home. Goodbye and good luck." I picked up my bag and was departing when I heard the commotion outside.

Someone was screaming, "What are you waiting for? Move it! Move it! Get off the bus. I said move it!"

I moved as fast as I could, but the guy in front of me was having trouble maneuvering a big suitcase down the aisle, and I started trying to help him.

"Are you going to take all day in there? Do you not understand what I am saying? Move it now! Get out here, and stand at attention, now!" We finally managed to get off the bus, got into line, and stood tall. A sailor in a blue uniform headed our way.

"You two apparently don't understand English," he yelled at us, standing about two inches from me and looking down. "I hope this isn't a sign of things to come."

He walked up and down the line and shook his head. "I pity the poor company commander who is going to have to train you guys. You look pathetic and helpless. But not my problem. Now, do you see those green benches? When I tell you, go over there and sit down. Don't talk. Just sit. Do you think you can do that? Now go, double time, move it, move it, move it."

There must have been twenty benches, and each probably could fit ten guys. I took a seat on the first one I came to. The other guys settled quickly too, but we were all over the place. After what seemed hours, another sailor came out of the building.

"Listen up," he said. "Take out your orders and give them to me when I come by." We did what we were told. "Smoking lamp is lit. Smoke 'em if you got 'em." And he left. I lit up along with eight others, took a long drag, exhaled, and let myself relax. Another sailor came out.

"Smoking lamp is out," he said. "Put out those cigarettes." *What? It's only been 30 seconds.* "I said put them out now! No, not on the ground. Put them out, and get rid of those butts." Like everyone else, I looked around; there was nowhere to put them out or throw them away. The sailor stared at us. Was this a test? Realizing I only had one choice, I put the cigarette out on the bottom of my shoe and placed the still-warm butt in my pants pocket. I thought this might be a good time to quit smoking.

"I am Second Class Petty Officer Capra," the sailor said. "Do you have a problem with each other? Why are you spread out all over? Get yourselves together as a group on these two benches here. Don't be bashful; come on, move it." We must have been getting tired of being yelled at; we responded immediately.

"Good. Now stand at attention." We jumped. "I am sure you are full of questions." We all shook our heads. "Well, I don't care. You are in the Navy now, and I doubt any of you are smart enough to ask anything worth my time to answer. From now on, you listen and do what you're told. Do you understand?"

One guy said, "What if—" and was quickly cut off. That sailor got right in his face.

"You deaf?" he shouted. "I said *no* questions. From now on, I do the thinking for you. I will tell you what you need and when you need it. Do you understand that?" He got no reply. He looked at the rest of us, then went back to the front. Until this happened, I was about to ask if I could call my parents and tell them where I was. I decided that could wait.

"You will be on these benches until there are enough of you to form a company. That magic number is eighty. Just before your arrival, Boot Camp Company 219 was formed and moved out. You may be here only a few hours or up to several days. You will always remain on these benches unless someone in authority tells you to move. For now, I am that authority. Understood?" We were learning it was best just to nod. Only this time, that didn't work.

"I can't hear you. I said, is that understood?"

"Yes," we all said.

"Yes what?"

"Yes, sir," some of us said.

"I'm not a sir. I'm Petty Officer Capra. You will refer to me as Petty Officer Capra. Now is that understood?"

"Yes, Petty Officer Capra," we all finally said.

"I can't hear you!"

"Yes, Petty Officer Capra," we yelled.

"Good. We're making progress already. Now, I am going to give you five minutes to take a head break. In the building on your left, you will find a head. You are not allowed in that building. That is Headquarters. Understood?"

"Yes, Petty Officer Capra."

"In the building behind you there is a head for your use. Whenever I say head break, that is where you will go. Don't worry about your belongings; they are perfectly safe here on the benches. Is that understood?"

"Yes, Petty Officer Capra."

When he said, "Go," we ran into the building and found a cavernous lavatory with a long trough on the wall. I found a trash can and got rid of that cigarette butt in my pocket. Feeling much better, I ran back with all the others. Capra wasn't there, but we stood at attention anyway. I was starting to understand what this hurry up and wait meant—and totally losing track of time.

Finally, Capra returned. "Okay. Let's get you fed. Behind me is a table with boxes containing your meals. You have ten minutes to eat."

Our meal consisted of a ham and cheese sandwich, two saltine crackers, an apple, and a carton of milk. It wasn't that bad if you could handle warm milk. We finished in under ten minutes; with no trash can in sight, we held our trash in our laps. Capra came out, and we jumped to attention.

"Very good. It's getting late, so let's get you settled in for the night. When I tell you, go back in the building behind you, wash up, brush your teeth, and use the head. Take your trash with you to the cans inside. You can take with you what you need from the personal belongings you brought. If you didn't bring these items with you, use water and brush your teeth with your fingers. When you're done, return to your space on the bench. This is your bed until you become a company and move out. It's a beautiful night, so enjoy it. Now, go."

I found my soap dish, toothbrush, toothpaste, and towel and

headed into the building. Starting to clean up, I noticed a few guys standing around and realized they didn't bring anything with them. Seemed like a good time to introduce myself.

"Hi, guys. I'm Rich Herman. If you want, you can share my soap, and you can put some toothpaste on your finger to brush. My dad and I do that all the time when we go fishing. And I have no problem letting you use my towel once I'm done."

One guy, the one I had tried to help get off the bus, came forward. "Thanks. I'm Walt Janko. I didn't bring bathroom stuff. My recruiter said I'd be given everything I need when I got here. Guess not, huh? I'll be good if I could just have some toothpaste on my finger." I gave it to him. "I'm from Ames, Iowa, by the way. And thanks for helping me off the bus. At least you tried." We shook hands.

"Minneapolis, Minnesota," I said, "almost neighbors."

Another guy, wearing dirty jeans and a black shirt with tennis shoes that looked like they were about to fall apart, stood nearby, looking lost. "Hey," I called. "Would you like anything to clean up a bit?"

"Naw. I'm fine. I can wait." He seemed confused, but I decided not to push it. And his voice seemed kind of strange. Accent?

Before long, we went back out and found our spots on the benches. He was kidding when he said we would be sleeping here, wasn't he? On a wooden bench?

Capra came out. "Okay, I see you're all back and in your spots for the night." So we were here for the night. Some guys wore only pants and shirts and didn't have any bag with them. At least I had my winter coat and a suitcase. "If during the night you have an emergency, or think you have an emergency, you can leave your spot, come up here and ring this bell on the post. A duty petty officer will come to see what you need. Make sure you don't waste his time. Understood? I said, understood?"

"Yes, Petty Officer Capra."

"Good. Sleep, you're going to need it." With that he was gone.

All eleven of us looked at each other. Told not to bring any jewelry, I'd left my watch at home, so I had no idea what time it was, but it wasn't even totally dark. I had to admit I was tired, though, so I put my suitcase on the bench and swung my feet on top of it. Then I folded my jacket, made it into a pillow, and laid my head down.

I closed my eyes to think about all that had happened in one day. That's all I remember.

I woke to the loudest noise in my ears—in what felt like the middle of the night. "Reveille, reveille, reveille," a guy holding a horn was yelling. "You have just experienced the sound of the Klaxon, gentlemen, and you better get used to it." Then we heard, "Attention on deck." We stood, half asleep, and saw Petty Officer Capra coming.

"You didn't think you were going to sleep all day, did you?" he said.

"No, Petty Officer Capra," we shouted back.

"You look like crap. I can't believe you think you're good enough to become United States sailors. It seems like every group that comes here looks worse than the last. What's the Navy coming to? Listen up. You have ten minutes to go to the head and then report back to your assigned spots."

When we returned, he continued. "This morning I am going to march you to the mess hall. You will form into two lines, the first with you six," he pointed them out, "and the second with you other five. We will run there at my pace, and if you can't keep up, we will let you sit where you are until the rest of us finish, and you can join us on the way back. Fall in." We did so, but not into two lines. I couldn't tell what we were trying to do. I figured something had to be done, so I spoke up.

"Hey, guys, listen up. You six are line one. Get behind Janko there. The rest of us fall in behind to make line two." Surprisingly, no one said anything, and it wasn't perfect, but soon we had two lines.

"Who are you?" Capra asked as he got in my face.

"Richard Herman, Petty Officer Capra."

"No, you're not. You're Herman. The Navy took away your first name. Now, who are you?"

"Herman, Petty Officer Capra." I made my first mistake, I thought.

"So, Herman. Can you even see with those glasses?"

"Yes, Petty Officer Capra." I was afraid my glasses would be a problem.

"Do you think you can lead this group better than me?"

"No, Petty Officer Capra."

"Then why did you tell them what to do?"

"I was just trying to help, Petty Officer Capra."

"Oh, so you think I need help, Herman?"

"No, Petty Officer Capra." Now I knew I'd made my first mistake. Why couldn't I have stayed quiet?

"Then, in the future, Herman, don't start telling my people what to do until I ask you to. Understood?"

"Yes, Petty Officer Capra."

"Good. Now. It seems they did what you said, Herman, so you come out here and lead them to chow. Follow me, and double time," he said. I fell in behind him, and everyone started running. We had double-timed about 100 yards when it happened.

"Can't run no more," I heard. We turned and saw one of our guys on all fours. It was the guy in the jeans and black shirt who didn't want any of my bathroom stuff. We stopped.

"I didn't tell you to stop," Capra yelled. "Everyone, run in place." He went back to where the guy sat breathing heavily. "What's your name?"

"Billy Blunck, sir." What kind of accent was that? I'd never heard anyone speak so slow.

"I'm not a sir, Blunck, I'm Petty Officer Capra, and you don't have a first name either. Just like Herman. Understood?"

"Yes, sir, Officer Capper, sir."

"Are you messing with me, Blunck? Do you think you're funny?"

"No, ain't never been funny. Officer Capp."

I thought Capra was going to lose it. Then, although obviously frustrated, he said, "Why did you stop? We just got started, Blunck."

"Tired. Can't I just sit here a while?"

"Aren't you hungry, Blunck?"

"I can wait." Exactly what he told me about cleaning up.

Capra's face turned beet red. We kept running in place, but it was hard not to laugh. Could Blunck be that stupid? Capra finally said, "You go over there, Blunck, and sit on that bench. We will pick you up on the way back. Do you think you can do that, Blunck?"

"Yes, Officer Crapper." And he headed for the bench. Capra opened his mouth, then shook his head and turned to the rest of us. "Double time, march." We left Blunck sitting there looking confused, as he had since he arrived.

In about a half-mile, Capra stopped us outside a wooden

building; from the smell, I could tell this was the mess hall. "You now have only ten minutes to eat because Blunck took up five of them. You are being fed first this morning because you are nobodies, and no one else on this base wants to eat or be associated with you. You can take what you want to eat, but make sure you eat everything you take. When you are done, you will fall in out here in two lines again. Behind Herman. Understood?"

"Yes, Petty Officer Capra."

I couldn't believe the chow line before us. I loaded a tray with scrambled eggs, bacon, a sausage patty, and oatmeal. I passed on the pancakes and French toast but added toast and several pats of butter.

When I finished, I saw a clock for the first time. It was 4:45 in the morning. I realized that we must be nearing the ten minutes, so for some reason I called out, "Come on, guys, time's up. Let's not give Petty Officer Capra any reason to get mad at us." I headed out as fast as I could and found the spot to line up, and everyone fell in behind me without saying a word.

"Nine minutes," Capra said. "At least you guys were paying attention. Let's go. Forward, march." Off we went at double time. I was glad to see Blunck still sitting on the bench. I was starting to feel sorry for him. "Fall in, Blunck," I heard. This time he did as he was told, and we made it back to the green benches, just as the sun was coming up.

"There are only eleven of you, so you can just sit here until some more join you," Capra said. "No use wasting my time until there are enough of you to make my time worthwhile. Unlike you, I have important duties to attend to. You know where the head is, and you are free to go there, and only there, when you need to, and then return to your spot on the bench. You may talk among yourselves, but keep it down. You will be given smoke breaks throughout the day. Then, and only then, are you to light up. If, for any reason, and I mean any reason, the duty petty officer needs to come out and tell you to quiet down or stop doing something he doesn't like, you will lose your new privileges. Am I understood?"

"Yes, Petty Officer Capra." And he left.

Later, a sailor came out from Headquarters, wearing a green belt with a club on it and an armband that said POOW, whatever that meant. He said, "Smoke 'em if you got 'em." None of us moved. He laughed. "It's okay, I won't be back for a while. Also, I put a butt can over under the bell for you to use. I better not see one ash or butt on this ground when I come back." He went back into Headquarters. A few guys lit up, but I decided not to take the chance. I thought I'd try to meet everyone and walked over to where Janko was standing.

"Morning, Janko. I guess we all made it through the night. You able to sleep in the cold?"

"Wasn't that bad," he said. "Actually, warmer than home is sometimes. And it's already getting warm. How about you?"

"I was out like a light, so guess it didn't bother me much either. Say, you want to go meet Blunck? He doesn't seem right. I think we should check and make sure he's okay." We walked over.

"Hey, Blunck, remember us? I'm Herman, and this is Janko."

"Yeah. You're the guy with no first name."

I let that go. "We just wanted to say hi and make sure you're okay. You feeling all right now?"

He looked at me and then Janko. "I'm fine. Just got tuckered out, that's all. We don't run much at home."

"Where's home, Blunck?" Janko asked.

"Jackson, Mississippi."

"Aren't you hungry?" I asked.

"Naw. I can wait." Apparently, he was used to waiting a lot back home.

"I can't believe that guy broke my knife," another voice said. The guy from the front of the bus had walked up. "My brother gave that to me. Man, he's going to want a piece of that Marine when I tell him." I wasn't going to say anything, but Janko held out his hand and introduced himself. The guy looked at him a second, then shook hands. "Frank Clay, from L.A."

"I'm Gary Gossett, Seattle," the guy with long hair said as he joined the group. "I feel like an idiot. Just glad I remembered I had those LSD pills on me before that Marine found them. Been to jail before, don't want to go back."

"Jail, no big thing," Clay said, sounding almost proud of it. "That's why I'm here. Been there a couple times. Last month, beat up a guy, and judge told me I could either join the military or go away for a couple years to one of his houses. My brothers talked me into joining the Navy."

We heard a door slam and saw the sailor with POOW on his arm coming. "The smoking lamp is out. Put out all your cigarettes. No more talking. I just got word that Earl is on his way with a bunch of new guys."

Finally, we saw Earl's bus pulling up. The sailor with POOW on his arm headed that way, and as soon as the bus doors opened, he started screaming. "What are you waiting for? Move it! Move it! Get off the bus. I said move it!" That sure sounded familiar.

About thirty guys got off and came over to the benches. A long time later, Capra came out again. "Everyone, ten-hut! I am Petty Officer Capra. Do you have a problem with each other? Why are you spread out all over? Get yourselves together as a group on these four benches here."

He gave the same speech as yesterday about not asking questions. He announced we had forty-three men and a company would be formed when there were eighty; until then, we'd stay on the benches unless someone in authority said to move. "For now, I am that authority," he said. "Understood?"

The new guys nodded, looking surprised when the rest of us yelled, "Yes, Petty Officer Capra."

"I said, understood?" he shouted.

"Yes, Petty Officer Capra," all of us answered.

He gave us a five-minute break. Miraculously, everyone was back on the benches well before he returned. "Ten-hut," he said. "You are a group of nobodies." This sounded familiar. "You are *not* civilians anymore. You are *not* sailors. You are *nobody*! This means no one wants to eat with you. So I am going to march you to the Mess Hall, where you will be given fifteen minutes to eat. When I tell you to fall in, make four lines of ten. The remaining two, fall in behind as best you can. I say the remaining two, because Herman is going to lead you from the front. He is also going to get you into your lines, so do as he says. Herman, get out here."

I ran to his side, wondering what I had gotten myself into. "Now, fall out and get into formation. Herman, let me know when they're ready." And he went and sat on a bench. Meanwhile, forty-two guys stood, not moving.

"You guys in this row," I said, pointing to the first row, "make line one. You guys in this row, fall in behind." They did. "Good, now this row, you're next, and then you guys here. Just stand behind the guy in front of you. And, Janko, get Blunck, and fall in behind as the last two guys. Make sure he, and anyone else in front of you, makes it to the Mess Hall." Janko smiled, grabbed Blunck, and fell in. Finally, we had the lines, and I turned and said, "Ready, Petty Officer Capra."

"I'd say they're far from ready, Herman. I don't know if this group will ever be ready. It's getting late, so we'll leave it there and head to chow."

This time we made the whole half-mile without losing anyone. When Capra told us to halt, I looked around and saw about half the guys bent over, breathing hard. Then I saw Janko coming with Blunck and several others. Capra was watching but said nothing until everyone settled down. He walked back and stared at the latecomers before saying, "Nice of you to join us for lunch today, Blunck. I didn't think you could run this far."

"Hungry. Do what ya gotta do, sir."

"Blunck, for the last time, I am not a sir. I am Petty Officer Capra. Now say after me, Petty Officer Capra."

"Petty Officer Capra."

"Finally. Now remember that from now on. Understood?"

"Yes, Petty Officer Capra ... sir."

Laughter broke out, until Capra, his face bright red, shouted, "One more laugh and no chow." Complete quiet. "Now, you have twelve minutes to eat, thanks to the time just wasted once again by Blunck. Herman will lead you through the chow line."

After lunch and the march back to the benches, Capra told us he would be away for a while, and the petty officer of the watch would be in charge. "You will be allowed to use the head when you need to; otherwise, remain on your bench. You can talk to each other, but no smoking unless the petty officer of the watch lights the smoking lamp." Aha, it dawned on me—that's what POOW stood for.

I saw Janko heading my way. "Hey, Herman," he said. "Good move having me take up the rear to watch Blunck and those other guys. Two of them said they wanted to quit, so I sort of helped them along."

I smiled. "Thanks. I figured we didn't need any more time off our chow time. And, man, Blunck must have been starving. I think we better try and help him for a while."

Another sailor in blue came out and announced that the smoking lamp was lit. "Don't worry, I'll leave it lit for a while, unless you give me reason to put it out." There must have been thirty guys lighting up. I decided to stick with quitting.

"Hey, Janko, let's go meet some guys." He nodded and followed me. I noticed two guys sitting together, dressed exactly the same and wearing cowboy hats. I stuck my hand out to the bigger guy. "Hi, I'm Herman from Minneapolis, Minnesota, and this is Janko from Ames, Iowa."

The guy, who had to be at least six-three, shook my hand. "Ted Wyler," he said, "and this is my twin brother, Tommy. We're from Boise, Idaho. Nice to meet you." They must have seen the blank look on Janko's and my faces. Twin brother? Tommy was about five-six, half Ted's size. They both started to laugh. "Yeah, we get that all the time. We're not identical twins, we're fraternal twins. Tommy just hasn't started growing yet."

"I can still kick your butt, big bro'," Tommy said, jumping up and slapping him on the head. They both laughed harder, which made us join in.

"Hey, Janko." We turned and saw Blunck standing there. "That was nice of you to help me today. Ain't nobody done that before."

"No problem, Blunck," Janko said. "I think we all better start taking care of each other if we ever think we're going to make it through boot camp. Hey, this is Ted and Tommy Wyler from Boise."

"You big," Blunck said to Ted.

"Naw. You should see our daddy, Big Buck. He makes me look small. Tommy here, he takes after our momma." And Tommy jumped up again and slapped him on the head. Blunck even laughed now. "Back on our ranch, we don't worry much about your size, it's your toughness," Ted said. "Gotta pull your weight. That's why Tommy being a shrimp don't matter—he's tough as nails." Tommy smiled and flexed his bicep, which now was as big as my thigh.

"You don't know tough till you been to L.A.," Clay said as he and Gossett approached. I didn't like how he said it and looked at Ted, who just smiled.

"Just a different kind of tough probably," Janko said quickly and got between everyone.

The sailor returned. "Smoking lamp is out," he said. "Take a head break if you need one and then back to your bench and no talking."

I was getting tired of these benches and hoped another bus would come soon. We still needed thirty-seven more guys to make up a group—no, not a group, a company. After a couple more hours, Capra appeared. "Ten-hut. No more buses today. The petty officer of the watch will be coming out soon with your dinner."

We stayed at attention. Finally, the tall sailor from yesterday with the POOW armband came out, followed by two sailors carrying big paper bags. The POOW told us to come up and get the box dinners and that we'd have ten minutes. Again—a ham and cheese sandwich, saltine crackers, an apple, and a carton of warm milk.

The POOW finally returned. "It's getting late, so let's get you settled in for the night." He repeated last night's speech about washing up.

Grabbing what I needed, I headed into the building. Janko caught up with me. I found a spot at a sink and started to clean up. I handed the toothpaste to Janko, who smiled and put some on his finger. When I finished washing, I gave him the soap, and he cleaned up too. After we both dried off using my towel, we looked around at the other guys.

"Hey, Blunck," I said. "Want to use any of my stuff?"

"Naw. I can wait, Herman." *Should have guessed, he can wait.*

Deciding not to push, I said, "Whenever you're ready." It seemed a lot of guys could just wait. How could they not clean up?

When we were back outside, the POOW walked around, apparently counting to make sure all forty-three were still here. He instructed us about ringing the bell if there was an emergency. "A duty petty officer will come see what you need. Don't waste his time. Understood?" Getting no response, he yelled, "Understood?"

"Yes, Petty Officer."

The night passed as uneventfully as the one before.

"Reveille, reveille, reveille," someone shouted, and there went that Klaxon again. "Attention on deck." Everyone stood and tried to wake up. Capra came out of Headquarters with the POOW.

Capra looked us over and said, "You all look like crap. It seems like every new group that comes here looks worse than the last. What's the Navy coming to? Listen up. You have ten minutes to go to the head and then report back to your assigned spots." We got back and stood waiting until Capra returned and said, "When I tell you, fall out, and form up exactly like you did yesterday. Herman, front and center." I ran forward. "I have important duties to attend to. The petty officer of the watch and Herman will lead you to chow. I do not expect any reports of problems. Fall out."

After breakfast. we returned to Headquarters and saw a lot of new guys sitting on the green benches. The POOW called, "Halt," and we stopped, although not without running into each other. He shouted, "Ten-hut," and left us. I was trying to count how many more guys there were. It didn't look like thirty-seven, and all I could think about was another day on these benches. And another day I probably couldn't call and tell Mom and Dad where I was.

Capra and the POOW came out and stood in front of the benches. "If I point to you, fall out," Capra said. "Give your orders to the petty officer of the watch, and get in line at attention behind those already standing there."

He started pointing, and new guys began falling in with our group. After a dozen or so joined us, Capra said to those remaining, "If you're still sitting on the bench, pick up your belongings and move over to the far left. I'll be with you shortly."

He then came and addressed our group. "Your lucky day. I just received word that I was to start forming companies with sixty personnel. There are sixty of you. I will now be informing your company commander that you are available."

He gave us a ten-minute head break, and we made it back to our spots in time. I suspected everyone was thinking the same thing. Inform our company commander? What would he be like? Did this mean we'd finally get off these benches? Were we going to get to sleep indoors and take a shower? It seemed like hours before the Headquarters door opened, and the POOW came our way.

"You sixty identified already as a company. When I tell you, fall out, and form six lines with ten of you in each line. Start with this bench here," he pointed to row one, "and so on. Take your belongings with you. Fall out." We gathered our things, and as before, Janko and I helped some guys get into line. Couldn't these guys count? Then I saw Janko lead Blunck to his spot and realized I answered my own question. Finally, the POOW seemed satisfied and went back into headquarters.

My heart pounded. The door to Headquarters opened, and the POOW came out. "Attention on deck. Company commander arriving."

CHAPTER 6

I GOT MY FIRST LOOK AT OUR COMPANY COMMANDER. He wore a blue uniform with a white sailor's hat pushed forward on his head all the way down to his eyes. He had red stripes on his left sleeve, a red rope hanging around the shoulder, and a bunch of medals on his chest. He didn't seem to be looking at us at all, and then he stopped and turned. I stared straight ahead and felt as though he was looking right at me.

"I am First Class Petty Officer Sabin," he said. "I am your company commander, and you will refer to me as Petty Officer Sabin. You are now officially Company 1966-220 and will be referred to as Company 220. Understood?"

"Yes, Petty Officer Sabin," about half of us replied. The other half got the petty officer right, but I had no idea what came after that.

"That's Petty Officer Sabin, spelled S-A-B-I-N, for those of you that can spell, and I didn't hear you."

"Yes, Petty Officer Sabin," we yelled, getting it right that time.

"Recruit Janko, front and center." Wow, I wondered what Janko did and how he knew his name. Janko ran forward and stood at attention in front of Sabin, who was about three inches shorter. "I did a quick scan of records and saw that you have some college behind you, and you also worked as an assistant scoutmaster back home. Is this correct?"

"Yes, Petty Officer Sabin," Janko said.

"You are now my recruit chief petty officer, RCPO, for Company 220. I will explain your duties later. Fall in behind me." Janko, looking confused, did so. "Recruit Masuda, front and center." A little guy, shorter than me and maybe Japanese, ran forward. "Your record showed you have some college and also five brothers. You are now my recruit leading petty officer, RLPO, for Company 220. Fall in next to Janko.

"Recruit Ward, front and center." A guy from the last bus to join us ran up and stood at attention. About my height and very muscular, he was wearing a cowboy hat even bigger than the Wylers' hats. Sabin said, "I saw in your record that you were the State of Texas High School Wrestling and Weightlifting Champ at 165 pounds. You are now the master at arms, MAA, for Company 220."

Sabin went on, "Now, I need a volunteer to be the company yeoman. This is the toughest job, and I don't have time to do a thorough review of all your records to try and figure out who may be qualified. If you can type and think you're smart enough to keep up with my demands, step forward."

For some reason I will never understand, I stepped forward. Sabin looked shocked. "Front and center, recruit." I ran up and stood at attention. "What's your name, recruit?"

"Herman, Petty Officer Sabin."

"You're the one who thought you were better than Petty Officer Capra at leading the recruits to Mess Hall?"

"No, Petty Officer Sabin. Just tried to help." I could see Janko behind Sabin, shaking his head for me to shut up.

Sabin looked down and got right in my face. "Herman, Navy petty officers don't need your help. Understood?"

"Yes, Petty Officer Sabin." How many times did I hear to never volunteer? And why did I want the hardest job?

"Well, you got gonads, Herman, I'll give you that. And if I remember your record correctly, you also have some college behind you. Okay, you are now the Company 220 yeoman. Fall in behind me." I was glad to get behind him and away from that stare. I stood next to Masuda, who gave me a thumbs-up. Janko and Ward showed no emotion and looked straight ahead.

"Company 220," Sabin said, walking up and down the lines, "it's time to join the Navy. RCPO Janko, RLPO Masuda, MAA Ward, Yeoman Herman, go get your belongings and come back here to the front." We did so. "RCPO Janko, you stand in front, RLPO Masuda, one step behind him, MAA Ward, one step behind and to their left,

Yeoman Herman, one step behind and to their right. The rest of you remain in your line and follow RCPO Janko, who will follow me." He called out, "Company, ten-hut, forward, march. Double time."

We marched about three blocks before Sabin called, "Halt," at an old wooden building with a barber pole outside. Sabin, walking back and seeing total disarray, yelled, "Ten-hut." I looked back and found it hard not to laugh. Guys were panting, shirts were hanging out, and they were nowhere near in straight lines.

"Company 220," Sabin said, "it's time to start looking like recruits. You will fall in line and enter the barber shop one by one. Tell the barber how you would like your hair cut, and, when done, fall back into ranks."

When the barber put the sheet around me, I said, "I'd like a crew-cut, please." I felt the clippers run down the top left side of my head a couple of times, then the middle and the right. He stopped and said, "What's that lump on your head?" I didn't answer, and he continued running the clippers around the sides and back of my head, then said, "Next." It had taken about one minute, and, as I left, I rubbed my head and realized all my hair was gone. I looked at Janko and Ward, and they were bald too. So much for telling the barber how you wanted it cut.

"That's better," Sabin said when the company was back in ranks. "That hippie hair doesn't belong in my Navy." He then marched us off to the Mess Hall. "By now you know the drill. You have twenty minutes to eat. I'm giving you an extra five minutes so you can use the head and wash up before getting into the chow line. When finished eating, fall back in ranks." He was right about one thing—we had this routine down pat.

After lunch, we marched several blocks to an old white building that looked like a warehouse. Six cement tables stood out front, with about ten clotheslines on the left and the same on the right. "This is your new home. RCPO Janko, you are assigned the bottom rack of the first bunk on the right. RLPO Masuda, you have the top rack above him. MAA Ward, you have the top rack of the first bunk on the left, and, Yeoman Herman, you take the bottom rack below MAA Ward. All others will be occupied by the rest of you. When I say enter, you will do so orderly. Place your belongings, if you have some, on what will be your rack, and stand at attention before it,"

Sabin ordered.

I saw what turned out to be thirty bunk beds inside a massive room. I placed my suitcase on my rack, which had a bare mattress, pillow, cardboard box, and silver bucket on it, and fell in at attention. I started looking for Blunck and hoped he would be able to find a rack okay. I glanced at Janko and realized he was probably doing the same thing. We both spotted Ted and Tommy Wyler, who had taken a bunk bed together, and big Ted had Blunck next to him. He saw us and gave the thumbs-up. Janko smiled, and we all nodded to each other.

"Get away from my rack," someone said. We all turned and saw Frank Clay. He had pushed one of the other guys and was glaring at him as if hoping he'd throw a punch. Sabin came in, but before he could say anything, Ward had run down the floor and spun Clay around.

"Stand at attention and shut up," Ward quietly said, looking up at Clay. Evidently Clay realized Ward was no one to be messed with and did as he was told. Ward quickly and quietly returned to our bunk and stood at attention, winking at me.

Sabin walked to the center of the room. "I think you all have just met and understand the duties of our master at arms. Listen to him. He is to maintain order among the ranks, and, as long as he does his job, you won't have me getting up close and personal. And, believe me, you do not want that to happen. Understood?"

"Yes, Petty Officer Sabin," we shouted back. No doubt in my mind, we all had learned a valuable lesson.

"RCPO Janko, RLPO Masuda, MAA Ward, Yeoman Herman, follow me; everyone else, stand at ease." We followed Sabin out into a hallway and into what must be his office. "I brought you four in here to explain your duties. MAA Ward, you already demonstrated what I expect from my MAA. The first few days are always the hardest but, once everyone realizes you have the authority to keep them in line, without physical abuse, mind you, everything will go much smoother. I expect you to be tough, but never lay a hand on them. That I see, anyway." With that, he smiled.

"RCPO Janko, you are the designated leader of these misfits. I will explain to the company that if they have a problem, they are to come to you. You will solve the issue unless you feel it needs my attention.

If you bring it to me, make damn sure it's important enough for me to get involved. I expect you to keep everyone informed and up to speed on what is required of them. If I see or think you can't handle the responsibility, I will have you replaced by RLPO Masuda, who is your second in command. Now, do you understand your duties?"

"Yes, Petty Officer Sabin," they replied.

"Good. I need to spend a little longer with Herman as his duties are a lot more involved. You three go out there and make sure the company is behaving themselves." They left.

"Okay, Yeoman Herman." Then he stared at me. "What's that lump on your head?"

"Just a small cyst, Petty Officer Sabin. Been there most of my life."

"All right, if you say so. Let's see if you have what it takes to be my yeoman." My stomach wasn't feeling so good. "First, you need to take these forms," he handed me a handful of papers, "and fill in all the charts with the names of everyone in the company. Here on my desk are all sixty records, which I now give you access to for the performance of your duties. All this information is to remain between you and me—is that clear?"

"Yes, Petty Officer Sabin."

"Good. As my yeoman, you will hear and see a lot about what goes on around here, and it better remain with you. If I ever get an inkling that you shared any information with someone not authorized, I will immediately place you on report, remove you from your duties, and have you thrown in the brig. Do I make myself clear, and do you accept this responsibility?"

"Yes, Petty Officer Sabin." What else could I say?

"It's a big job, and I rely on my yeoman to make sure my ass is covered on every little administrative detail. You will make out all muster sheets, meal chits, watch bills, lists of demerits, and the list goes on and on. Do you think you can handle that?" He held up his hand. "Before you answer, you need to know that all this is in addition to handling all the duties that every other recruit has, with a few exceptions, which I'll explain later. No other special treatment. You're just another recruit who volunteered to take on more. Now, is all that understood, and do you still want to be my yeoman?"

"Yes, Petty Officer Sabin."

"Okay, let's join the rest of the company."

We walked out and into the bunk area—and absolute silence. I fell in beside my rack and noticed Ward was gone, and so was Janko. Looking down the row of bunks, I saw them standing in front of Clay and Gossett, who apparently were bunkmates. Sabin walked down there and said, "Problem here?"

"No, Petty Officer Sabin," Janko sounded off. "There was still a little confusion on how sleeping assignments were made. MAA Ward and I have explained the situation, and everything's fine now." Clay seemed about to say something but, looking around, decided to nod instead. I figured it was only a matter of time before he'd do something especially dumb.

"Good," Sabin said. "Nice to see you guys are getting along so nicely. Now, for all of you. RCPO Janko is your leader. If you have a question or would like to make any comment, you will do it through him. He is your go-between to get to me. If he has trouble with any of you understanding what he expects of this company, MAA Ward will help him explain. RLPO Masuda is second in command and will act in his absence. Yeoman Herman is about to become your best friend or your greatest enemy." *Did he have to say that?*

"Yeoman Herman makes out the duty roster. What is that? You will soon find out. Yeoman Herman will also keep track of all demerits. What's a demerit? You will soon find out. If you do anything that requires documentation, Yeoman Herman will keep track of that. What requires documentation? You will soon find out. Hopefully, you get the idea. Now, before we move on, does anyone have a question they would like to ask me?" With that, he started walking and looking at every recruit. I hoped no one raised their hand. Finally, Sabin announced we would have a head break and then fall back into ranks outside.

When I got outside, Masuda was standing with Janko, so I went over, extended my hand and introduced myself. We shook, and he said, "Kenny Masuda. Nice to meet the guy who has no first name and likes to volunteer. I'm from DC, look Japanese, but that's only because my parents are, and, yes, I am as tall as I'm going to get at five-four." He laughed, and Janko and I joined him. I liked this guy immediately. Then we saw Petty Officer Sabin coming.

We learned we were about to march to the outfitting station

and receive bedding and our initial seabag items. "When you have received all your items, you will form back up in ranks outside," Sabin said.

After running for about three blocks, we reached the building where we formed two lines, as instructed. Inside, table after table held linens. A man in civilian clothes handed us a green seabag as we came by and called out, "Take two sheets, two pillowcases, two blankets, three towels, three washcloths, and proceed to the next room."

The next room had tables filled with clothing. At the first table, the processor asked, "Waist size?" Before I could answer, he gave me three pairs of blue pants, four pairs of white pants, three blue shirts, and four pullover white tops.

At the next table, the processor said, "Shoe size?" Based on the first table, I said nothing. "Well," he said, "it's your feet, sailor, and if I were you, I'd want shoes that fit." Maybe he actually cared.

"Size nine," I replied.

"That's better. Here is one pair of size nine boondockers, one pair of size nine tennis shoes, and one pair of shower shoes that should fit. Next."

The next processor didn't ask anything, looked at me, and loaded me up. "Seven T-shirts, seven skivvies, twelve pairs of socks, twelve hankies, one blue belt, one white belt, one raincoat, one blue jacket, one blue knit hat, and a blue ball cap. Move to the next table, grab a douche kit, and depart."

Janko and I left at the same time and fell in, holding all our new belongings. After the rest of the company joined us, Janko surprised me by yelling, "Put all your belongings into your seabags."

He looked at me and whispered, "Petty Officer Sabin told me to do that to see how they respond." I nodded, and after stowing everything, which wasn't easy, I joined Janko in watching everyone following his order.

Sabin came out and shouted, "Company, ten-hut. Pick up your seabags, forward, march. Double time." And we ran back, with a lot of effort hauling our new belongings, to the barracks. We were ordered to stow our gear, take a head break, then fall back in. Sabin told Janko, Masuda, Ward, and me to come to his office after the head break.

"Now, listen up," he said to us. "I'm going to explain to Yeoman

Herman his first duties, and you three must be able to cover for him if he's not able to perform them." He looked directly at me.

"I am giving you a pad of sheets for various duties, one of which is for nightly security watches. You need to assign a man to each two-hour period. You'll need to develop a system to fairly assign watches to everyone in the company except yourself. This is one of those exceptions I told you about. You'll be too busy with your yeoman duties. I will explain other responsibilities to everyone later."

He continued, "Second. A chow chit must be filled out for every meal. You present this to the duty MAA when entering the chow hall. If you want everyone to eat, make sure there are no mistakes. And learn to sign my name, Yeoman Herman—I don't want to be bothered with doing this crap." He smiled and signed the chit, then had me sign his name a couple times to practice.

We went to early chow and marched back to our barracks. I was hoping that maybe tonight we'd finally be able to call home. This, however, was not about to happen.

"Company, ten-hut," Sabin said. "When I tell you, remove the following from your seabag—one blanket, two sheets, one pillowcase, one t-shirt, one pair skivvies, one towel, one washcloth, shower shoes, and douche kit. Then store your seabag under your bunks. No talking. Go."

While removing my items, I heard the noise level getting louder and louder. Apparently, a lot of guys were having problems getting their things out and started talking. Then it happened.

"Company, ten-hut," Sabin screamed. It was the loudest he had ever yelled, and everyone jumped to attention. He looked like a whole different person as he marched down the room and stood in front of Janko. His face blazed red, and the veins in his neck stood out. "RCPO Janko. Did I give this company permission to speak?"

"No, Petty Officer Sabin," Janko replied.

"Then why do I hear them?" He went down to the first rack and threw everything on the racks onto the floor. He moved to the next set of bunks and did the same, keeping on until all the bunks were empty and everyone's belongings were on the deck. He then stood in front of one of the guys and said, "Do *you* have anything you want to say?" The guy, trembling, shook his head no.

"I can't hear you, recruit. I said, do you have anything to say?"

"No, Petty Officer Sabin," he finally managed to get out.

He walked down and stood before Ted Wyler. Looking up, he shouted, "How about you? You look like the biggest piece of crap I have in this company. Do you have anything you'd like to say?"

"No, Petty Officer Sabin." And then someone laughed.

Sabin stepped over to Tommy Wyler, who was smiling. "You finding this funny, recruit?"

"Yes, Petty Officer Sabin. I've never seen anyone talk to my brother like that before."

"Brother? You must be the Wylers." He looked up at Ted and then down at Tommy. "I thought you were twins? Well, seeing this is so funny, drop and give me fifty pushups, little Wyler."

"Yes, Petty Officer Sabin." Tommy dropped and did fifty pushups without breaking a sweat.

Sabin continued down the aisle and finally stopped in front of Ward. "From now on, MAA Ward, I expect you to take charge and make sure the recruits follow my orders. No talking means no talking. Do you understand?"

"Yes, Petty Officer Sabin."

"You have lost your last chance at a smoke break for quite a while." I definitely was glad I'd quit. "Now, pick up your items and put them where they belong."

There wasn't a sound made as we collected our things. I looked around and saw a lot of guys quietly helping each other, and the Wylers were taking care of Blunck. Ted didn't seem affected at all by being yelled at, and Tommy was smiling and constantly poking him in the ribs.

When everyone seemed to be done, Sabin, a lot calmer now, said, "You all have a cardboard box. Inside you will find paper, an envelope, and a pencil. Everyone is going to write to someone. Your parents, guardian, relative, girlfriend, or whoever. This one time, your letter will be monitored to be sure you followed directions and that someone is being contacted. For some of you, like Yeoman Herman, who thought he was going to Great Lakes, this will be your opportunity to let your family know where you are." I was startled to realize he knew all along I was probably worrying about this.

"This letter will be placed in the box with all the belongings, including the cigarettes, you brought with you. Everything, except suitcases, goes into the box. Suitcases will be stored until you leave. *Everything else* in the box. We will get the box mailed for you and will include in it written instructions on your mailing address and what to do in case of emergencies. Okay, begin writing. You can talk, but keep it down."

I never considered I wouldn't be able to call Mom and Dad. I couldn't believe they were going to find out where I was from a letter received inside a cardboard box with all my belongings, but I wrote a short letter explaining I was in San Diego and I was okay. I had nothing more to say because I didn't know anything. I was sure they'd understand. When I finished, I looked around the room, and Janko and Masuda were doing the same. We saw several guys just sitting there, so I walked over and said, "Let's see if we can help. I'll check on Blunck first."

"Great," Janko said, "I'll go this way. Masuda, how about you go over there?"

"On my way." Masuda headed to the racks farther down.

"Hey, Blunck, how you doing?" I said.

"Hey, Herman. I'm not so good at writin'."

"Let me help you. Who do you want to know where you are?"

"Don't think anyone cares. 'Cept maybe Meemaw."

"Who is Meemaw?"

"She took care of me sometimes. She's my Daddy's momma." *Oh, his grandmother. Meemaw must be a Southern thing.*

"Got it. Let's let Meemaw know where you are then. Just say, 'Meemaw, I am here in Navy boot camp and doing okay.' You have her address, right?" Getting a blank stare, I said, "Where does Meemaw get her mail?" He smiled and took a piece of paper out of his pocket. It listed Fannie Mae Blunck, Route 2, Road C, Jackson, Miss. 39200. I helped him write a note to her and get his envelope addressed.

Once everyone seemed to be done, I went and stood by Ward and said, loud enough for Janko and Masuda to hear, "I think we may have more than we can handle with Blunck." They nodded, but before they could say anything, Sabin returned.

"Okay. When I tell you, strip down, and put everything in your box with the letter on top. Then, put on your shower shoes, take your towel, washcloth, douche kit, and hit the head. You will shave off all facial hair. *All.* No sideburns, mustaches, or any facial hair. If I don't think you got it all, I will show you how to shave properly. Trust me, you don't want to make me help. You will then brush your teeth, shower, and take care of any other business you need to. When you return, put on your skivvies and t-shirt, and stand at parade rest in your shower shoes. Go."

After three days in the same clothes, you didn't have to tell me twice. I undressed and put those clothes into the box with everything I'd brought with me. All the showers were taken, so I found an empty sink and opened my douche kit, finding soap, razor, shaving cream, and other necessities. It felt great to shave, and finally I enjoyed a hot shower. Toweling down, I saw Blunck just standing there.

"Hey, Blunck. Great to be able to clean up, right?"

"I can wait," he said. Not this time. He was pretty dirty and starting to smell fairly bad, but then again, we all were.

"Yeah, but now is a good time, and we don't know when we'll get a chance to again. Here, let me help you get that stuff out of your douche kit." With a little prodding, Blunck finally shaved, got his teeth brushed, and headed to the shower. I went back out and got into my underwear feeling like a new person. Janko and Masuda were headed my way.

"Hey, Herman," Janko said, "I think Ward could use our help." I followed them into the head, where Ward, with a towel wrapped around him, had five guys standing against a wall.

"Look, guys," Ward said. "Petty Officer Sabin made it clear, no facial hair allowed, and all five of you still have hair showing. I'm not trying to be a hard ass, but if you don't shave better, I'm going to help you before Petty Officer Sabin sees you and we all get into trouble."

"Not going to happen, dude," Frank Clay said. I should have known it would be him, and, yeah, there was Gary Gossett among the other four. "I've had it with you, Ward," Clay continued, walking toward him, "thinking you somebody being the MAA. Well, I don't give a rat's ass, and you can take a hike."

What happened next took place so fast I wasn't sure what I saw, but Clay lay on the deck out cold. A crowd was forming, getting pretty loud; Janko stepped forward.

"Show is over, guys," Janko said. "Back to what you were doing." He started walking them out. Gossett and the other three were heading to the sinks, presumably to shave better.

Masuda knelt and asked, "Clay, you okay?" Clay moaned, trying to sit up. Ward stood there like nothing had happened. Then I saw the Wyler boys coming.

"What did we miss?" Tommy Wyler said. "Damn, Ted, looks like Clay fell in the shower." He was laughing; Ted only shook his head.

Ted helped Masuda get Clay to his feet and slapped Clay on the shoulder. "My brother has that right, Clay?" he said. "You fall in the shower?" Clay, still dazed, looked at him and the rest of us, then nodded.

"Good answer, Clay," Ted continued. "We're like family now and have to look out for one another. I'm sure glad Ward was here to see you're doing things right. And it looks like you can continue shaving now, don't you think? We all want to look good for Petty Officer Sabin, don't we?" Clay, his lip bleeding, shook his head and headed to the sink to improve on his shave. At that moment, I felt Janko, Masuda, Ward, the Wyler brothers, and I had become good friends who could turn to each other when needed.

When Sabin returned, he walked up and down the aisles looking at each of us. He stopped in front of Clay to take an extra good look before moving to the center of the barracks. "Not inspection-ready, but not bad for your first cleanup. I do see that one of you took a fall in the shower and want to encourage you all to be careful in the future. Not following the rules can lead to accidents, so let this be a warning to all."

He continued, "When I tell you, make up your racks and stow your belongings. When you are done, sit on your racks so I know everyone is finished. Begin."

I took a sheet and started to make my rack. From what I'd seen during the day, this might be a big problem for some of the group, so I hurried as fast as I could. Looking around, I wasn't surprised to see a complete fiasco. Sixty guys, in nothing but their underwear, and it was obvious some of them had never made a bed in their life. Janko and I set out to help, and I saw Masuda helping Blunck. The Wyler brothers were at it as usual, with Tommy jumping up smacking Ted in the back of the head a few times. Before long, the scene became hilarious, and most of us were cracking up. It seemed everyone, even Clay and Gossett, had joined in laughing. I thought this was the first time we were actually in it as a group. Eventually, we got all the racks made.

"Ten-hut," Petty Officer Sabin yelled. "By now, I hope you realize you have no more freedom. There's no calling mommy and daddy. You belong to me and the U.S. Navy. When I tell you to sit, you sit. When I tell you to stand, you stand. When I tell you to jump, you ask how high. From what I've seen so far, most of you will not have what it takes to become a sailor."

He was walking the aisles, glancing at our racks, shaking his head, and looking none too pleased. "Looking at your so-called made-up racks makes my point. It is up to you to prove me wrong. No one, and I mean *no one*, gets a free ride. It takes more than being strong to be a sailor. It takes more than being smart to be a sailor. You are in this together, and the sooner you figure that out, the better your chance to survive." He paused, letting us think about that for a minute.

"You are here for twelve weeks, broken down into four phases. Since you arrived, you have been in Phase One, processing. Phase Two is your initial training, Phase Three is service week, and Phase Four, advanced training leading to graduation. Each phase has goals to achieve. So, what is the goal of Phase One? For the next ten days, you will be doing in-depth preparation for boot camp, which will begin with Phase Two," he said.

"That starts Thursday, April 28, which will be your Week One Day One, referred to as One-One. For those of you who survive, graduation will be Friday, July 1." After one last look around, he said, "Company 220. Lights out in five minutes," turned, and walked out.

I wasted no time getting to the head and back to my rack. The loudspeaker announced, "Taps, Taps, lights out," and the room went dark. I felt a chill throughout my body. The effects from entering that recruiting office with "The Letter" last December were sinking in. Then I heard the bugle playing "Taps." It had a nice ring to it. I smiled and fell sound asleep.

CHAPTER 7

April 27, 1966, San Diego

COMPANY, TEN-HUT, PARADE REST," PETTY OFFICER Sabin shouted. We stood at the base of our bunks that afternoon waiting anxiously for word on what was going on. Dismissed from marching practice early today, we had gone to early chow, then were told to get showered and be by our racks in thirty minutes.

"Today marked the end of your processing," Sabin said. "Much to my surprise, all of you have made it through and will commence Day One-One tomorrow." Although no one made a sound, you could sense the excitement.

"What you have experienced so far is nothing compared to what lies ahead. The next couple of weeks, you will continue to march and drill every day. You will be introduced to your first ship and learn seamanship, damage control, firefighting, and naval terminology. I have brought you in early tonight so you can have some personal time to write your families and prepare any items you think need attention. You can move about and talk among yourselves, but keep it down. I want you fully rested in the morning." He departed.

"Listen up," Janko said. "Before you get started, I want to say a few words. We've had our ups and downs these past ten days, and I think we've all learned a lot about each other and what can and cannot be accepted. For one thing, all of us are advancing, so it proves what we can do as a team. I for one am proud to be part of this company and want to make it the best that Petty Officer Sabin has ever had."

"We're with you, RCPO Janko," Ted Wyler shouted. One thing we learned so far was to address our company leaders by their title, not just last name.

Things were making a little more sense to me now. Earlier today, Sabin had me in the office to go over all the paperwork on each recruit. He said it was his first formal evaluation, and he even discussed some of his concerns with me. "I've come to trust you," he said, "but I want to remind you that what is said in here is between you and me."

"Yes, Petty Officer Sabin."

"Good. I want to be fair to every recruit. Sometimes that means I have to let one go in order to protect the others and our company as a whole. I still have my doubts about Blunck. I don't know if we can make a sailor out of him or not. I know you and the others are helping, but at some point, he has to be on his own. I see that look on your face. Okay, for now I will allow him to advance, but he's on a short leash. I am also concerned about Fox, Howell, Osgood, and Sax. They seem to be struggling to keep up. I want you to start a new demerit chart for every recruit, so everyone starts fresh with zero. If I don't, some will never make it." He smiled. "Any comments?"

"Yes, Petty Officer Sabin. I agree."

He laughed. "To the point, Herman, I like that. By the way, you are also my eyes and ears when I'm not here, and if Janko, Masuda, or Ward express any concerns, I expect you to tell me. One thing I hope to teach you all is, as a leader you are only as good as those around you. Remember that."

That evening, I decided it was a good time to catch Mom and Dad up on what had been happening.

Apr 27, 1966

Hi Mom and Dad,

I finally have a chance to write. Hope you are doing ok, I am. You should have gotten the package with my letter and you know I am in San Diego, not Great Lakes. Wild, huh? It's hot here during the day and cold at night. Saw the mountains and a palm tree for the first time. Now I just see the base we are on.

I'm in a boot camp company with 59 other guys and we have bunks in a big room in an old building. We all got our heads shaved, and we received a seabag full of uniforms and everything else we need here. Our leader is called the Company Commander and his name is Petty Officer Sabin. I volunteered, I know you said not to, Dad, and I am now his Yeoman, or secretary. We get fed three meals a day and they're great. We go to bed at twenty hundred (8 p.m. civilian time) and they get us up at oh four hundred (4 a.m. civilian time). We only use military time now. It seems early for bed but I'm always asleep in minutes. You hear lights out and then a bugle plays "Taps." I like that. My bunk mate is Lyle Ward. He's from Texas and talks slow. Two other guys I met and like are Janko, he's from Iowa, and Masuda, a little Japanese guy from Washington, DC. I guess I'm rambling and you're wondering what we do.

Today we finished what they call stage one, and tomorrow we start actual boot camp. It is called week one, day one. Oh Mom, we graduate July 1 so maybe you can mark your calendar and let everyone know I'll be home around then. Thanks. Anyway, we have been busy getting prepared for tomorrow. I can't write everything so will just give you the good stuff.

We march everywhere. Always double time. Every day we spend two hours practicing in formation and learn all kinds of commands. Everyone carries a rifle except me. As Yeoman, I carry a bayonet and clipboard. I felt stupid at first but getting used to it. Anyway, we do all this practice just to perform on graduation day.

Another big deal is our racks and clothes. Our bunks have to be made a certain way and if it isn't perfect Petty Officer Sabin throws everything on the floor and you start over. Some guys always need help. And our uniforms. We spent half a day just stenciling them and the other half on how to fold them. Everything, even socks, have to be folded a certain way or they get tossed. Oh, and every time there is something wrong you get a demerit. I go with Petty Officer Sabin when he inspects and have to keep track of all demerits and record them. I have a desk in his office to do paperwork. Tomorrow, when we start actual boot camp other Petty Officers will be doing inspections and if you get too many demerits you can get set back and start all over or even get kicked out.

We had another physical. Ready for this? I'm now five-eight, 141 pounds. The biggest guy is six-four, 246 pounds, and his twin brother, yep, twin, is five-six, 168 pounds. They're from Idaho and are fun. The doctor did tell me I will need to get that cyst on my head removed after boot camp. I was afraid they would do it now and I would have to start all over, but he said it could wait for now.

Oh yeah, we got all kinds of shots. It was cool because most of them we got with an air gun. First time I ever saw one of those and I liked it. One shot, though, we got in the thigh. It was in a huge syringe and had the biggest needle I've ever seen. They say it's to prevent every disease *known to man. It reminded me of the glucose shot I got every six months to test for diabetes because of Louie. How is he by the way?*

Oh, this is important. They got us up one morning at oh three hundred, yeah, 3 a.m., and marched us about a mile and then had us take a bunch of written tests. Petty Officer Sabin said these would determine what we will do in the Navy. We find out how we did in a couple weeks so I'll let you know.

We did have one fun thing. We had swim tests and I found out you have to be able to swim 50 yards in order to graduate. I had no problem but 14 of our guys had to have help and failed. Anyway, they have to give up free time and take lessons. I thought everyone knew how to swim. They do in Minnesota. One of the guys from California jumped in and just sank. He told me they live near and play in the ocean all the time, but they ride waves and not many learn to swim. Crazy huh?

Well, I want to get this ready to mail. Oh, Mom, can you send stamps?

Love, Rich

I put my letter on the table by the office with all the others. I didn't think I said anything in my letter to upset Mom and Dad. I left out the bad stuff and didn't tell them any details. A lot sure had happened.

The first morning, Sabin took us for our swim test, where we had to jump from a height of thirty feet into the water and swim fifty yards. I was looking forward to it, but I could tell some guys weren't. There was a bin full of swimsuits, and, after each getting one that fit just well enough it wouldn't fall off, we went to the pool. One by one, we went up a ladder and, when told, jumped in, and swam the length of the pool.

The line was going pretty well when it suddenly stopped. A recruit on the platform stood frozen in place. It was Clay, scared to death. Then, out of nowhere, Blunck appeared behind him. I didn't know what he said, but Clay quickly jumped and, after a few seconds, came thrashing to the top. A sailor on the side of the pool held out a pole and pulled him in. Clay sat there shaking. The sailor went to him, and they went into the locker room.

All eyes were on Blunck. Standing at the top, he said, "Can I go now?" Then, he didn't jump, he *dove* into the pool and swam the fifty yards like a fish. Everyone started clapping and yelling, "Blunck, Blunck, Blunck."

"Company, ten-hut," Sabin yelled. He went down to the end of the pool and got in Blunck's face. "What the hell was that, Blunck? You think you're some kind of Olympic diver or something? Did you not think you could break your neck? Well?"

"That's how I do it at home, Petty Officer Sabin."

"I don't care how you do it at home, Blunck. You're in the Navy now, or have you not figured that out yet? You do it my way. Understood?"

"Yes, Petty Officer Sabin. Do you want me to do it again?" Everyone laughed, which didn't sit well with Sabin.

"No, I do not want you to do it again. And don't you ever pull a stunt like that again. Understood?"

"Yes, Petty Officer Sabin."

"Everyone, at ease. Continue with the swim testing." Sabin went back to the ladder, but on the way, he smiled at me and mouthed, "That was beautiful." Yes, it was. Way to go, Blunck.

Later that day, we were introduced to the "grinder"—an area several blocks square with a tar surface. We soon found out we would spend two hours a day learning how to march properly and to answer drill commands—all in preparation for one thing, graduation. We also learned that some punishments required reporting to and running around the grinder. In other words, the grinder became a big part of our lives.

Back at the barracks, Sabin called us to attention. "One of the most important duties you perform in the Navy is protecting your shipmates," he said. "Tonight, you are going to start standing security watches. One watch will guard outside and the other inside the barracks area. Each watch is two hours." He announced that I would post a Watch Bill on the bulletin board each morning with assignments, Janko would set the watch each night, and Ward would instruct recruits on conducting the watch.

I saw Blunck heading toward his bunk. "Hey, Blunck," I called.

"Oh, hey, Herman."

"I've been meaning to ask you about that day at the pool. Where did you learn to swim like that? And what did you say to Clay to get him to jump?"

"That's nothin'. Been doin' that since I was a kid. Back home it's higher than that where we dive into the quarry. Water deep so you swim or drown. That's how we take a bath most of the time. And I just told Clay he had a big spider on his back."

I laughed. That explained a lot. "Did you write Meemaw tonight? Want some help?"

"Nah. Tell ya the truth, don't wanna bother her. She can't read, and if I write she gonna have to bother someone and ask them to read it to her. She knows I okay. Thanks, Herman. Real nice to offer."

"No problem, Blunck. How's everything else going?"

"Don't know. I sure get yelled at a lot, and I feel bad for you guys if I trouble."

"No problem, Blunck. We're a team. Now, go get some rest."

I thought about what Petty Officer Sabin said we would be doing starting tomorrow. I also thought about the recruits he was concerned about making it through. At least they now had zero demerits. Sabin had told me not everyone was cut out to be a sailor. That didn't mean I couldn't help them do their best.

CHAPTER 8

May 18, 1966, San Diego

WE WERE PREPARING FOR ANOTHER INSPECTION when we heard, "Petty officers, in my office." Sabin now referred to Janko, Masuda, Ward, and me as his petty officers. We responded quickly; this was going to be a very important get-together. "Today marks the end of Phase Two, and by 1200, I will inform Division Headquarters who did and didn't make the cut to continue," Sabin said.

Right after reveille, I had put all of the company personnel sheets on his desk to review. I stayed up late the night before to make sure all the academic grades, demerits, and personal comments were recorded properly. I was so keyed up when I finished, I couldn't sleep, so I wrote home.

May 17, 1966

Hi Mom and Dad,

Before I forget, thanks for writing and sending the stamps. It's great to get mail. I've heard from Mar and Uncle Sherm too. I feel bad for all of the guys who never hear their name at mail call.

Tomorrow is a big day because Phase 2 is ending, and we find out who will and who won't advance. I pretty much know because I keep the records but the final say is Petty Officer Sabin. We lost one guy who had an outstanding arrest warrant for a felony. One day he was just hauled away. A couple guys are in trouble because they failed some written exams or have a lot of demerits and then there is the one guy, I told you about, who just can't do anything right. I really like and try to help him but one thing I am learning is not everyone can make it in the military.

We still do a lot of marching and learning drills to perform at graduation. We are getting pretty good at it too. And we do a lot of physical stuff like push-ups, sit-ups and even some weightlifting. I think I'm in better shape now than I was when I wrestled. Did I tell you Ward was the Texas state wrestling champion at 165 lbs? He thought it was great I was runner-up in Minnesota at 103 lbs. I'm a lot bigger than that now.

I'm learning a new language too. Not really, but it seems like it. Navy lingo. Hatches for doors, deck for floor, head for bathroom, and all sorts of neat stuff. We also had our first experience of being on board a ship and learning firefighting, stopping flooding and manning battle stations. (Don't panic, Mom). It's unbelievable how complicated it is living on a ship. Better get used to it, huh?

One thing I am enjoying is learning all the history of the Navy and its customs. The other day we learned all about Core Values—Honor, Courage and Commitment. I know when the day was over, I sure had a lot of pride to be an American and working on being a U.S. sailor. Hope that doesn't sound too corny. Just the way I feel.

Well, it's almost midnight and I better get some sleep. Be Good and Take Care.

Love, Rich

I put the letter with the outgoing mail. I would never write them everything that happened here as they'd probably worry. Plenty had happened—some of it bad, but a lot of it funny.

The first day of Phase Two, Sabin ordered us to fall out and muster in front of our bunks in five minutes. We were standing by when we heard, "Ten-hut," from a tall, skinny petty officer. "I am First Class Petty Officer Waters, Company 181 commander, and I will be conducting your first personnel inspection."

He walked around for a few minutes before stopping in front of me. "If you're assigned this rack, then you are the company yeoman. Get your demerit board, and log in whatever I tell you. Do you understand?"

"Yes, Petty Officer Waters," I replied.

"We'll start with you." He inspected my bunk and every piece of clothing in my locker. Next, he inspected Ward, Masuda, and Janko. When he started with the other recruits, all hell broke loose. The first rack he came to, he yelled, "Blanket folded wrong, sheet folded wrong, socks on bucket wrong. You getting all this, Yeoman?"

"Yes, Petty Officer Waters." I was writing as fast as I could.

He went to the locker, took out every piece of clothing and, before throwing it on the floor, yelled, "Folded wrong." This happened to all fifty-six recruits he inspected. "RCPO, go get your company commander." Janko ran off, and in less than a minute, he returned with Sabin.

"You wanted to see me, Petty Officer Waters?" Sabin asked.

"Your recruits are pitiful, Petty Officer Sabin. You have a lot of work ahead of you, and it's obvious you won't be winning any awards with these losers. I don't think many of this group will ever see graduation. I sure don't want them in my Navy." And he walked out smiling.

"Company 220, ten-hut," Sabin shouted. "Pick up and restow your belongings. Petty Officers, when you're finished, report to my office, and the rest of you keep working to make sure you have corrected all demerits."

As Waters hadn't disturbed any of our gear, the four of us soon went to Sabin's office. "Well, you have now witnessed what inspections are going to be like from now on," he said. "Yeoman Herman, how many demerits did you log in?"

"I haven't had time to add them up yet, but well over 100 per recruit."

"Figures, that asshole Waters was getting payback for when I inspected his company a few weeks ago. Company 181 is the first in our brigade of forty scheduled to graduate July 1, and we are the last. He's pissed because his company will put in almost a week longer than us, because that's how long it takes to form up 2,400 recruits. Anyway, I know it's a lot of work, Yeoman Herman, but get them all logged in as soon as you can, because your demerit book is also subject to inspection."

I didn't need to hear that. A lot more paperwork and one more thing to keep track of. I could almost see Dad pointing his finger, reminding me that I volunteered even when he told me never to do so.

"This is just a taste of what can be expected, Petty Officers, and I look to you to help me get everyone through. Plus, unlike what Waters said, I expect to win a lot of honors with the company. Understood?"

"Yes, Petty Officer Sabin," we all replied. He always had a way to get us fired up.

I got back to my rack and was thinking how crazy the morning had been, when I noticed two sailors in whites with hard hats, sidearms, and chief master at arms (CMAA) banners on their arms enter the barracks. They marched straight into Sabin's office.

"MAA Ward, Yeoman Herman, and recruit Gossett, my office," Sabin called out. As the three of us entered, one of the CMAAs took out a pair of handcuffs, spun Gossett around, and put them on him.

"Recruit Gossett, you're under military arrest. You are being taken into custody and transported to the brig, pending disposition of an outstanding arrest warrant from the city of Spokane, Washington, for breaking and entering, robbery, and the cause of bodily harm," one CMAA said. "Petty Officer Sabin, we will take all his paperwork and personal belongings at this time."

"Yeoman Herman," Sabin said, "provide the records. MAA Ward, take a pillowcase, go get Gossett's personal effects, and return to the office. And before you take this lowlife away, one question, Gossett. How did you ever think you could get away with being a wanted fugitive and join the Navy?"

Gossett, now shaking and crying, replied, "While I was visiting a cousin in Spokane, I got high on LSD one night and broke into a house. It was a stupid mistake. I was hoping that the police there wouldn't find me in Seattle, especially if I left town and joined the Navy. I would like to stay in the Navy."

"You have to be kidding me, you piece of crap," Sabin said. "I want you marched out of here with the handcuffs showing, so I can make an example out of you. There is no room in my Navy for druggies, especially ones who commit felonies."

Ward returned with the belongings, and the CMAAs marched Gossett out, almost dragging him through the door. There wasn't a sound in the barracks when Sabin turned and said, "For anyone who thinks they can use drugs and use it as an excuse for committing crimes and be in my Navy, you have just witnessed someone who has thrown their life away and will be spending some hard time in federal prison. Let this be a lesson for you. Personnel inspection in five minutes."

There wasn't another day quite that dramatic, but there were days that would never be forgotten. One was when we boarded the training ship USS Recruit (TDE-1). We got to open and close hatches (doors), go up ladders from one deck (floor) to another, tie up the ship with lines (ropes), talk on shipboard phones, learn about firefighting equipment, and see where sailors work and sleep onboard while at sea.

Another unforgettable event came in the middle of the night. Shouting from outside the barracks awakened everyone; then the door flew open. Little Wyler was pushed into the room by Petty Officer Waters, who yelled, "Get me Petty Officer Sabin now." Janko headed that way, and the light in Sabin's office came on. All of us were up now; whatever was happening didn't sound good.

"What's going on?" Sabin said.

"I want this recruit put on report for disrespect, dereliction of duty, and I'll think of some more things," a furious Waters said.

"Wait a minute, Waters," Sabin said. Shocked, I realized he used the name with no title. "First, get your hand off my recruit, and, second, no one is getting put on report until I find out what is going on."

"This recruit was disrespectful to me while on watch, and I want him to pay for it."

"Disrespectful how?"

"I was heading to my barracks, and he challenged who I was. Then he was out of line and disrespected me."

Sabin looked down at Wyler. "That's a serious charge, recruit Wyler. Tell me exactly what happened."

"Yes, Petty Officer Sabin," Wyler said calmly. "I was standing security watch outside when I heard someone coming. I called out to halt and identify yourself. I then heard someone say, 'It's Superman,' so I said, 'Well, fly your super ass over here and be identified.' The next thing I know is Petty Officer Waters grabbed me, and, well, here we are." Everyone tried to keep from laughing, but Sabin couldn't control himself and cracked up. Then Waters got even more infuriated.

"Sabin, I demand you put him on report." *Last name only again.*

"Waters, I'm not putting anyone on report for standing his watch and challenging a potential intruder. I will talk to him and deal with it; now please get out of here."

"You haven't heard the end of this," Waters shouted. "That recruit doesn't belong here, and I'm going to see to it he is set back to start all over." He stormed out. I had the feeling we would be seeing more of him, unfortunately.

We spent more time in the classroom than I thought we would. Our instructors were all sailors and very good. Most of them were in the classroom with us; however, we did get some lectures on a cool new system the Navy was trying called Closed Circuit Television (CCTV). Instructors in rooms all over the base and other commands—one onboard a ship in the Pacific—came to us on a TV screen.

We had personnel inspections every day, and, after that Day One-One disaster, we got a lot better and the demerits a lot fewer. However, one thing became clear as I logged in our results each day. It was the same guys, and always Blunck, getting the bad marks. I was sitting in the office with Janko, Masuda, and Ward when Sabin entered.

"My job is to train recruits and prepare them for joining the active duty forces where the Navy needs them," he told us. "Part of this job is to weed out those I think need extra help before they move to the next stage. As you know, recruit Gossett, a druggie and felon, will be gone forever. I have also recommended three more to be removed from the company and reevaluated. I'm proud of how you all have worked together trying to get everyone in the company through, and this is no reflection of those efforts. I want you to know that recruit Tommy Wyler is not on the list. I will probably hear about it, but I think he's worth keeping, and I'm willing to go to bat for him. The three recruits on the list are Fox, Osgood, and Blunck." He paused.

I was hoping Janko would speak up first, and he did. "I believe that is a very fair list, Petty Officer Sabin, and I think we are all relieved you are keeping recruit Little Wyler. Sorry, that's what we call him."

We laughed, and Sabin said, "Keep that between us. Yeah, it was a tough call, but the Navy needs guys like him, and I don't care what Petty Officer Waters tries to pull, I'll fight to keep him. I'm also keeping recruits Clay, Howell, and Sax. They will remain on my short leash, but I think they have a chance to turn things around with your help. And, guys, I'm sorry about recruit Blunck, but he just isn't fit for the military, and it would be unfair to keep him any longer. He did his best and can go home with his head held high. I know you'll all make him know that."

He sent Ward to bring in the three recruits. "Recruit Blunck, recruit Fox, and recruit Osgood, you will not be going forward with Company 220," Sabin said. "I am recommending you be reevaluated by an assessment team who will determine your future with the Navy. I want to let you know that I am proud of your efforts these past few weeks, I have put remarks to reflect that in your records, and I wish you well. Please pack your seabags, and accompany Yeoman Herman to headquarters."

"Yes, Petty Officer Sabin," they all replied.

He instructed me to escort the recruits, when packed, and deliver his decision to headquarters, waiting for a reply before returning. He handed me the list of recruits who would be advancing to Phase Three.

In the barracks, I found everyone standing and watching. As the packing began, each recruit came over and shook hands with Blunck, Fox, and Osgood, and I even saw a few hugs.

It was a quiet march to Headquarters, and when we were just about there, Blunck stopped. "I'm sorry," he said, "for being a problem, Herman, and I want to thank you for everything you done for me. You been so nice."

"It was my pleasure, Blunck. You're a great guy and a good friend. You go home and be proud of what you have done, and you can tell Meemaw I said hello. I think you're going to be a lot happier back home with your family."

With a big smile, he picked me up and hugged me. We continued with nothing else being said.

About an hour later, I returned and handed Sabin the reply from Headquarters, and he addressed the company. "Congratulations, men, if you are in this room, it means you have successfully completed Phase Two and will commence Phase Three, service week." A loud cheer went up before we quickly got back to attention.

"During service week, also known as Hell Week, you will be working the galley," Sabin said. "You'll also meet with a specialist to go over your exam scores to determine where you may be best suited to work in the Navy. Yeoman Herman will post all these assignments on the bulletin board tomorrow. I don't say this often, but you are making me proud to be your commander. I expect even more from you in the coming weeks, and I expect Company 220 to be the winningest company of awards ever given. You are going to find service week one of the hardest there is in boot camp. Tonight, I want you to take some time to write your loved ones and relax. Tomorrow, your petty officers, minus Yeoman Herman, will lead you in sports challenges for the day. Have some fun. Dismissed."

The room exploded with cheers. "Petty Officer Sabin, we're number one! Petty Officer Sabin, we're number one!"

As the celebrating went on, I slipped out into the office. The reason I'd miss the sports the next day was that I had to meet with the galley CMAA and work out assignments, then meet with the leading assignment specialist to work on scheduling interviews. More paperwork would involve recording the results of all interviews and submitting the final "Dream Sheets" on where each recruit would like to be assigned upon graduation. That night, I focused on the individual interviews. Every guy had worked hard to make the cut and advance to Phase Three. I felt responsible to make sure he was prepared, as his next four years in the Navy could be determined here. I worked until I thought each record was thoroughly ready— finally realizing it was past lights out.

CHAPTER 9

THE NIGHT BEFORE SERVICE WEEK STARTED, SABIN met with us petty officers, and we discussed the galley assignments and the interviews with the assignment specialists. Each of us went over our particular responsibilities for this tough week. At the end of the meeting, Sabin sent me and Ward out to stand by the bulletin board so I could answer any questions about the recruits' assignments.

I waited while Ward told everyone what was going on. I was smiling when Ward came up. "I spread the word," he said. "Now let's see if anyone comes up here. What you smiling about?"

"Nothing," I said. "Just glad we're about to get this week started so we can get it over."

Ward nodded in agreement. "Be careful what you wish for," he added. I didn't know how accurate this comment would be until the next day.

At the end of our bunks, each of us had a bucket hung to hold our washed socks to dry, along with our scrub brush. The next morning when reveille sounded, for some reason I jumped up, hitting my head on the bucket. At first, I didn't think it was a big deal, then I felt the blood run down my forehead and start to get into my eye. I sat on the edge of my rack, and suddenly Petty Officer Sabin was standing before me.

"What the hell happened, Herman?" he asked.

"Just hit my head, but I think I cut that cyst," I replied weakly. I wasn't feeling so good.

"MAA Ward, help him get dressed and over to sick bay. Stay with him until he's seen, then report back to me."

"I need to get everyone to their assignments," I said.

"RCPO Janko and RLPO Masuda will take over until you return, Yeoman Herman," Sabin said, "It's called teamwork. Just get yourself taken care of. Now go."

We made it to sick bay, and Ward helped me in. A sailor was taking my information when the blood and white fluid started to gush forward.

"What the hell, corpsman to the front desk," I heard someone yell.

A sailor in whites came running out, took one look at me, and said, "Get him to Bay Number One, *now*!" The next thing I knew, I was lying on a bed, and some guy was looking at my head.

"I'm Doctor Lindsey. How long have you had that cyst on your head?" he asked.

"Long as I remember."

"Well, it seems to be cut pretty bad, so I'm going to remove it. It isn't too big, so it shouldn't be a problem, and I don't think you'll need any anesthetic. I'll just get hold of it and cut the roots. Should come right out. Okay with you?"

"Sure." Did I have a choice?

I felt the doctor putting what looked like tweezers into my head and pull. Then I saw a bright white light, and excruciating pain hit me.

"Oh shit!" the doctor said. "This thing is huge, and his scalp has split. Corpsman, get a bandage on that now. Stop the bleeding. Damn, never seen anything like this."

I lay there while the corpsman held one bandage after another to my head. The pain was still unbelievable.

"You doing okay, son?" the doctor asked. "Sorry about that. That cyst appeared small on the surface, but it was filling with fluid and growing fast beneath the scalp. It was just a matter of time before it became a real problem and could have even affected your brain. You're lucky you cut it today—who knows what might have happened if it continued to grow? Would you like to see it?" He held up a jar containing what looked like a small brain about the size of a golf ball with a bunch of tentacles floating around it. I threw up.

I must have passed out, and when I woke with a throbbing headache, Sabin stood by my bed talking to the doctor.

"Look, Petty Officer Sabin," Doctor Lindsey said, "as I told MAA Ward to tell you, recruit Herman has a hole in his head. It can't be stitched and must heal from the inside out. He will need his bandages changed twice a day and cannot do any physical exercise for at least ten days. As his doctor, I recommend he be set back for two weeks and placed in another company. What's the big deal anyway? You have hundreds, if not thousands, of recruits come through here, and you have set back your fair share, I hear."

"Recruit Herman is not just any recruit, Doctor Lindsey," Sabin said. "He is an essential part of my company and has worked hard since day one. Honestly, he is not only the best yeoman I have ever had, he is one of the best sailors, and I want him to return to the company and be the example to others on what can be achieved through hard work and that we look after our own. It's what we're all about, Doc."

"Tell you what," the doctor said. "He has to be here twice a day for a bandage change and wound check, and he must be on light duty until I clear him. I'm trusting you, Petty Officer Sabin." Then he laughed. "I don't think in five years as head of this medical facility, I have ever heard of a company commander marching into this clinic and going out of his way to help a recruit. Corpsman, get me the paperwork to sign so these two can get back to what they're supposed to be doing." He then looked straight at me. "Don't let us down, recruit Herman."

When we got back to the barracks, Sabin said, "We're going to do exactly what the doctor ordered, Herman. Don't let what you heard back there affect your head. I did what I needed to get you back here. I just didn't want to break in a new yeoman. Now go get some rest. We clear?"

"Yes, Petty Officer Sabin." I tried not to let him see me smile.
May 25, 1966

Hi Mom and Dad,

Today is the last day of Phase III, Service Week, and I thought I'd tell you what has happened since I wrote you last week. First, everything is fine and I'm ok. Remember that cyst on my head that I've had forever? Well, 2 days after I wrote you it broke open and I had to have it removed. It was a mess and it turned out to be bigger than anyone thought. Anyway, the doctor pulled it out and it left a hole in my head, so I had to go to sick bay every morning and night to get it checked and new packing put in. Each time they put a little less and it healed from the inside. The doctor said I was lucky it didn't get any bigger before it was removed, so that's a good thing. I was worried because the doctor wanted to set me back 2 weeks to heal, which means I would have left Company 220 and started over. But guess what? My Company Commander, Petty Officer Sabin, told the doctor that he wanted me to stay in 220 because I was doing so well and he needed me as his Yeoman. The doctor said ok, and was I ever happy. I don't remember anyone ever doing something like that for me before, so I really owe Petty Officer Sabin. I was on light duty so all the guys pitched in and I think we're all a lot closer now.

Now, some important stuff. Remember I told you we took a bunch of tests at 3 in the morning and that they would determine what we do in the Navy? This past week we got our results to review and then everyone met with a person who helped us decide what we may be good at. I scored high in math, clerical and radio. I had low scores in mechanical, shop practices and foreign language. After talking with the specialist, I asked for administrative jobs like yeoman or something in communications. Petty Officer Sabin said the Navy is going to put me where they want me, but it's nice to ask anyway. We won't find anything out now until we get orders the week before we graduate.

Oh yeah, I saw the doctor today, and I'm all healed up and back to full duty. I'm glad because today is the end of Service Week and tomorrow, we start Phase IV, which is our advanced training. We're also going to be getting fitted with all our dress uniforms and have pictures taken. Should be fun.

Be Good and Take Care.

Love, Rich

The last evening of service week, I was finishing my letter home when I heard the guys coming, so I placed the envelope in the mail, then followed Sabin into the office.

"I've been cleared for full duty, Petty Officer Sabin," I said, handing him the paperwork from the doctor.

"That's great," he said. "It looks like you can join in for Phase Four after all. Congratulations. Now, have RCPO Janko get everyone together in five minutes"

Within minutes, we stood at attention. "At ease," Sabin said. "Well, guys. You did it. You survived service week and—"

"Attention on deck." We all jumped to attention, including Petty Officer Sabin, and saw a chief petty officer at the door. "Division Commander, arriving." I wasn't sure if this was a good or a bad thing.

Sabin walked forward and saluted our division commander, Lt. Lewis. "Company 220, standing by for inspection, SIR."

"At ease, recruits," Lt. Lewis said. He stopped in the middle of the room. "Gather round." We were a little hesitant, but Janko took charge and moved forward and knelt down. We all followed. Lt. Lewis looked down at Janko. "Petty Officer Sabin, this must be RCPO Janko I've heard so much about. Natural leader."

"Yes, sir," Sabin said, with pride in his voice.

"Recruits," Lt. Lewis continued, "Not often in my job as your division commander do I get to see the recruits unless it's for a negative reason. Today, I get to visit your company for a positive one. Petty Officer Sabin, Company 220 is the first company in the last two years to meet one hundred percent of their duty assignments during service week. The galley commander and his staff even requested that your company be given another week so that they can enjoy another seven days of smooth operations. Like that is going to happen." Everyone laughed and clapped.

"Also, Company 220 is the first company this year that had every recruit show up for his appointment with an assignment specialist on time. I had my aide, Chief Doty, look into it and he learned that your Yeoman Herman apparently went above and beyond and, along with your other petty officers, made sure each recruit was counseled on trying to get a job they may like. Petty Officer Sabin, I came here to personally congratulate you on the progress you and Company 220 have made so far. I look forward to hearing what else you achieve as you enter Phase Four tomorrow."

After the lieutenant and chief had departed, Sabin said, "Well, guys, that is a first. The division commander never comes to the recruits. It's always the other way around. You can be very proud of that. Now, where was I before we were interrupted?" He paused for the laughter.

"Tomorrow you start Phase Four, advanced training. Word is going to pass around fast that the division commander came here today, and all eyes will be on you. Don't let up. Tonight, I am going to give you free time; I hope you all write home. Before I dismiss you, I have some more good news. Not only has Yeoman Herman been found fit for full duty, tomorrow he will be authorized to start giving out phone chits so you can all call home."

Sabin left, and the room erupted in cheers and back slapping. Little Wyler jumped on his brother's back and started riding him around the barracks like a horse, slapping him on the butt and head.

My own head was still sore and healing, so I took it easy. I wished Petty Officer Sabin had waited before saying anything about phone chits, but the guys deserved to know, even if it meant I'd be hounded by everyone thinking they should be first.

After evening chow, everyone kept themselves busy getting their gear folded and uniforms looking good. I got an idea and asked Janko, Masuda, and Ward to join me in the office.

"Hey, guys," I said. "You heard Petty Officer Sabin tell everyone I had the phone chits and could start giving them out. I know everyone wants to be first, and I don't want to be accused of showing favoritism." I described my idea. When we returned to the barracks,

Janko announced I would explain the plan and that all the petty officers agreed with it.

"I have fifty-six pieces of paper here with the numbers one through fifty-six," I said. "I also have a master phone list with everyone's name. You'll come up one at a time, pull a number, and I'll record that by your name. Everyone has the same chance to get number one as they do number fifty-six. After we're done, you may trade numbers, and I will adjust the master list. When headquarters provides me the times calls will be authorized, I'll assign the times and let you know. Any questions?"

"You rock, Yeoman Herman. Let's do it," someone yelled. We drew numbers, some made trades, and within an hour I had a Master Phone Call List. I headed to the office to do never-ending paperwork. When Sabin stopped by, I told him what we had done, and he just shook his head.

"You're something else," he said, looking over the list. "Why hadn't anyone else ever thought of something like this? Usually, fights break out over getting a phone chit, and someone is always complaining. What, you got number forty-three?" He laughed.

"I know. RCPO Janko got thirty-one, so I think everyone knows it was fair. The funny draw, though, was when Big Wyler got number eight, and Little Wyler got number fifty-one and threatened him if he didn't trade. It was hilarious. We sure are glad you stood up to Petty Officer Waters and fought to keep Little Wyler."

"You'll find the longer you hang around this outfit that you get a feel for those that are going to make great sailors and shipmates," he said. "Why don't you knock off for the night, grab a shower, and get some rest? Tomorrow is the start of busy weeks, and I think you're still a little shaky."

"Thanks, Petty Officer Sabin. Think I'll take you up on that."

CHAPTER 10

July 1966, San Diego

THE LAST FEW WEEKS FLEW BY, AND NOW, ONE WEEK from graduation, the company was doing field day in preparation for our final graded barracks inspection. Earlier, Petty Officer Sabin had me place all the recruit service records on his desk, and he was in there all morning. He directed Janko, Masuda, and Ward to supervise the field day and had me stand by to answer any questions.

June 1, 1966

Hi Mom and Dad,

I'm finally getting a chance to write. First, thanks for the letters, they mean a lot. You asked about when I will call home. My turn should be next week but, I won't know exactly what time so hope someone is home when I call. I don't know how much time I have right now so will tell you what I can about what we are doing.

We always march and drill and do lots of physical training so won't bore you with that anymore. It is paying off though and I think I'm getting bigger every day. One fun thing we did was we went to the rifle range and were trained to be marksmen. We took the bus so we were off base for the first time. We shot an M-1, which is just a little bigger than the 30 ought 6 we use hunting so I didn't have any trouble qualifying at 200 yards. Then we went to fire fighting. They put us in a building and then set it on fire and we had to put it out. It wasn't easy but we did it.

I sure have a lot more respect for firemen now. I'll tell you more about it when I come home.

We got our last shots too. Or I should say guys going to ships or overseas got them. I didn't get any, and Petty Officer Sabin said that was because I was guaranteed a school when I enlisted so will receive orders somewhere in the States. I'd forgotten about that.

We spend a lot of time in classrooms too. There's actually a final written exam we take. It's 150 questions and you have to score 75 to pass. They show us a lot of films about living on a ship. It's like living in your own little city and it takes all kinds of different jobs, called ratings, to make it work. Just learning the names of all the equipment onboard and what it's used for is hard. And we learn all about the history of the Navy and all the great battles and leaders there have been. I enjoy the history.

Want to get this in mail so will close for now. Be Good and Take Care.

Love, Rich

Jun 10, 1966

Hi Home,

It was great talking to you and I was so happy you were both there. I guess I rambled so hope you didn't get too confused on everything I talked about.

Only two weeks before graduation and we're all getting pretty excited. Remember I told you about all the written tests we had coming? Well, everyone passed so far and we are in the running for top Academic Company. Petty Officer Sabin said we would be his first company to ever do that. He confided in me that any recruit that is set back before Phase 3 doesn't count for overall company performance or his record, but now they do. We want him to win Top Commander. A couple guys were close to failing so some of us helped them study and I guess that paid off. We still have one final written exam to take so wish us luck. And my bunkmate Ward spent a lot of his off time helping guys get their lockers and uniforms squared away, and that worked too because we had very few demerits on the barracks and personnel inspection and passed with flying colors.

Oh, that water survival training I told you we were going to have. I had a good time and I learned that almost every piece of our uniform is designed so that it could help save our lives if we ever abandon ship. We had to jump into the pool again from 30 feet, only this time in our dungarees. We practiced taking off our pants and tying the bottoms of the legs together. Then we trapped air in the legs and used them as a flotation device. We turned our hats inside out and trapped air in them, then our shirts. By the time I was done I could use everything to float for hours while waiting to be rescued. A couple guys had a hard time but some of us helped them and we all got through it. The instructor told us this is exactly what we could expect in real life because someone was bound to be hurt and need help. We all felt great when we got out of the pool and were hugging each other. It was neat.

Like I told you, we got our dress uniforms back from the tailor shop and had our pictures taken. I'll send you some copies. And I got paid for the first time. I got $30 and paid for the pictures, tailoring of my uniform to get the stripes put on right, and for our company book called The Anchor. We get paid again before graduation and I'll use that for my plane tickets home. Still think I will fly standby so I can save my money. I'll let you know the flight info when I get it. Getting close now.

Be Good and Take Care.

Love, Rich

I snapped to when I heard Petty Officer Sabin say, "Yeoman Herman, come in here," and I entered the office.

"I've gone through all these records, and they look excellent. The only thing missing now is the last scores, which we won't have until

Monday afternoon after your final exams. Speaking of which, I was hoping you may be able to help here." He explained his concerns about a few recruits with poor grades and that he was hoping this company would be the one where everyone passed the final exam. I told him I would think of something if he'd give me an hour or so.

Later, Sabin brought the other petty officers into the office. "I trust that the barracks is ready for inspection tomorrow," he said. "I don't want any surprises." Janko, Masuda, and Ward all gave a thumbs-up. "Good. Before graduation there is one last obstacle, the final written exam. Yeoman Herman and I want to discuss something with you." He had me lay out my plan and asked them for their help.

Sabin entered the barracks soon afterward. "At ease, men. Gather round and get comfortable. A week from today, all of you who pass your final written exam will graduate. You have been a great company, and I hope to see every recruit pass. I have discussed this with your petty officers, and they have asked that all planned activities for the rest of the day and tomorrow, except security watches, be suspended and that free time be given to study for the exam. Yeoman Herman has figured out the best way to achieve this goal and will lay out the plan when I depart."

I began, "I have gone through all test scores from day one and broken down the areas we'll be tested on. I've assigned a tutor who has shown strength on the subject and have listed the recruits that need help on the subject and given them times for study with the tutor. You may be surprised at some of the tutors. Like Clay." I saw quite a few startled faces. "Clay has the best scores and demonstrated the best knowledge of firefighting and damage control, so makes sense he helps those who are weak. Agree?"

"What? I don't know how to teach," Clay said.

"Just answer their questions, Clay," Janko said. "It'll really help out."

You could almost see the confidence rise in Clay, and he smiled. "For all that you guys have done for me, I'll do my best." Everyone started clapping.

"Okay, one more thing," I said. "We have a chance to win the

Academic Award, which is the top award given in boot camp. This is important to Petty Officer Sabin. I think we all will agree he's been a great company commander, and I, for one, want to see him beat out Petty Officer Waters for top honor. Now, I'm going to post the lists. Let's do this."

For the rest of the weekend, with the exception of chow, head breaks, and sleep, we studied in our assigned groups. We had our final exam Monday, and that afternoon everyone anxiously awaited the results. We were preparing for tomorrow's last graded barracks inspection, but you could feel the tension in the room, and no one was putting a lot of effort into cleaning. Finally, Sabin walked in, showing no expression at all.

"Ten-hut, at ease," he said. "First of all, I want you to know that I think you all tried your best and worked hard getting ready for your exams. You may not know it, but I've never had a company where all recruits pass. Wait, did I say *never*? Not anymore. You did it! You all passed and have won the Academic Award."

The room exploded with shouts, "We're number one!"

Finally, Sabin said, "Not only did you all pass, the exam officer said you also scored the highest mark ever recorded in firefighting and damage control."

The guys mobbed Clay and were slapping him on the back while I explained to Sabin about his being the company tutor for that area. Sabin said, "Recruit Clay, front and center." Reluctantly, Clay stepped forward. "We're proud of you, recruit Clay, and it just shows what you are capable of."

Suddenly, Little Wyler walked up to Clay. He said, "Thank you, Clay," and then jumped up and smacked him on the back of the head. Even Sabin joined in the laughter.

"Okay, recruits," Sabin finally said. "I'm putting RCPO Janko in charge to make sure the barracks is ready for tomorrow's inspection, and, when he is satisfied, he will give you the rest of the night for free time."

Before departing, he handed me the exam results to enter into the recruits' records. I updated all the records. No surprise, Janko scored the highest and Masuda second. I did okay, the fifth highest. After I finished, I came back in the barracks and wrote a note home.

Jun 20, 1966

Hi Folks

Just a quick note to let you know we did it. We had our final exam and everyone passed. I came in fifth. Our company also won the Academic Award which is the highest one given. Tomorrow we have our final barracks inspection and then we spend the next few days practicing for graduation Friday and getting our uniforms ready. I wish you could be here but I know that's not possible. It is supposed to be in the nineties so we're going to be miserable in dress blues and just hope no one passes out marching.

Sunday, we get our first liberty pass. This means we get four hours to go off base on our own. We can either go to the San Diego Zoo or a place called Balboa Park. Most guys are going to the zoo because they say it's the best in the world. I can't tell anyone, but Petty Officer Sabin and his girlfriend are taking me to the beach to let me swim in the ocean. He couldn't believe I'd never seen the ocean so thought I'd like to jump in. Anyway, he said as long as I didn't tell anyone he could sneak me out. Should be fun.

All for now. We should get orders soon so will let you know where I am going.

Be Good and Take Care.

Love, Rich

After our final inspection, Sabin had us all fall in by our bunks. "Good news. Your orders have arrived," he said. "I'm going to sort them out with Yeoman Herman and then hand them out. Take your time reading them, and I will be available to go over them with you individually. I'm canceling this afternoon's graduation practice and giving you free time to look over your orders, talk to me, and then write home or start making plans."

Entering the office, I could hardly wait to see my orders but knew I had to record all the others, so I had him hold onto mine until I was done. Finally, as he left the office with the other orders, he handed me mine and said, "Congratulations, you're going to be a radioman." I didn't know what that meant.

I looked at the words on the paper: *Report to Naval Training Center San Diego, Ca., 17 July 1966 for further transfer to Radioman A School upon completion of Basic Electronics School, San Diego Ca.* Sabin returned and said, "Radioman is a good rating, and you can advance fast. I think you'll like it, and you're coming back here for about six months of schools, so that's great."

I nodded but didn't say anything. The rest of the afternoon, Sabin talked to everyone about their orders. Turned out only seven of us got schools, so I was happy I was one of them. Janko got Yeoman School, my first choice; Masuda would be going to a language school; Ward got shore duty in Seattle.

Friday came, and on a gorgeous, hot, sunny day, we graduated. We marched and performed our drills flawlessly. Finally, all the companies formed up and came to attention before the viewing platform, where we rendered honors to our commanding officer. He gave a speech, and our company was recognized, along with others, with several awards. Then, Petty Officer Sabin was called forward, and he was presented the Academic Flag, the top award given.

Jun 27, 1966

Hi There

So much has happened I don't know where to start. We all survived the heat and have graduated. It was a grand ceremony and there must have been a thousand people watching. During the ceremony, the Academic Flag was handed to Petty Officer Sabin and I got to march with it because I am the company Yeoman. That was great, but I think the highlight of the day was when we got back to the barracks and before we were dismissed our Division Officer came in and gave out the Top

Recruit award to Little Wyler. I told you about him and his twin brother. Anyway, it was neat.

Now, the big news. I got my orders! I am going to Radioman School for 18 weeks here in San Diego. It's not the occupation I asked for as my first choice, but Petty Officer Sabin said it's a very good rating and I can move up fast. I was disappointed at first but now I'm happy with it. The school starts in August but I have to report back here by 17 July.

I've decided to pay full fare to fly home. I don't want to take a chance and not get a flight right away and end up sitting at the airport. I know it's expensive, $105, but I'm anxious to get home. I'll work out the money with you, Mom, when I'm home.

We had our final physicals and received approval to accept our orders. Are you sitting down? I weigh 162 pounds and I'm 5'11". Yep, I've gained over 40 pounds and grown about five inches since I joined the Navy. You always said you grew late, Dad, so I guess it's a Herman thing. Eleven weeks of eating great and working out every day pays off. Anyway, look for the new me when I get home.

The next couple days we'll be making plane reservations, getting our records updated for emergency data and making sure all the paperwork is correct, and I'm even attending classes on pay and benefits and how to manage my money. It's amazing how many guys have never written a check or had a savings account. We also will attend classes on "Conduct Ashore" and "Personal Responsibilities." So, I'll be busy.

I'll let you know my flight arrangements as soon as I make them.

Be Good and Take Care.

Love, Rich

Hard to believe, it was my last night of boot camp. The day was filled with saying goodbye to everyone. I was going to miss some of these guys. Janko, Masuda, Ward, and I had been through a lot in a short time. I would even miss Clay. Of all the guys here, he seemed to have changed the most; I liked him now. And the Wyler twins. I had so many stories to tell about them. And, of course, Petty Officer Sabin. When I was in the office packing everything up and sealing everyone's records, he came in and told me to close the door.

"Herman, I don't usually get too close to my recruits, but you're one of a kind. I want you to know something. There is a good chance I'll be selected for advancement to chief when the board meets next month. I'm young, have a good record, and graduating a class like Company 220 will definitely help. Being a chief is what I want more than anything. I think if you stick around long enough, you will make chief with no problem. I also want you to consider something else. Officer programs.

"I have never had a recruit who is so well rounded," he said. "Not only are you an admin whiz, everyone likes you and, more importantly, respects you. You're fair, yet don't take crap from anyone. You can take a lot of credit for the success of this company. Yeah, the other petty officers too, but they seem to follow your lead. Anyway, just wanted you to know, and if you ever decide to make the Navy a career and need a letter of recommendation, just ask." I thanked him, we shook hands, and he left.

Eleven weeks ago, I came to San Diego a civilian, not knowing what to expect. Now, I'd be leaving as a U.S. Navy seaman apprentice, E-2, in my dress blue uniform. I couldn't wait to get off that plane. I'd called to tell Mom the flight time, and she said they would be there to pick me up. I felt I would have a hard time sleeping tonight. I thought about what Sabin had said. Making the Navy a career had never entered my head, let alone being a chief petty officer or even an officer. Someone could actually do this for twenty or even thirty years?

CHAPTER 11

July 1, 1966, Minneapolis

I WAS SO EXCITED I COULD HARDLY STAND IT BUT waited to get off the plane to make my parents wonder if I made the flight. Good thing I paid full fare. Being the Fourth of July weekend, planes were packed. Finally, I decided it was time.

As I walked into the terminal, I saw Mom and Dad looking for me. And there were Irving and Margy, Mom's brother and wife, who helped raise me; I had stayed with them a lot when my parents commuted to Rochester, while Louie was at Mayo Clinic. Their daughter Jackie, my favorite cousin, only one year younger than me, was here too, with her husband, Gary. No one appeared to recognize me, and I walked right past them. As they kept looking at the door, I said, "Hi, guys." Jackie turned first and came running to hug me.

"I didn't see you," she said. "Wow, have you changed."

"Where's Sonya?" I asked. Their daughter was born about a month before I left for boot camp.

"Aunt Agda and Aunt Betty are spoiling her—you'll see her Sunday."

"Hey, little guy," said Gary, standing about six-foot-three and 250 pounds. He shook my hand, smiling. "You finally grew up." Everyone laughed.

The whole family started hugging me, and tears were flowing. "You have grown." Dad said, looking me straight in the eye.

"It's great to be home," I said. "Can't wait to get to the house and tell everyone about boot camp and catch up. Anyone else here?"

Mom hooked her arm into mine. "Louie is at work, and Mar

and Jim will try and make it up this weekend," she said. Marlys and Jim now lived in Milwaukee. I hoped this was far enough away they didn't have to deal with Louie's problems as I had.

On Sunday, most of our friends and relatives came to the open house held in my honor. Harry Newsom and his wife, Gladys, even showed up. Harry was a bully in the CCC camp when he and my dad met. My dad stood up to him and got his butt kicked, but they had been best friends since that day. Their son, Mark, was in the Navy stationed in Norfolk, Virginia. They hoped we might run into each other someday. Like what were the odds of that happening?

Uncle Sherm didn't show, and I missed not being able to talk to him. He and Denise had gotten married last month, and I didn't even know until now. Maybe they were too busy to see me.

Missing from the get-together were my closest friends. Darrell was off on one of his many adventures, this time in Alaska. Although Darrell had that kind of personality that draws everyone to him and was instantly liked, he was a true loner, and I was probably his only close friend. Tommy Gilmore, who bought my 1957 Chevy and became a good buddy, had been drafted and was at basic training in Kentucky. And Todd had joined the Marines a month after I joined the Navy and was at boot camp in San Diego. I'd wanted him to go with me, but Todd wanted to be a Marine.

One night, Dad came into my room and said, "I know you think I'm upset that you joined the Navy, but I want you to know your mother and I are proud of you. When you pick me up from work tomorrow, would you mind coming a little early and wear your uniform? I'd like the guys to see you."

"Absolutely," I said.

Wearing my dress blues, I parked the family car by the loading dock the next day at George A. Clark & Sons, one of the country's largest suppliers of wholesale pump and well parts. Whenever here, I always felt I was visiting an immense hardware store. Dad had been with them twenty-six years and was warehouse manager. All of his guys were hard-working, blue-collar members of the Teamsters Union; most were of Polish or Italian descent. They'd lived through or grown up during the Depression and were proud to be Americans. Leo Bozack, Dad's foreman, was the first to see me and almost crushed me with his bear hug. It took us nearly an hour to greet everyone, and on the way home, I could tell Dad enjoyed showing me off.

My leave ended all too soon. After fourteen days, I flew back to San Diego to attend Basic Electricity and Electronics Preparations (BEEP) School. I adjusted easily to the school schedule. I hooked up with Petty Officer Sabin, and we got together several times and played golf or bowled. He was a lot better golfer than me, but he couldn't match me on the lanes.

I graduated from BEEP school with honors September 2 and started Radioman "A" School the following Monday. The first thing I had to learn was Morse Code. I remembered Dad trying to teach me when I was in scouting, but I never tried very hard. Now, I wished I had. We started by yelling out the alphabet with dits and dahs. "Dit dah, *alpha*," we would yell. "Dah dit, *bravo*," and on through all twenty-six letters. We did this for hours; after a while I wanted to scream, and some did. Eventually, we started listening to the code through earphones and typing it out on a typewriter. Here, I had a big advantage because I took typing in high school; I quickly picked up speed.

Our days were split into learning code and the Radioman Rating, which included electronics, equipment, and messaging. Over the next fourteen weeks, I became proficient and led the class copying code, at twenty-four words per minute. After taking the exam, I was advanced to seaman, an E-3, getting a twenty-dollar-a-month pay raise.

The next day I received my transfer orders to USS Cambria (APA-36), Norfolk, Virginia. I had to report December 30, 1966. I called home that night and told them the good news about my advancement, and they were happy for me. Then I told them about my orders to a ship homeported in Norfolk.

I graduated with honors, second in class overall, on December 9, earning the designator for radioman, RM. I left for home on leave the next day wearing dress blues with three white slanted stripes and a lightning insignia above on my left arm. I was now Radioman Seaman (RMSN) Herman.

It was good to be home for the holidays. Once again, Darrell was gone. His dad said he was in Mexico and wasn't sure when he would be back. I wondered what he did for money. I probably didn't want to know. Tommy Gilmore was in advanced Army training somewhere and couldn't get furlough. I worried for him because I knew he could be headed for Vietnam. His mother said she would tell him I called.

Todd, now a lance corporal stationed in Seattle, Washington, came home on leave two days after me, and I went with his parents to meet him at the airport. We hadn't managed to get together while in San Diego, so we caught up on the ride home, telling each other what it was like being a sailor and Marine. Later, he left to see his girlfriend, Pam, and said he'd give me a call.

I got that call two days later, and Todd said he and Pam were having some problems. Since junior high school, they'd been on again, off again, so I didn't think much of it. He said he had met a girl at the bowling alley and asked her out. She said she'd go, but only with another couple; if he had someone to go with her roommate, it was a date. I had to laugh. I lost count of the times in high school when Pam would ask me to go with her best friend so her parents would allow her to date Todd. I told him sure, set it up.

That evening, hoping to impress our dates, Todd and I wore our dress uniforms. With hats in hand, we knocked on the apartment door. A tall, good-looking blonde opened the door, called for her friend, and then the two of them burst out laughing. The blonde said, "You don't think we're going to go out with you looking like that, do you? If I knew you were in the military, I wouldn't have said yes. We don't date baby-killers." She slammed the door.

Todd was fiery red. Knowing his temper, I said, "Come on, let's get out of here. We don't need them, Todd. Besides, you got Pam. Just think of Pam." The veins in his temple were about to burst, so I dragged him away. Luckily, I was driving. He never said a word on the way home. When we got there, I got us a beer and finally managed a laugh.

"You know, I've heard of that happening before. It's just the way things are, Todd. I knew when I got my draft notice and decided to join the Navy, and you knew when you joined the Marines, it was a choice. Well, I'm proud of our choices and proud to wear these uniforms. The hell with them."

"I know," Todd finally said. "It just hit me hard, that's all, and makes me mad. Stupid bitches. Sorry I got you into this mess."

"What, and let you have all the fun? Let's have another beer, and why don't you give Pam a call."

The next day I picked Dad up at work. I wore my dress uniform and, just like in July, was mobbed and cheered when I arrived. I wished Todd could have been with me and experienced the feeling of pride I had being with these guys. They loved the fact I was in the Navy and defending their country. On the way home, Dad, who rarely showed emotion, had a tear in his eye when he asked if I would come visit his men whenever I came home. I grasped his hand and said, "Absolutely, it'll be our tradition."

Another tradition, already established in our family, took place Christmas morning. Like most, it started with a simple idea. Louie, needing constant medical care as a child, had been living at Mayo Hospital in Rochester. One year when I was about six, doctors allowed him to come home for Christmas. Mom and Dad made the ninety-mile trip on Christmas Eve to pick him up and brought him home for two days. Wanting to make his short stay meaningful, Mom invited relatives and close friends over for brunch on Christmas morning, which became an annual affair.

Although Louie lived at home now and was doing well, Mom and Dad still hosted an open house from six to eleven o'clock for anyone that could make it. In Minnesota, being December, this meant weather permitting. Over the years, it grew, and about fifty to sixty showed up. Mom always had two toasters and about five griddles going with pancakes, eggs, bacon, sausage, and hash browns. Dad made and served his Tom and Jerry drinks, brandy-laced eggnog, Bloody Marys, screwdrivers, and beer. Mar, Louie, and I served and picked up dishes, and everyone helped wash them to keep up. People came and went, had a good time, and no one went away hungry. Although a morning affair, not everyone left walking straight either.

This year was no different. The Newsoms came and, when they heard I was headed for Norfolk, gave me Mark's address and phone number. I told them I'd give him a call. He was older and had almost eight years in the Navy already, so I wasn't so sure he'd want to hear from me, but I didn't tell them that.

On Wednesday, Mom said, "It's too bad you have to leave Friday. Why would they want you to report in on a holiday weekend?"

She had a good point. New Year's Eve was Saturday. I'd love to be home New Year's Day and go over to Margy and Irv's to watch the bowl games on their new color TV. *Maybe if I called …* I got my orders and found the phone number to call if I had any questions. My hand was shaking when I dialed.

"Norfolk Fleet Locator," someone answered, "how may I direct your call?"

"USS Cambria, please." I said.

"One moment." I was on hold forever.

"Quarterdeck, USS Cambria, Petty Officer of the Deck, how may I help you?" I heard.

"My name is RMSN Herman, and I have orders to report this Friday. I'm calling to see if I can talk to someone about staying on leave until Monday."

I heard laughing. "Stand by. Let me get the duty officer."

About three minutes later I heard, "Command Duty Officer."

"Yes, sir," I said. "This is RMSN Herman, and I have orders to report by Friday. I was wondering, it being a holiday weekend and all, if I could extend my leave and report in Monday?"

"Is this a joke? Is someone messing with me? You better not let me catch you if you are."

"No, sir. I thought I'd ask."

"Herman, right? Well, let me tell you something, Herman. No, no, no, you can't extend. This ship has commitments and needs you to report as ordered. Now carry out your orders, and make sure your ass is onboard on time. Do you understand?"

"Yes, sir. Understand. See you Friday." He hung up before I could ask him how I got to the ship from the airport. I wasn't about to call back.

"What did they say?" Mom asked.

"Just that I'm needed, Mom."

I arrived at the Minneapolis Airport December 30, and checked in two hours before my scheduled flight to Chicago. My orders said I should report to the USS Cambria by midnight, or 2359, so I hoped my connecting flight to Norfolk wasn't delayed. Guess it was a little late to worry about that now.

Waiting for my flight, I reflected on the past year. I heard my flight number, boarded, buckled up, and looked out the window. I was here because of "The Letter" a year ago. I made my choice, and now, no regrets, no looking back. I wondered what lay ahead. The plane taxied and took off.

CHAPTER 12

December 30, 1966, Norfolk, Virginia

IN THE AIRPORT TERMINAL, I FOUND MY SEABAG AND looked for a phone. I spotted a sign and remembered being told in boot camp that if you were ever traveling and needed help, look for the United Services Organization (USO). I headed that way.

An older lady, wearing a hat with a small American flag flying on top, greeted me, and I told her I had to report to my ship in a few hours and didn't know how to get there. She showed me the phone I could use, and I dialed the number on my orders.

"Quarterdeck, USS Cambria, Officer of the Deck," someone answered a few minutes later.

"Yes, sir, this is RMSN Herman. I have orders to report in by 2359 tonight, and I'm at the airport. What should I do?"

The voice told me to look for the bus going to Norfolk Naval Station, show the driver my orders, and ask him to take me to receiving. "When you get there, call, and I'll have the next vehicle making a run to the base pick you up. Got that?"

"Yes, sir." I hung up, thanked the lady with the neat hat, and walked outside.

The bus came and, after about six stops picking up and dropping off sailors, reached the receiving station. They called the ship and let them know I was there. In about an hour, a seaman wearing an armband reading Duty Driver came in the door.

"Someone named Herman here?" he yelled.

"Yes, that's me," I said and grabbed my seabag.

"I'm Menard," he said. "Let's go."

We got into an old gray van and drove several minutes before he said, "I'm YNSN Menard, and I'm the executive officer's yeoman. Everyone calls him the XO. You can call me Menard. Why are you reporting in today? Why didn't you call for an extension until Monday so you could stay home for New Year's?"

"I did call Wednesday," I said. "The command duty officer said to report in as ordered because the ship had commitments and needed me onboard."

"What? What idiot said that? Wait, Wednesday. Oh, that was Lt. Cmdr. Fortune who was CDO. Fortune got stuck with CDO duty because the XO, my boss, who is a great guy, gave maximum holiday leave to officers and forced him to stand duty. Fortune, what an asshole. Wait until I tell the XO. He put out the word to all the CDOs to extend reporting in dates and leaves, if requested, until next Monday. Commitments, huh? The ship is in the shipyard for repairs and couldn't get underway before next week anyway. The XO isn't going to be happy."

I wished now I hadn't said anything. "So how long have you been on Cambria, and do you like it?" I said, changing the subject and hoping he'd forget about it.

"I've been onboard just over a year, and it's not so bad. Of course, working for the XO, I get out of a lot of the crappy jobs. A lot of guys hate it though, because it's an old ship with terrible living spaces and food. And, because we're an amphibious ship, we carry Marines to train when we deploy, and they're always in the way. All they do is lie around, do exercises, and clean their guns. You'll see. Do you have a rating, Herman?"

"Yes, I'm a radioman."

"That'll help, as you'll go to the communications division. You'll start out in X Division like everyone else and do crap work for a while."

I saw a sign saying Portsmouth Naval Shipyard, and Menard had me show my ID to a gate guard, then we drove down a bunch of piers. I realized it was after 2300, and I was cutting it close to report in on time.

"Here we are, home sweet home," Menard said. I got out, grabbed my seabag, and looked at a long metal stairway going up to the deck of a colossal gray ship. "Just head up the brow to the quarterdeck, and salute the OOD to get onboard. See you later, Herman." He drove off.

I walked up the brow, and, finally reaching the top and remembering from boot camp training, I saluted and said, "Request permission to come aboard, sir."

A sailor with an OOD armband said, "Come aboard. Who are you?"

"RMSN Herman, reporting as ordered." I handed him my orders.

"Cutting it pretty close, aren't you, Herman?" the OOD asked. Before I could reply, he said, "Petty Officer of the Watch, log in Herman as reporting for duty at 2345, 30 December 1966. Then get the duty X Division guy up here."

"Logging it in," the POOW said. "Hoss has the duty tonight."

"Stand by over there, Herman," the OOD said. "Hoss will get you settled until Monday. I don't know why you just didn't call for an extension of leave like everyone else. Would have saved us the time and paperwork."

I didn't say anything this time. I was still hoping Menard would forget I told him I had tried to extend. About twenty minutes later, a big guy in old dungaree pants with his shirt hanging out approached the quarterdeck. "What the hell you get me up for," he said to the OOD.

"New shipmate," the OOD said. "RMSN Herman checking in. Get him settled in until Monday, will you, Hoss? And no lip. Just do it."

"Screw you," Hoss said and flipped the OOD the bird. He waved me over. "Let's go. Can't believe you're checking in after midnight. It's New Year's Eve now, for Christ sake."

I followed Hoss through a hatch—he had to duck— and down about four decks, then down a narrow passageway. He stopped and opened a hatch. "You can bunk in here for the weekend. You'll find bedding in the corner. You're the only one in X Division, so take any rack. I can't believe you didn't call in for an extension of leave until Monday like everyone else. Why anyone would want to spend New Year's on this piece of shit is beyond me. Any questions? What was your name? German?"

"Herman," I said. "Just one question. Where's the head?"

"At the back of the compartment. You're the only one, so whatever mess you make, you clean up. Now go to bed." He started to leave.

"One more thing, Hoss," I said.

Before I could ask my question, he turned and threw a knife at me. It went past my head and stuck in a locker behind me. I froze and stared at him. He glared at me, saying, "You said you had one question, not two." He walked over and took the knife out of the locker. "Welcome to Cambria, asshole." He left.

I found an old gray blanket and some rolled-up sheets and made up a rack in the back corner. I cleaned up and somehow managed a couple of hours sleep. When I woke, I put on a pair of dungarees and sat there thinking. It was like a bad dream, and I was still shaken up. He actually threw a knife by my head. I heard some announcements over the loudspeaker and didn't do anything but sit. Then I heard, "Liberty for the off-going duty section." I wasn't sure what I should do when the hatch opened.

"RMSN Herman. You in here?" A sailor in dungarees entered. "You Herman?"

"Yes," I said.

"You didn't muster on the quarterdeck this morning. The OOD sent me to find you and make sure you're here. Why didn't you muster?"

"I didn't know I was supposed to, so I was just sitting here," I said, feeling stupid.

"What? When you checked in last night, weren't you told to muster? Oh, wait, Hoss had duty, didn't he? Oh, Christ. Did he throw a knife at you? Figures. Okay, I'm Seaman Gandy. No problem, that's just Hoss welcoming you onboard. Don't worry about it. He hardly ever hits anyone." He looked at me and burst out laughing. "I'm kidding, Hoss could throw that knife at you a hundred times and never hit you, unless he wanted to." He laughed some more. "Come on, Herman, let's get you mustered, I'll cover for you being late, and then get you some chow."

Gandy led me to the quarterdeck, talked to the OOD, and signed me in, then took me down about five decks, showed me the mess decks, and talked the duty cook into giving me some cereal and toast. "I don't know why you didn't call in for an extension," Gandy said. "You're here now, so let me show you around a little bit so you can at least find your bunk and the chow hall today." As we walked, we talked about our hometowns, families, and living on the ship. He had to stand watch somewhere, so he led me back at the compartment I was bunking in and left.

After about an hour, I went topside to see if I could find the quarterdeck on my own so I could make muster on time at 2100. Then I worked my way around a few decks, going down one ladder at a time, to make sure I could find the mess decks and then back to my compartment. The ship was much bigger than I could have imagined, and I didn't want to get too far away, fearing I'd get lost.

I thought about calling home but decided I didn't want my family to know how terrible my first two days had been and what I found out when I arrived. Every person I met said the same thing. "Why didn't ..." I was starting to realize that if I had called any other day, when Lt. Cmdr. Fortune wasn't CDO, I'd be home right now. Instead, here I was on New Year's Eve 1966, not knowing anyone or having anywhere to go. No, let the family enjoy their time; I'd write when I was settled in and feeling better, hopefully.

Just before midnight, I went topside and watched as fireworks went off. I decided to make a wish—that 1967 and my life on Cambria would start better than 1966 ended. Then I heard the countdown over the ship's announcing system, ringing in the new year. I yelled, "Happy New Year 1967."

CHAPTER 13

January 2, 1967, USS Cambria, Norfolk

I WAS GLAD TO SEE MONDAY ARRIVE AND HAVE THE New Year's weekend behind me. I mustered on the quarterdeck at 0700, and the OOD told me to hang loose in the X Division compartment until someone came for me. It turned out to be almost three hours before the hatch opened and a guy in khakis came in.

"I'm Chief Palm. You must be Herman." He shook my hand. "I'm the X Division chief, and that means you report to me. I see you're an RMSN, so eventually the communications division will come to get you. That could be anywhere from four to eleven weeks. Until then, you work for me. I just got back from leave last night, along with about a hundred other guys, so things are a little hectic. Guys are checking in, trying to figure out duty sections, and it's mass confusion everywhere. Plus, the CO wants to get us out of drydock and out to sea this week, so all the officers are running around like chickens with their heads cut off. On top of that, we have a crew of about 530 enlisted sailors, and fifty-nine are AWOL. I'm not going to assign you to do anything today. Just stay out of everyone's way, and I'll be back tomorrow. Any questions?"

Before I could say anything, he added, "Good, welcome aboard. See you tomorrow."

I stood there, baffled. *What? Did I hear right? Ten percent of the crew AWOL? That doesn't sound good. Four to eleven weeks before I go to my division? Yeah, sure was a good thing I reported in on time. What did I tell Mom? I was needed? What a crock.* Looking out the hatch, I saw sailors everywhere in the passageway running around yelling. Chief Palm was right about one thing, mass confusion.

He returned Tuesday morning with my orders and records in hand. He took me to the personnel office and handed me over to a petty officer, saying they'd get my paperwork started. Before leaving, he said, "Check in with me tonight before liberty call, and I'll see how you're doing."

After an hour of paperwork, the petty officer handed me a blank check-in sheet and said he would call for someone to take me around. About fifteen minutes later, Gandy walked in. "Hey, Herman, let's get you checked in."

"Hi, Gandy," I said. It was like seeing a friend.

"I see you survived the weekend," he said. "What's your impression of Cambria so far?"

"It's a lot bigger than I expected, and I was afraid I'd get lost."

Gandy laughed, "Yeah, we're about 500 feet long, sixty feet wide, and ten stories high. With officers, there's about 600 of us. When we deploy, we get more sailors onboard, and then we load up with Marines. It gets pretty crowded by the time we sail to the Mediterranean. Don't worry, you'll learn your way around in no time. Now, give me your check-in sheet."

According to Gandy, most places could care less about checking you in. He put a bunch of initials on some of the lines as I watched him. "Don't worry, I'll tell you what you need to know," he said. "Now, let's do Disbursing first to make sure you get paid." He led me all around, and, by the end of the day, I was checked in, except for my division and an interview with the XO, which Gandy said I would be called for some day in the future.

"So how did it go, Herman?" Chief Palm asked.

"Good." I showed him my check-in sheet.

He looked at it and chuckled. "I can tell SN Gandy helped check you in. Only he could do it in one day. I won't even ask how many places he signed off. That's fine, and I see no reason why you can't go on liberty." He handed me a small blue card with my name on it. "This is your liberty pass. You can only hit the beach in dress blues, and the personnel office should have given you a paper on rules of where you can and can't go. Be sure to follow them. See you tomorrow."

Looking at the liberty card, I felt excited. Except for those few hours in boot camp, I'd never been on liberty before. I didn't have anywhere to go but decided to get my blues on and leave the ship. On the quarterdeck, I nervously showed my ID and liberty card to the junior officer of the deck (JOOD) and said, "Request permission to leave the ship."

He looked me over, nodded, and saluted. "Permission granted." I saluted, stood on top of the brow, faced aft, and saluted the flag before walking down the brow. My first liberty and I was on top of the world.

I felt like a different person Wednesday morning, even though I hadn't done much the previous night. I'd found a diner at the end of the pier and had a burger, fries, and a Coke, then found a small drugstore and bought a paperback to read. I was back aboard ship by 1900. Big first liberty.

"Herman, you here?" Chief Palm called out.

"Yes, Chief."

"Well, I don't like it, but the XO wants to see you this morning. Unusual because it's usually several weeks before he sees new crew members. Your lucky day, I guess. Stay put, and his yeoman will come get you when it's time."

"Hey, Herman," Menard said about fifteen minutes later. "Let's go meet the XO. I bet old Chief Palm is pissed. He likes having new crew members in his little division for as long as he can so he can have a gofer. You know, go for this and go for that. Anyway, I told the XO about you calling for extension and Fortune saying no. I was right—he wasn't happy. He's having Fortune in this afternoon to explain. I told the XO you were an RMSN coming from school, and he said schedule you for an interview. I decided today would be good."

"Thanks, Menard," I said. I wasn't so sure I meant it.

Menard took me into an area marked Officers Country. The

deck went from gray metal to nice blue tiles. He took off his cover, motioning me to do the same. We came to a hatch, and he knocked, saying, "XO, YNSN Menard, sir, with RMSN Herman."

"Enter," we heard from inside. Menard opened the hatch and ushered me in. "Thanks, Yeoman. That'll be all for now. I'll call when I'm done talking to RMSN Herman."

"Yes, sir," Menard said and stepped out.

"Sit down, Herman," the XO, a guy about my size, said. "Welcome aboard Cambria. Although I understand you got off to a rough start, being turned down for extension of your leave. Unfortunate, but water under the dam. Did everything else go all right with your arrival?"

"Yes, sir," I said. I already had a chief mad at me and an officer in trouble, so I wasn't about to say anything.

"Good. You've come at a good time, Herman. We're about to get out of the shipyard." He smiled and said, "Tell me a little about yourself."

"Well, sir, I'm from Minnesota." I was surprised how relaxed I was; I liked the XO immediately. We talked for about ten minutes, then he picked up my record, and I figured it was time to listen.

"I've reviewed your record," he said, "and it looks like you've been a hot runner ever since joining the Navy. You were at the top of your class in Radioman School and already show leadership skills. I firmly believe in rewarding deserving personnel, so here's what I'm going to do. I'm going to deem you eligible and recommend you for the E-4 exam next month. I see no benefit having you spend time in X Division, although Chief Palm would disagree, so let's get you transferred to your division immediately."

He signed a couple of papers, then called out, "Yeoman Menard, call CR Division and tell Lt. Martin I want to see him." He turned and smiled. "Welcome aboard again. Don't let me down."

"Lt. Martin, reporting as ordered, sir," an officer standing outside the hatch said a minute later.

"Come in, Lieutenant. This is RMSN Herman. He arrived over the weekend, and I don't want him wasting time in X Division. With our busy schedule coming up, I'm sure you're anxious to get him settled in your division as soon as possible. RMSN Herman, Lt. Martin will be your division officer."

Martin looked confused. "Yes, sir, and welcome aboard, RMSN Herman. What should I do about the regular check-in process, XO?"

"Lieutenant, I just told you he is checked in and assigned to your division. Go make it happen." The XO sounded a little upset.

"Yes, sir, thank you, sir. Come with me, RMSN Herman," an embarrassed lieutenant said.

We walked down the passageway, leaving Officer Country, and I wondered who I was going to piss off next. Without doing anything, I seemed to be causing trouble. One person had already thrown a knife at me. I had one officer being called in to explain to the XO why I wasn't granted my leave extension, and I had a chief who was pissed because the XO called me for my interview. I could only imagine how mad he'd be when he found out I was leaving his division already. Then, my own division officer had been embarrassed in front of the XO because of me.

Suddenly Lt. Martin, a little shorter and about fifty pounds heavier than me, stopped. "I was given a heads-up about you, Herman," he said. "This morning at breakfast, I heard Fortune say he had to answer to the XO this afternoon for not letting some complaining new radioman have leave extension over the holiday weekend. I figured he was only bitching as usual, but now I'm not so sure. Is that what you are, Herman, a whiner? Did you whine to the XO to get out of X Division, although everyone else has to go through it. Well?"

"No, sir," I said quickly. "I didn't say a word to anyone or complain about anything. It all just sort of happened."

"Well," he said, "I don't like problems. I hope you don't cause any more for me. Let's get to radio, and I'll turn you over to your leading petty officer, and the LPO can get someone to get you checked out of X Division and into CR Division."

We went up about five decks and entered a space marked CR Division on the hatch. "Petty Officer Fisher," Martin called out.

"Yes, sir," said an older-looking guy in dungarees with a coffee cup in one hand and a cigarette in the other.

"This is RMSN Herman, and the XO said he's to check into our division today. Make it happen." Martin left.

"Yes, sir," Fisher said. He took a swig of coffee and put out his cigarette. Immediately, he lit another and sat down. I figured he must be close to fifty; he needed a shave, looked dirty, and smelled like booze. I stood silently, not wanting to make a bad impression if this was my LPO.

A seaman came in and said, "Hey, Fisher, is this the new guy?" Fisher nodded, as if he could care less about anything. "Okay, I'll take care of him and we'll be back before liberty call." Fisher nodded.

"I'm RMSN Bruce Nash," the new arrival said, shaking my hand. "We all go by last names, so just call me Nash. Herman, right? Let's go get you checked out of X Division and settled into CR Division." Once through the hatch and away from earshot, he said, "Welcome aboard. I've been onboard almost a year. We're a pretty good division. Don't pay any attention to Fisher. He's a lousy drunk and an even worse leader. Tomorrow morning, when we muster, you'll meet most of the other guys, and it won't take you long to figure out who is in charge."

Chief Palm wasn't around, so Nash had me pick up my gear and leave the X Division compartment. He took me to what would be my new home for the next three years, CR Division berthing.

The compartment, three decks below the waterline, was not at all what I expected. The racks, flat canvas material with about a two-inch mattress, were six high, about two feet apart, and hung on a chain. Nash explained our Communications Department was lucky and had the whole berthing space to ourselves: thirty-four radiomen, CR Division, and fifteen signalmen, CS Division. He showed me to an empty rack, the fourth highest in one stack, and then to my locker.

Next, we went up the ladder one deck, and he showed me where the head was. "Okay," he said. "Do you think you can find your way back to your rack and then to radio?"

"Sure, no problem."

"Good. Be up in radio around 1630, and we'll get a couple of liberty passes from Fisher." Nash took off, and I headed back to the compartment to stow my stuff.

Amazingly, I found radio with no problem. Inside, I saw Fisher at a desk holding a cup of coffee and cigarette in the same hand, and no one else around.

"Herman, right?" he said. "First day on board and I suppose you want liberty. Well, what the hell, you aren't assigned a duty section yet, so why not. Here's a liberty card, stay out of trouble, and be here at 0700 in the morning for Division Quarters. Can you handle that?"

"Yes, and thank you, Petty Officer Fisher," I said.

I decided to leave ship and give Mark Newsom a call. I hadn't seen or talked to him in years but figured the worst that could happen was he'd say he was too busy. At least I could tell everyone back home we tried to get together.

I found a phone booth, hesitated, then dialed the number. After two rings I heard, "Hello."

"Hi," I said. "This is Rich Herman, and I was calling for Mark Newsom."

"Oh, yeah. This is Mark. I was wondering when you were going to call. You on your ship now?"

"Yes, I checked in last Friday. Your mom and dad gave me your number. Hope you don't mind me calling."

"Not at all," he said. "Tell you what, getting together during the week is kind of hard, and I have plans for this weekend. Why don't you call me the end of next week and we'll try and get together?"

"Sounds good," I said, feeling a little more comfortable. "My ship is supposed to get out of the yards soon, and I'm not sure when I'll be able to call. But thanks, and as soon as I can, I will."

"Sounds good, Rich," he said. "And I mean it. Give me a call. I'll show you around. By the way, do you bowl or play softball? I'm always looking for someone for my teams."

"Let's just say I have bowled some and enjoy softball."

"Great. I look forward to your call," he said and hung up.

I headed back to the ship, took a shower, shined my shoes, and got my best dungarees ready for tomorrow. After figuring how to get up to my rack, about ten feet high, I climbed in about 2130.

Some guys came down the ladder, and they were obviously drunk. Two of them were complaining about being cheated in some pool game. I heard them say next time they were going to take Chesney with them and kick everyone's ass. The more they talked, the louder they got, until finally, some guy in his rack across the compartment told them to get to bed before he got up and kicked their ass. I heard no more from anyone and wondered who that was. And who was Chesney? I figured in time I'd find out.

CHAPTER 14

HEY, HERMAN," I HEARD. I TURNED, AND IT WAS RMSN Nash. "Thought you may like some company, this being your first morning going to Division Quarters and all."

"Thanks, Nash, and yes, I would," I replied honestly.

From the berthing department, we went up eight decks to get to the weather decks outside our division spaces on the oh-five level. A bunch of guys were smoking and hanging around outside when we walked up, and Nash introduced me as a new member of the division. I got a lot of looks and a few head nods, but no one said anything or offered to shake hands.

"I think he's going to be a good one, guys," Nash continued. "He's already pissed off Fortune and Chief Palm." Suddenly, everyone laughed and started shaking my hand.

"Put out the cigarettes and fall in," Fisher yelled. He had a cigarette in his hand and looked drunk. "We have a new man reporting in. RMSN Herman, where are you?"

"Here," someone said. *What?* "Right here, Fisher," a guy down the line said and stepped forward. I looked at him, and he had a big smile and winked at me. "Glad to be aboard." He stepped back in line. I was so shocked I did nothing. Everyone was trying not to laugh.

"Is that you, Herman?" Fisher asked. He looked confused, then continued. "Okay, guys, the captain announced we'll be getting underway in a few days. We need to be ready for a couple days sea trials, and then we're heading for Reftra down at Gitmo. We have a lot to get done, so everyone be ready to bust some butt. First, we'll need a full supply run. RM3 Cooper is the supply petty officer and will coordinate loading out. Cooper, you ready?"

"I sure am, Fisher," the same guy who answered for me said, stepping forward. Fisher shook his head.

"You're Cooper? I thought you said you were Herman."

"What?" Cooper said. "Why would I do that? Herman is the new guy down there." He pointed toward me. Nash nudged me, and I stepped out.

"I'm Herman, Fisher." I said. Fisher looked at me, then Cooper, and then me again.

"Oh, got it." he said. Everyone was starting to laugh. "Okay, welcome aboard again, Herman, and everyone stand by to get your marching orders from Petty Officer Kupp." Fisher went through the hatch into the division spaces.

"Settle down," a second-class petty officer with a heavy accent said, stepping in front of ranks. "Good job, Cooper. You've managed to really screw up Fisher this time. When did you and Herman plan this little gem?"

"We didn't," Cooper said. "When I saw Herman looked a lot like me, I thought I'd mess with Fisher. He's drunk again, and I figured he wouldn't know the difference. I was right." He walked down and shook my hand. "I'm Jeff Cooper, and this is Tom Kupp, our real leading petty officer. Fisher is a drunk, and no one pays attention to him. Welcome aboard, Herman, and thanks for playing along."

"I wasn't sure what was happening so just played dumb," I said. I took a closer look, amazed at how much Cooper and I looked alike.

"What's this Nash said about you, Fortune, and old Chief Palm?" Kupp asked. Most of the division was huddled around now, and it was obvious Kupp was in charge. Like Nash said, I'd quickly learn who ran things.

I gave an overview of not getting leave extension, Menard telling the XO about it, and then the XO apparently chewing out Fortune. I said Chief Palm was upset because the XO pulled me out of X Division and assigned me to this division so fast. "That's about it."

"Well," said Kupp, "Nash was right, and you are off to a great start getting those two pissed at you." Laughing, he slapped me on the back. "And I love it. Don't worry. You're one of us now. Come on and meet the guys."

He introduced me to everyone, thanked Nash for taking care of me so far, and told Cooper to take me under his wing for a few days. I knew I wouldn't remember most of the guys' names, but I did get to meet RM2 Chesney. I also recognized the voice of the guy in the compartment who told the drunks to go to bed or he'd kick their ass. RM2 Ferraro.

"Listen up," Kupp said. "Cooper has over a hundred supply chits ready to go. It's going to be an all-hands working party. No moaning or groaning. Let's do it and be done by the end of the day. Cooper, take charge."

"Okay, guys," Cooper said. "Chesney, Ferraro, Damon, Hawkins, and Stark will lead the work groups. Petty Officer Kupp will be in main radio to solve any disputes, and I'll be in the teletype maintenance shop with Herman, to coordinate and monitor events." He handed out the chits to the group leaders. "Hit it, boys."

I was surprised at how smoothly things went. No one complained, and soon they were all gone. I followed Cooper into the teletype repair space, where he went over to a coffeepot, poured two cups, and handed me one. "Figure you'd take a cup black, and, if you didn't, you would after a few weeks at sea," he said smiling. "Now, we have a few minutes before they start coming back with supplies, so let's chat. Where you from?"

"Minnesota," I said. "From everyone's accents, I have a feeling I'm the only one."

"Accents?" Cooper said. "You got the accent. Naw, kidding. I'm from Chesterfield, Pennsylvania, just outside Philly. Now Kupp, he's from the Bronx, New York, and proud of it. Chesney, the good-looking one with the muscles, is from Boston, and Ferraro, the mean-looking one, is from New Jersey. They're probably the accents you're talking about. I'll let you make up your own mind about people, but a heads-up. Because Fisher is always useless, except as a code operator, Kupp has taken charge and is good at it. Chesney is quiet but gets things done, and Ferraro is, just let's say, respected by all. Those three have been onboard the longest and are a tight group. If any of the radiomen get in trouble, all three are right there. If you screw up, you answer to them."

"I kind of figured that out; thanks for letting me know I was right," I said. "Fisher said we were doing sea trials and going to Gitmo for Reftra. What's all that?"

"Sea trials," he said, "is going to sea for a few days after being in shipyard and working the kinks and cobwebs out. Gitmo for Reftra means we're going to Guantanamo Bay, Cuba, for refresher training. It's three weeks of nothing but training, training, and training. Trust me, by the time we return to Norfolk, you're going to realize what the real Navy is like."

"What do you think I'll be doing?"

He seemed to think, then said, "You said you topped your class on copying Morse code, so being new and not qualified on anything yet, you'll probably be assigned as a CW operator. I'll talk to Kupp and see if he'll put us in the same section, and I can look out for you. If we're lucky, Damon will be in our section. He's a great guy and good at training people." The hatch opened, and Ferraro came in.

"Here you go, Cooper," he said. "Sixty cases teletype paper being brought up. It was slow at supply storage because all the divisions are loading out and everyone wants to be first, but Chesney took the LPO down there aside, and all of a sudden we went to the head of the line." He laughed and went back out.

Cooper grinned at me. "Told you, Chesney gets things done."

About 1100, Kupp came in and said the chow hall was opening up lines for sandwich and beverage pick-up so no one had to stop the loadout to go eat. He told us to keep going and he'd have chow delivered. Supplies kept arriving steadily, and by 1700, we were done. Kupp put the word out to muster on the weather decks outside radio. Cooper had me stand with a couple of guys between us. We stood at parade rest a few moments, and Fisher came out. He looked terrible.

"Petty Officer Cooper," Fisher said, "step forward." As arranged, I stepped forward. Fisher looked at me, shook his head, and continued.

"Congratulations, Cooper, the division completed loadout in one day. Good job." I waved to everyone, all of whom cracked up, and fell back into ranks. Fisher went on, "We go to sea soon; make sure you're ready. Any questions, ask Petty Officer Kupp. Liberty cards are on my desk. Dismissed."

I went on liberty with Cooper and learned he'd been on Cambria over a year and had about two more to go. The more we talked, the more it became apparent that we not only looked alike, but also had a lot in common.

Lying in my rack that night, I felt relaxed for the first time since leaving home last Friday. I had a good first day in my new division and met some nice guys. I was looking forward to my first underway. At least I thought I was—and now at least I had something to write home about.

"Taps, Taps, lights out." The bugle played.

CHAPTER 15

January 9, 1967, on Cambria

A LONG HORN BLAST FILLED THE AIR, FOLLOWED BY "Underway," heard over the ship's announcing system, the 1MC. My first time at sea had begun. I was both excited and apprehensive, not sure what to expect or how I would react—and hoping I wouldn't get seasick.

Over the last few days, I'd gotten to know the guys a lot better. Cooper showed me around radio, explained all the different equipment I would be learning to operate, and gave me a tour of the officer stateroom locations and departments that I'd be delivering messages to. The final night, Kupp posted the duty roster for our underway shakedown. There would be only two sections, Port and Starboard, with twelve hours on, twelve hours off watch.

My first watch assignment was CW operator. True to his word, Cooper got me assigned to the Port section along with him and Damon. Our section assumed duty first, and I was sitting at my position when Ferraro, our watch supervisor, came over.

"Okay, Herman?" he asked.

"Yeah, I'm doing great."

Suddenly, RM3 Reddy ran by. He had a brown paper bag tied around his neck and was carrying a pack of crackers.

"Damn TJ." Ferraro laughed. "Reddy gets seasick as soon as he hears underway, but he'll go stand his watch and before long, after eating a pack of crackers, will be fine. Never complains and never misses his watch. Now, let's get you set. I want you to sit here and copy the code on this channel." He plugged a set of earphones into a receiver and put them on my head. "Copy everything you hear, and someone will pick it up for me to review. Got that?"

"Got it." Sounded easy enough. I started typing out what I heard. Turned out it was the stock market. Seemed odd, but I did what I was told.

I looked over and saw Fisher was listening to code too. I said, "Hey, RM1, you copying this too?" Immediately, his ball cap hit me in the face, and the metal first-class insignia split my lip.

"Knock it off, Fisher," Ferraro said. "Herman, you all right?"

"Yeah," I said with my lip bleeding. *What was that all about?* Fisher picked up his hat and went to refill his coffee cup.

"Just don't say anything to that drunk," Ferraro said. "This is his last underway, and then he's getting transferred to shore duty to retire. Good riddance."

Fisher returned, sat down, and typed out everything that had been sent since he threw the hat. I was shocked. That meant he was able to translate, from memory, over one hundred words that were sent while he was away from the desk. During this time, I'd missed everything and started copying with what was on the air now. I was an excellent CW operator, and I couldn't figure out how anyone could do what Fisher had done. He might be a drunk, but I had to admire this.

"Herman," Ferraro said a few minutes later. "Secure from copying CW. That's enough stock exchange stuff for the old man to read. I need you to bring this message to Lt. Cmdr. Fortune. Make sure you have him initial that he read it before you leave."

"Will do." Taking the message board, I left radio, found Fortune's stateroom, and knocked on the door. "Message for you, sir."

"Enter," I heard someone say. I did so, and a big guy looked at me and the name on my shirt. "So you're Herman. Give me the message." He glared at me. "Do you know how much trouble you got me into, Herman? The XO reamed me good because of your complaining. Well, let me tell you something. I don't like whining smartass sailors, and I'm going to be watching you. You make the smallest mistake, and I'm going to make your life miserable. You understand me?"

"Yes, sir." I decided it was best to let it go, get the message signed, and get out of there.

He read the message, initialed it, and handed it back, but held onto the board. "Watch your step, Herman." He slowly let go, and I left.

"Anything to report?" Ferraro asked when I returned.

"Yeah. He said, 'Watch your step, Herman.' I definitely need to avoid Lt. Cmdr. Fortune. He hates me."

"He's an asshole. Even the other officers don't like him. Sorry about that. I'm making you messenger of the watch, but I won't have you go see Fortune again. When not out on a message run, I want you to team up with Cooper and have him start you out qualifying on some of the beginning positions."

When the Starboard section relieved us, I went out on the weather deck outside radio and gazed at the sea. Everywhere, all I saw was water, no land in sight. The sun had set, and the moon glistened on the water. An amazing sight—and one I knew would always be remembered.

Staying attached to Cooper while at sea, I learned as much as I could. By the end of the underway, I had a lot of qualification signatures. I didn't spend a lot of time with Damon, but, when I did, I enjoyed learning from him and understood why Cooper wanted him in our section.

When we returned from sea trials, we went to the ammunition piers and loaded weapons. Then we tied up at the piers at the Norfolk Naval Base. No more shipyard. We'd have a week in port before going to Gitmo, so I gave Mark Newsom a call.

The following Tuesday, I arrived at 1800 at the Enlisted Club on base, where Mark suggested we meet. I arrived early because I didn't think he was too keen on meeting, and I wanted to make a good impression. I hadn't seen him for years and wasn't sure I'd recognize him, but when I saw a guy walking my way, I knew him immediately.

"Hey, Mark," I said, standing and extending my hand.

He smiled. "Hey, Rich, damn, I didn't recognize you. Last time I saw you, you were about five feet tall. Didn't expect you to be almost as tall as me." He shook my hand, then we both sat. "Do you drink beer?"

"I'm a Herman, aren't I?"

"Good point. Let me get us a couple of Falstaffs." He returned and handed me a bottle. "You look great. Radioman, huh? Good rating. On USS Cambria. Don't know anyone on board. So what's your schedule?"

"We get underway for Gitmo Friday. Come back for a couple of weeks and deploy for the Med. What do you do?"

"As you can see, I'm a first class personnelman. Stationed here at a helicopter squadron on the Air Station. Been here eight years and live with two other guys off base in a big house. I'll have you over one day."

We caught up on family and what we both liked to do. Mark was in two bowling leagues and played on a softball team in the city league. It was obvious he was good at both sports, and suddenly I wasn't so sure I could make either team, although I said nothing. He also had a part-time job bartending at the Petty Officer's Club and was going steady with one of the waitresses, Patti. We talked a couple of hours, and he gave me a ride back to the ship. We planned to get together again when I came back from Gitmo.

"Tell you what, Rich," he said, "when you get back, I'll introduce you to Patti. I also have a confession to make. I wanted to meet you at this club tonight, because, quite honestly, I only met you to get my parents off my back. I figured you'd still be that little kid, and I wasn't looking forward to you knowing me too well or expecting me to be your big brother. I admit I was wrong, and I'm looking forward to your call."

"Thanks, Mark. I was a little nervous too, meeting an old man and all." I laughed and was glad to see he did too. "Looking forward to meeting Patti, and maybe you can teach me how to bowl." He waved and drove off.

Minnesota was an hour earlier than Virginia, so I called home and filled my parents in on my first underway and our upcoming schedule. I wanted them to know I'd be busy and not to expect to hear from me that often. I finished by telling them about meeting Mark, and they seemed excited to know I'd be seeing him more while stationed here. When I said goodbye, I felt they were happy I'd called him—and maybe Mark was right, someone did expect him to be my big brother.

CHAPTER 16

February 19, 1967, on Cambria

IT WAS ALMOST MIDNIGHT, AND I WAS AT MY FAVORITE
place on the ship, the fantail. Here, I could look out over the ocean
with no land in sight and reflect on what had been and what would be.
Tomorrow we'd be home from our training at Guantanamo Bay. We'd
spend the next five weeks in port, preparing for our Mediterranean
deployment and giving the crew some deserved rest and relaxation.
So much had happened the past four weeks. It seemed I had been
surviving on about four hours sleep a day, yet, though tired, I felt
fantastic and raring to go. I'd been so busy I hadn't even had time to
write home. I would make sure I took time to do that. So much to
tell my family. Especially about RM3 David Damon, my first mentor
or sea daddy.

The day we got underway, Lt. Martin held division quarters to
cover some general information and explain our mission. He started
by telling us that Fisher had been transferred early because of health
reasons (which we found out later meant he was at a hospital for
alcohol abuse) and that Kupp was officially our leading petty officer.
He outlined our objectives and what was expected of us, then turned
us over to Kupp and left.

"Okay, guys," Kupp said. "You heard the lieutenant. We're in our
watch bill rotation, and most of you have been through this before.
Let's work together, train our butts off, and make this the best division
on the ship. Now that I'm officially the LPO, I will be talking to all
of you individually about setting your goals for this Reftra and our
Med deployment. RM3 Cooper and RMSN Herman, stand fast; the

rest of you, dismissed." Everyone fell out, and Kupp came over to Cooper and me.

"The reason I wanted to talk to you two is," he looked around to be sure no one heard, "Lt. Martin got word this morning from the XO that he's recommended Herman for the Advancement Exam next week and wants all the paperwork for his signature by tomorrow." I had forgotten the XO saying that when he interviewed me, until now.

Cooper looked shocked, and Kupp went on, "I know, surprised the lieutenant and me too. Anyway, I'm the training petty officer, but you do all my admin stuff, Cooper, so do what you have to, and get me what I need. Damn, I don't know how, Herman, but the XO sure likes you. The problem is, when the guys junior to you find out you're taking the exam a year ahead of them, it could be a problem, so we want this kept quiet for now. Got it?"

"No problem, Kupp. Way to go, Herman," Cooper said as he punched my arm. "And, as I think about it, I'm not that surprised. Herman has a great record so far, and the XO likes hot runners. Plus, Fortune did him wrong, and you know the XO is probably using this to get to him. The CO will back the XO, so Fortune loses again. I love it." He and Kupp both laughed.

I only smiled, while thinking this was just one more thing Lt. Cmdr. Fortune would hold against me, and now some of the guys in the division also might not trust me.

"Don't worry, Herman," Kupp said. "Cooper and I know how to keep a secret and won't tell anyone. If, by some chance, you pass and make third class, it won't be until April, and by then no one should care. And, Cooper, make sure when he's on watch he doesn't have to go see Fortune with messages or anything. Eventually, it'll all calm down, I hope. Now, new subject." He looked at me. "Cooper asked that I put you in the same section as him and Damon. I did this because, if the XO is right, then let's get you trained by the best. I'll tell Ferraro I want Damon to train you on watch and Cooper to train you for duties off watch. The rest is up to you. Any questions?"

"No, and thank you, guys. I think," I said. They both laughed, and I was still taking it all in when the ship's whistle blew, followed by a loud, long alarm.

"General quarters, general quarters. All hands man your battle stations," came over the ship's 1MC. Reftra officially began. It was time I went to work and started to prove I deserved the confidence so many had already shown in me.

We remained at battle stations, running drills, about three hours, then secured and went to regular watch duties. I was assigned as a CW operator again, and shortly after assuming the watch, someone tapped me on the shoulder. I turned around and found RM3 Damon standing there. Remembering him from sea trials, I was glad to see him.

"RM2 Kupp talked to me and RM2 Ferraro," he said, "and gave us our marching orders. He said I'm to train you, and that's what I'm going to do. Ferraro said you are mine except during general quarters, so let's get started. Take off the headphones and pay attention. There are eleven watch stations in each section, from watch supervisor down to messenger. Every, and I mean every, watch position is important, and don't ever forget it. A messenger may be a junior radioman, but if he screws up and is late or fails in delivering a message, or if he comes back and doesn't report to his supervisor something he is told to, the ship suffers and that means the mission suffers. Got that?"

"Yes," I said.

"Good. Always report to your supervisor everything that happens on a message run. You're not trained to know what is important, and he's experienced and is in charge to make decisions, so let him. He can only be as good as you let him, and he will never fault you for telling him something, only for not telling him something. Make sense?"

"Yes," I said, and that was the start of my training program. I could tell how much pride he had in being a part of this division, and it was rubbing off on me. I would never have thought how important a messenger was, and now I wanted to be sure I was a good one.

Damon was an excellent teacher, although his teaching style was unique. The best example of this was demonstrated during a watch during our last week at sea. I got signed off as a CW operator and qualified quickly as messenger, message typist, and copy distribution clerk. I thought my progress was good, but then, before returning to port, Damon surprised me by saying he wanted to me to start on some advanced qualifications. Little did I know it would be a lesson that would stay with me forever.

"Get an equipment operator qual card," Damon called.

"Right," I answered. Really? Equipment operator? That was a position for petty officers and guys who had been on board over a year. I knew better than to question him and went to see Cooper and get the card. Cooper, looking as surprised as I was, gave me the card, and I brought it to Damon, who was talking to RM2 Stark. I liked Stark and thought he was sharp. From Massachusetts, he was the sections frequency manager, which meant he was qualified almost everywhere in radio.

"Thanks, Stark," Damon said and turned to me. "Let's go to the transmitter room." He explained, "The equipment operator is responsible for tuning the transmitters and receivers to the frequency he is given, so that we maintain constant communications with the other ships and shore commands we are working with." We stopped in front of a rack of equipment. "This is a WRT-2 transmitter. I am going to show you how to tune it to the frequency Stark gave me. Pay attention."

I watched, trying to remember everything he said as he went from knob to knob. He went slowly and explained every move he made and why. When he was done, I thought that wasn't so hard. Then, he changed all the knobs and turned the transmitter off. "Okay, now you do it."

I turned on the transmitter and couldn't remember what to do first. I knew I had to do this and that but had forgotten the order. I said, "I'm not sure where to start."

"Well, congratulations," he said. "You got it turned on." He laughed. "Here, I'll get you started." He did the next step, and when I nodded, he turned off the transmitter again. "Try again."

This time I remembered the process and, although slow, I got the transmitter tuned properly and ready to be put online. I double-checked everything and turned to Damon. "WRT-2 number one ready to put online."

"Yes, it is," he said. "Not bad, and remember that speed is not as important as accuracy. The transmitter has to be tuned properly, or it is of no use. Now let's go back and tell Stark that he can put this equipment online when needed."

"Hey, Damon," Stark said a little while later, "I have a transmitter frequency change request. You want it?"

"Give it to Herman," Damon said.

"Herman," Stark hollered. "I need this frequency change. Put it on WRT-2 number three."

"Got it." Taking the form, I went to the transmitter room and turned on the WRT-2. I was in the process of tuning when, once again, I hit a stumbling block. Frustrated and knowing I was getting nowhere, I decided to call for help. Then, the transmitter door opened, and Damon came in.

"What's the problem?"

"I'm stuck," I replied and went to show him where I was having trouble. Suddenly, I was kicked so hard in the ass that I saw stars, and the pain caused me to go to my knees.

"Damn, Herman," Damon yelled. "Get up here." He pulled me to my feet and threw me against the transmitter. "One more time. Now, pay attention, and I'll walk you through it." Tears were running down my face, and I was shaking, but he walked me through the procedure one more time. "I hope it set in this time 'cause I'm not bailing you out again." He walked out.

I took a minute to compose myself before returning to radio and reporting to Stark that the transmitter was ready for use. He acknowledged and logged it on the status board. I saw Damon over in the corner, and he and Cooper were talking about eating scrapple, a Pennsylvania dish, I figured, and acting like nothing had happened. For me, my butt was so sore I couldn't sit down.

After watch, I was heading to the chow hall when Damon called out, "Herman, got a minute?" I joined him on the weather deck.

"You're probably wondering why I kicked you earlier," he started. "No, I'm not going to apologize, because I did you a favor. I guarantee you will never need help again setting up that transmitter. I may not have the best training style, but it is effective. However, that's not the reason I wanted to talk to you. I have never shared this with anyone, but I've decided to make you the first and tell you my philosophy of leadership." He looked at me as if he wanted that to sink in, then stared out to sea. There was dead silence for a few minutes.

"Look," he finally said. "During my almost four years in the Navy, I have found there's two different types of leaders. There's the guy who thinks he is smarter than everyone else and, to be successful, must make all the decisions and take all the credit. He keeps and trains people around him to be capable enough to make him look good, but also not good enough, so he can blame them when something goes wrong. It doesn't matter if he is on the job or on liberty, he is always a little better than everyone else.

"Then there are people like me," he said. "I believe in training people to be as good as me, let them make their own decisions, and get credit for them. If we fail, we fail as a team. When on liberty and off the ship, I try to respect everyone for who they are and not for what they look like or where they come from. Do you understand the difference?"

"Yeah, I think so."

He continued, "I'll be getting out and leaving the ship during our Med deployment. Until then, I believe it's my responsibility to train as many radiomen as I can. I also need to train my relief, and if I do it right, he'll be a better radioman than me. And I have picked you. Why? Because in you I see a young me, and in this short time I've known you, I see someone not only smart enough to take over but you have a way with people. Kupp, Ferraro, and Chesney, the 'Big Three,' all like you, and not many can say that. You have made friends with them, yet treat Stark and Reddy the same way. That's a gift. So, I will teach you everything I know, and, when you put that with what you know and pick up elsewhere, it will make you better than me. You will train your relief, and he will be better than you. Follow?"

"I don't get the part about Stark and Reddy," I said.

He laughed. "That's my point. If you haven't noticed, Stark and Reddy aren't exactly white, and a lot of guys will work with them but never accept them as shipmates because they're colored. I could care less, and, obviously, you don't either—but watch out, it could turn some against you. Just a fact of life. I'm betting you can handle it, and like I said, that's a gift. If you treat everyone the same on and off the ship, you will be a successful leader. Anything else?"

I thought for a minute. "I guess not. I'm a little shocked though. There's no way I can learn all this stuff in a couple of months, and I'm only an RMSN, so no one will pay attention to me."

"I know the XO saw potential, because he recommended you early for the third-class exam, and, if you make it, that'll help. What I'm going to do is groom you for the future. I'm going to give you all the tools to succeed. I'll bet by this time next year you'll be the mainstay of CR Division. Don't let me down." He smiled, slapped me on the back, and left.

I thought about that conversation as I sat on the fantail the night before we were to pull into port. Reveille was going to be at 0500, so I headed down below. I felt like the luckiest guy in the world. I understood what Damon was passing on to me and would do everything I could to become the leader he saw in me. I knew there would be ups and downs. I never could have guessed how many or what they would be.

CHAPTER 17

February 1967, Norfolk, Virginia

HELLO," A FEMALE VOICE ANSWERED.

"Is Mark Newsom there?" I asked. It had been a week since we returned from refresher training, and I had the weekend off.

"You must be Rich," she said. "I'm Patti. Hang on a second."

"Hey, Rich," Mark said. "You just met Patti. Are you off today?"

"Yes," I said.

"Okay, why don't we pick you up in about an hour, and you can go bowling with us? Still at Pier Seven?"

"Yes, that would be great. See you then."

Right on time, Mark pulled up at the head of the pier in his 1962 Ford Thunderbird. "Get in," he called out. "This is Patti." A petite brunette got out, smiling, and I hopped into the back seat. "First thing we're going to do is get you some civilian clothes to wear."

Only second-class petty officers and above were allowed civilian clothes onboard a ship, and they could wear them on and off on liberty. Being an RMSN, I wore my dress uniform. Embarrassed, I said, "I can't afford any right now, and you know I can't have them aboard ship Mark."

"I know," he said. "Think of it as a welcome gift from us. You can leave them at my place and change there when you're on liberty."

At the Navy Exchange, Patti helped me pick out a pair of pants and a shirt. We went to the bowling alley on base. When I got a pair of shoes and chose a ball, Mark and Patti had been joined by another couple.

"Rich," Mark said, "this is Daro and Betty, our best friends. Daro is a first class yeoman, and we bowl together in two leagues. Daro, this is my cousin Rich from back home. He's an RMSN on the Cambria."

"Nice to meet you," Daro said and introduced me to Betty, his wife.

"Hi," I said, shaking their hands. Had I heard Mark introduce me as his cousin?

"You told me you have bowled some?" Mark asked.

"Actually, I've bowled quite a bit," I said. Mark had been so nice, I couldn't try to fool him. "You know, Mark, family thing." He smiled.

"Hear that, Daro?" he said. "Thinks he can bowl. Well, let's see." He and Daro were in two tournaments coming up so were practicing as partners under tournament conditions. Betty didn't bowl, and Patti wasn't very good, but would act as my partner and an opposing team. Made perfect sense to me.

Mark and Daro were good bowlers; I learned Daro's tournament average was 192, and Mark's, 187. I told them I hadn't bowled for quite a while but could probably give them a run for their money. In the end, Daro rolled 624, Mark, 588, and I had a respectable 557 series. Patti didn't want to know her score.

"I'm impressed," Mark said on the way to his house. "You can bowl. When you get back from your Med cruise, I'll see if I can get you on one of my teams." We pulled in the driveway, and I followed him inside and was introduced to his roommates as his cousin.

When it came time to leave Sunday, I thanked everyone. As I was walking out with Mark, Patti gave me a hug and whispered in my ear, "I'm not coming. Mark wants to talk to you alone. Remember, you're always welcome here."

On the way to the ship, Mark said, "You're probably wondering why I introduced you as my cousin." Yes, I thought, I was. "I figure we've known each other our whole lives, and it's a lot easier than trying to tell the story about how our dads met in the CCC, beat each other up, became friends, and shared one pair of shoes." We both laughed. "Besides, I like the idea."

"Me too," I said.

"I wanted to talk a little bit about how you're doing. I've been around a long time and thought you might like to have someone to talk to off the ship. How are things going so far? How did Reftra go?"

"Good," I answered quickly. "I've made a couple friends and my qualifying seems to be going well." I then told him about my being put up for early advancement and how Damon seemed to have taken me under his wing.

"Wow, you are on the fast track, and I couldn't agree more about this Damon's take on leadership. One thing I would add though, Rich; not everyone is a leader. Some are followers, and the Navy, just like the real world, needs both. Remember this too—there has to be a balance between your job and life away from that job. Don't focus too much on one or the other. Your XO and Damon have tagged you as a leader and are going to expect a lot out of you between now and the end of your Mediterranean deployment. I'd recommend you take a few days leave before sailing and go home to have some fun. Come back fresh and be ready to hit it."

He pulled up to the pier. "It's been a pleasure having you out for the weekend, and we'll do that a lot while you're stationed here. Call anytime. Cousin!"

"Thanks, Mark," I said. "I'll try not to be a pest."

I boarded the ship and went to find Cooper, wanting to get his thoughts on taking leave before we deploy. I found him in berthing talking to Kupp.

"Hey, Herman," Cooper said. "Where you been all weekend?"

"Hi, Cooper, Kupp," I said. "I spent it with my cousin and his girlfriend. I'm glad I got you both here." I told them what Mark had said about taking leave. Kupp, as my LPO, would have to approve it first.

"Normally," Kupp said, "I'd say no, but I don't see any problem. Cooper and Damon both say you've been busting your butt and doing well. Put in your request."

"Now I've seen it all," Cooper said. "No one has ever gotten leave after only three months onboard. You getting soft, Kupp?"

Kupp looked at Cooper, who looked like he wished he'd kept

quiet. "No one has ever asked. Submit the request, Herman, I'll get it approved." He walked away.

I called Mom and immediately got yelled at for not writing for so long. When she finally let me talk, I told her about my leave. She was thrilled and said she would help pay for the ticket.

We decided to surprise Dad for his birthday, and I flew home the day before it, March 17, for my four-day leave. Mom and Louie picked me up, and after taking them home, I drove down to Clark's. I was going to continue the tradition we'd talked about, and I wore my dress uniform.

"Hey," I yelled out once I reached the third floor. "Anyone seen Clayton Herman?"

"Who wants me?" I heard my dad say. He came walking around the corner and stopped when he saw me. "Well, I'll be damned."

"Happy birthday, Dad." I walked toward him. As was his custom, he shook my hand but showed not much more emotion. "Any chance you can give me a tour of this place?"

We spent the next hour talking to what seemed everyone employed there, not only the warehouse but also the front office. Finally, Zeke Pearson, one of the higher-ups in management, told Dad to get out of there and go celebrate with his son. We did. As we got in the car, he looked at me and said, "Tradition. Thank you, son."

I didn't get to see my closest friends, though. Todd and Pam, married in February, were living in Washington state. Tom was either somewhere being trained or in Vietnam; his mother didn't want to talk about it. Darrell was gone somewhere out West. We had an open house Saturday afternoon to celebrate both Dad's birthday and my being home. I enjoyed seeing relatives and friends, and later, I went over to New Brighton to visit my cousin Jackie, who couldn't make it to the party.

On Sunday, Mar and Jim arrived and were in the kitchen with Dad and Louie. While I was giving hugs and handshakes, Dad got a beer and handed me one. Mom started to make dinner, pot roast with trimmings, when Marlys suddenly yelled, "Stop. Everyone, sit down." Mar never raises her voice, and Mom quickly took a seat.

Mar took Jim's hand and said, "Mom, Dad, you're going to be grandparents." Dad dropped his beer. Mom jumped up to hug Mar and Jim. Louie looked like he didn't know what that meant. Mom and Mar started talking, laughing, and crying at the same time. Jim sat and smiled, and Dad went for another beer. I didn't know who was the most excited. Everyone forgot about dinner.

Later that evening, after Mar and Jim left, it was like old times. Louie had gone to work, and at exactly seven o'clock, Mom lit a cigarette. Dad came into the living room, a drink in his hand for Mom and beers for me and him. He turned on the TV, and we started watching the *Ed Sullivan Show*. Out of the blue, he said, "I'm taking a day off. You leave tomorrow, Rich, and we may not see you again until who knows when. We need to spend some time together." I wondered where that had come from.

"Oh, Clayton," Mom said, "I think that's a great idea." She did? "I'll take the car in the morning and come home so we can take Rich to the airport." Mom had spoken, so that meant end of subject.

That last morning at home, Dad and I talked more than we ever had. We also consumed a lot more beer than we ever had. When Mom got home, she found us both laughing and obviously drunk. I knew she was mad, but, staying calm, she got me in the car and took me to the airport. I figured she was a little worried about me so went along to check in.

"Ticket, please," the woman at the counter said.

"Right here," I said. I reached into my peacoat, and it wasn't there. I checked out all the pockets. Nothing. I checked my bag. No ticket. I started laughing. "I think I forgot it at home."

"Well, no ticket, no checking bag, and no boarding plane. Next," the woman said.

"Wait a minute," Mom said. "He has to get on that plane and back to Norfolk."

"Sorry," the agent said. "If you want him on the plane, you need to buy another ticket. If you find the original one, you can make a claim for a refund in sixty days."

"This is ridiculous," Mom said. "Give him another ticket."

"Sixty-five dollars and eighty-nine cents, please," the woman said.

I watched Mom write and hand her a check. My bag was checked, and I was given a new ticket. I wasn't laughing anymore.

"You do realize that you will repay me for that ticket, don't you?" Mom asked.

"I'm sorry," I said. "The ticket must be on my dresser. I'm sure you'll find it and get a refund."

"I know, son." She gave me a big hug. "Now, catch your flight, and try to be more responsible from now on. And write. You're such a good writer, and we love your letters." She kissed my cheek, and I headed for the gate, feeling terrible and making a promise to myself never to let her down again. I would write my family often.

Back at the ship, I was stowing all my gear when I heard some guys coming down the ladder. The Big Three—Kupp, Ferraro and Chesney—returning from liberty and talking about a pool game. I thought I'd let Kupp know I was back and headed that way, when I noticed he had a cut over his left eye and big bruise on his cheek. Ferraro didn't look much better. Maybe this wasn't a good time; I turned and headed back to my locker.

"Hey, Herman," Kupp said. "How was your leave?"

"Great," I said, "I think it was safer than where you guys were too." I regretted that remark as soon as I said it.

"Don't say that," Ferraro said. "It hurts too much." Both he and Kupp were holding their faces, trying not to laugh. Chesney, as usual, showed no expression at all.

"It was worth it," Kupp went on. "Chesney made a three-bank shot on the eight ball and took fifty bucks from some Marine at a bar on the strip. The guy's buddies called him a cheating hustler. They shouldn't have said that, and we let them know."

"Yeah," Ferraro said. "We all know he's a hustler, but he doesn't cheat." Even Chesney started laughing now.

Kupp came over to me. "We got our sailing orders, and we'll be deploying March 30. Starting tomorrow, Squadron Six will be coming aboard, and we need to help their communications guys get settled. They have their own spaces behind radio."

"Squadron Six?" I said.

"Yeah," he said, "we're the Flag Ship for the squadron. When we deploy, it's with six ships, and the commodore and his staff sail onboard us. Usually, the communications guys include one officer, a senior and couple of junior enlisted guys. We also have about fifty Marine communications guys who will board after we get underway. They have their own radio room the deck below us. We help them too. Hope you're ready to start being a real sailor." He slapped me on the back, and they all headed for the showers.

In ten days, I'd be leaving on my first Mediterranean deployment. Thanks to the XO, Kupp, Cooper, and Damon, I knew what was expected of me. At least I thought I did. I wondered how the squadron and Marines would change that. I'd have to wait and see, but I felt ready. My cup was and would remain half full. I'd heard that somewhere.

CHAPTER 18

March 27, 1967, Norfolk

IT WAS THE MONDAY BEFORE SAILING WHEN THE squadron detachment showed up, and it didn't go smoothly. Kupp led morning quarters, and Lt. Martin and another lieutenant attended. Finishing up, Kupp said, "Lt. Martin has something for us today."

"Thank you, Petty Officer Kupp," Martin said. "I'd like to introduce Lt. Vargas." Vargas, who seemed much older, nodded. "He is the communications officer for Amphibious Squadron Six, and he and his team will be getting settled in today. I expect everyone to welcome them aboard and help to make the transition go smoothly."

"Thank you, Lt. Martin," Vargas said. "I know you're all thrilled to have us with you." Some of the guys laughed. "Fact is, we need a place to hang our hats, and you guys got the short straw." Everyone laughed. "Actually, it's just me and my leading radioman, RM1 Hill, who will be in your spaces. During war game operations, there will a communications watch officer assigned for message screening. RM1 Hill will work closely with LPO Kupp and all your watch supervisors to establish how best to meet our needs, and we'll try and make it as painless as possible. Trust me." This guy sounded great.

Then, the hatch opened, and a dark-skinned RM1, in perfectly pressed uniform, came out and joined Vargas. "Ah, there you are. This is my LPO, RM1 Hill." I could feel the tension immediately around me.

"Oh Christ," I heard Cooper whisper.

"I'm not taking orders from him," Ferraro said under his breath.

"Welcome aboard, Petty Officer Hill," Lt. Martin said. "Let's get to work. Carry on, Petty Officer Kupp."

We were dismissed from quarters, and Damon motioned for me to join him. I followed as he went over and extended his hand to RM1 Hill. "I'm RM3 Damon, and this is RMSN Herman. Welcome aboard."

"Thanks," Hill said and put a toothpick in his mouth.

Kupp joined us, saying, "Seeing as you already made friends, Damon, why don't you and Herman help Hill and his guys get settled." He waited for Damon to acknowledge, nodded to Hill, and left. No handshake.

"Will do," Damon said. He looked at me, and I could tell from his expression that he wanted to make sure I was aware of what was happening. I did, and it made me uncomfortable, but I needed to tread lightly here.

"What do you need first?" I asked Hill. With that, we departed and spent the day helping the squadron get set up.

On Wednesday, I was on the mess decks with RM1 Hill to attend a mandatory captain's call for all crew members who had never been on a Mediterranean Deployment aboard Cambria. Hill, although part of squadron and not ship's company, had asked if he could join me. Most guys were smoking and shooting the breeze when we heard a hatch open.

"Attention on deck," I heard. It was the XO, leading a captain who I assumed was the commanding officer. I had never seen the CO, or Old Man, as everyone called him, and was impressed by how big he was.

"At ease, men," the captain said. "Gentlemen, I haven't had the pleasure of meeting most of you but, I am your commanding officer, Captain Haines." He waited for everyone to settle, then continued. "We get underway tomorrow for what will be the first Mediterranean deployment for most of you. I firmly believe in work hard, play hard. I continuously hold conversations with the officers and chiefs about the role we play and what I expect from each department, division, and man onboard.

"During the deployment, I hope this great wisdom," he paused, and many of us laughed, "is passed down to each and every one of you. Today though, I want you to hear directly from the Old Man's mouth what our mission is. I do this because not only do I owe it to you, but, if I am going to hold you accountable, I want to make damn sure you know what you're being held accountable for." He looked out at us all, and no one made a sound.

"Regardless of what you hear," Capt. Haines continued, "Vietnam is no longer a small conflict somewhere in Asia. We are at war. I'd venture to say most of you are here because of it." I thought, yes, sir, the letter.

"Our ship is a troop transport vessel and part of the Amphibious Force, Atlantic. Ship's company is five hundred seventy men. We deploy with five other ships and the squadron commander's staff of over one hundred men, who are already onboard. Our primary mission is to train Marine forces on how best to fight a war through amphibious assault landings with follow-on support from sea. We train ourselves, and we train Marines. In two days, we will embark twelve hundred Marines," he said.

"For the next six months, Marines are going to be everywhere onboard our ship. It gets a little crowded, and sometimes, when we are working and training, they will seem to be getting in the way. Do you know what I say about that? Tough!" He looked out, and I swear I felt his eyes directly on me. "Does anyone venture a guess as to why I say that?" He waited but got no takers.

"Ninety percent of you, and I'm very proud of you for this, volunteered for Vietnam duty. Not everyone is needed in Vietnam, and the Navy has sent you here. It is here you will do your part, a very important part, to help the Navy meet its mission. In reality, about ten percent of us will ever see Vietnam. In contrast, the opposite is true of our Marine friends. Following this deployment, ninety percent WILL see action in Vietnam. I expect every one of you to remember that when you think the Marine cleaning his gun in the passageway is in your way. Inconvenient? Tough! *Never* forget what we are training for. *Never* forget our mission." He turned and nodded to the XO.

"Attention on deck," the XO called. He and the CO departed.

"Good pep talk," Hill said with a toothpick in his mouth. "First time I ever heard a CO do that. What do you think, Herman?"

"I was excited before—now I'm fired up. You been to the Med before?"

"Twice, both times on a destroyer. This will be my first time on an amphib carrying Marines. That's why I wanted to attend captain's call. Still trying to learn my job with the squadron." We both went up to radio.

"Hey, Herman," Kupp said when he saw me enter. "How was the CO's talk?"

"Great," I said. "I learned a lot. RM1 Hill said that was the first time he's seen a CO talk to the crew like that."

"Hill? Remember you work for me, Herman. Don't get too chummy with squadron guys. Especially someone like Hill."

"I know you're my boss, Kupp." I couldn't let it slide. "Hill seems like a good guy though."

"Whatever." I thought he wanted to say something else but changed his mind. "Go make sure you're ready to get underway tomorrow. I want you in dress blues to man the rail while we leave port. Look sharp."

"You got it." I headed down to berthing and checked my uniform.

Later, lying in my rack, I had a hard time getting settled. First major deployment. I looked forward to getting qualified at as many positions as I could. I was also wondering what ports we would visit. I hoped we'd be in port for my twenty-first birthday. I then started thinking about what the CO said and our mission. Work hard, play hard.

"Taps, Taps, lights out." The bugle played.

CHAPTER 19

April 17, 1967, Mediterranean Sea

A CALM NIGHT AT SEA, ONE OF THE FEW SINCE WE deployed March 30 from Norfolk, and I sat enjoying it on the fantail. So much had happened recently. I decided it was a good time to write home.

Apr 17, 1967

Hi Folks,

It is a beautiful night and I actually have a little time to myself so thought I'd catch you up on all that has happened since I called you. First, the important stuff. Three days ago was my first anniversary of joining the Navy. That night, I witnessed something very few people can ever claim, seeing two continents at the same time as we passed through the Strait of Gibraltar and sailed into the Mediterranean Sea. To the north, I saw Europe's southern Spain and to the south I saw Morocco of Northern Africa. How neat is that.

I guess the biggest news is I made Petty Officer Third Class. Remember I told you the XO recommended me a year early? Anyway, not only is it a nice pay raise but I now wear what's called a crow with a chevron on my left arm which indicates leadership. The ceremony was yesterday. It's a tradition that everyone senior to you can tack on your crow by punching you on arm so I'm pretty sore today. A good sore, though. Oh yeah, address my mail now to RM3 instead of RMSN.

Remember I told you I didn't know what to expect once we got underway. Well, it's been an experience I'll never forget. The day after we left, we went to Cherry Point, North Carolina, and picked up 1200 Marines. Until we get to the Med and start doing their training on beach assault from sea, there isn't much for them to do. All day long they lie around and clean their guns and kind of get in the way. I remember though, the CO saying their day will come.

We then met up with five other ships and started our transit across the Atlantic. We hit some heavy seas and I found out the power of the ocean. We're a big ship and it just tossed us around like we were a cork. I still haven't gotten seasick but a lot of the guys, and I think most of the Marines, have. One neat thing we did was fire our deck guns. They're called Mount 38's which means they fire shells five inches in diameter and 38 inches long. Every time one of the guns fired the whole ship shook. Loud too.

We stood Port and Starboard watches all the way across. That means 12 hours of watch followed by 12 hours off. We have a lot of drills every day and I think I'm getting about four hours a day sleep. I'm not complaining though. I'm learning a lot about my job and also the other guys in the division. We have ten days of Marine War Games coming up and then we're scheduled to pull into Toulon, France. I think I'll be going on liberty with Cooper and Stark. I seem to get along with them great and we're all petty officers now.

Something else that is neat is a military chaplain goes on all deployments and so he says a prayer every night. You know I'm not big on religion but I've enjoyed hearing him and I figure it can't hurt. Right?

Will close for now. Looking forward to our first mail call soon. Hope I get lots of letters.

Be Good and Take Care.

Love, Rich

I thought I'd covered the important stuff in the letter. As usual, I didn't go into detail on everything.

I told them the seas were rough. I didn't tell them that we took several rolls of forty-three degrees and that I later learned the Cambria was designed to handle no more than a forty-five-degree roll before capsizing. I didn't tell them that sometimes, even when tied down, equipment and supplies came flying through the air, and we suffered cuts and bruises. And Mom didn't need to hear that a sailor, on one of the smaller ships, had a medical problem and almost died because the weather was so bad a helicopter couldn't get him off the ship for a day. Luckily, he did survive.

I told them about the tradition of tacking on your new crow. They didn't need to know that some sailors took this as an opportunity to inflict real punishment. Some guys avoided eating for a day or two, so they wouldn't have to go through the chow line and face the pain. I chose to do it and get it over with. For the most part, it wasn't that bad until I saw the Big Three in radio. I'm not sure who hit the hardest, Kupp or Ferraro, but when Chesney hit me, it felt like the blood was going to go out the ends of my fingers, and the pain was almost unbearable. I tried not to show too much emotion, but later that night, my arm was numb, and I couldn't raise it. I guessed it was worth it though as, the next day, all three guys congratulated me again, said well-deserved, and I even got a smile out of Chesney.

I put the letter in my locker and went to relieve the watch. Entering radio, I located Damon. For the last couple of watches, Ferraro had told me not to relieve any watch station and tag along with Damon for training. During one of my breaks, I saw RM1 Hill and went to see how he was doing.

"Hey," I said. "You want to tack on my crow too? Everyone else has."

"No," he said. "How 'bout I just tap it and congratulate you? I'm sure you're pretty sore." He lightly touched the crow.

"Thanks, not sure I could take much more." We both laughed. "So, how are things with squadron?"

"Good. Lt. Vargas said the commodore is happy, and that's all that matters. Later today, the lieutenant and I are going to be briefing your senior guys on the upcoming war games exercise and what communication support we'll need. I don't think your LPO thinks much of me, but so far he's made things work smoothly."

"That's just Kupp," I said, trying to make light of the comment. I had noticed that Hill often got the cold shoulder from most of the guys. "Good luck with your brief." I saw Ferraro coming, and he didn't look happy.

"Herman," he said, "you lose Damon? Need me to find something for you to do?"

"No," I said, "going to find him now." I nodded to Hill and went toward the transmitter room. I knew that Ferraro was watching me, so I was glad to see Damon and headed that way. He went straight into the teacher mode. Our training got cut short when Damon was told to muster for the squadron brief. He had me tag along.

We entered the squadron comm office and joined Lt. Martin, a couple of officers I didn't recognize, and the Big Three. Once settled, Martin said, "Everyone from ship's company is here, Lt. Vargas." He identified Kupp, Ferraro, and Chesney as his watch supervisors, Damon as his top troubleshooter, and me as Damon's assistant. I couldn't believe I was here.

Vargas introduced three squadron officers who would be the communication watch officers for all exercises. "Like you, I hate briefings," he said, "but it's imperative that you hear this from me and RM1 Hill. For the ten days of this upcoming exercise, your primary mission will be to provide essential communications not only to the ship and squadron, but also to the embarked Marine commander and his forces afloat." He turned the brief over to Hill to explain the requirements and what was expected.

For the next hour, Hill covered the Communications Plan. He took questions, and any that he and Vargas couldn't answer were written down with assurances that the answer would be provided. I was impressed with Hill, but Vargas amazed me. He seemed to know more about naval communications than anyone in the room. It was hard to believe he was only a lieutenant, especially at his age.

"I think that about covers everything," Vargas said. "We'll get back to you on what's pending. Thank you all, and let's give these Marines what they need and have a good time doing it." I noticed that he did seem to be having a good time.

"Hey, Ferraro," Kupp said when we got back to our radio room, "turn the watch over to Cooper, and come join the rest of us." When Ferraro returned, he continued, "Well, I hate to admit it, but that was a good brief. Don't you dare tell Hill I said that. Now, let's take those requirements and get the circuits and operators identified."

For the next couple of hours, I watched as the guys put together a workable communications plan. We would be supporting twenty-seven separate communications circuits all at the same time. It was mind-boggling and exciting.

The day before the exercise, Lt. Martin gave the entire division a pep talk and had Kupp go over the comm plan and watch bill. At the end, he asked if there were any questions or comments.

"Yeah," Cooper spoke up, "I have a comment, but you don't want to hear it, so I'll keep my mouth shut." He was looking from Kupp to me.

"You're right," Kupp said, "I don't want to hear it." His look said he didn't want Cooper to push it. "Cooper, you, Herman, Stark, and Damon, stand fast. Everyone else, dismissed." Ferraro and Chesney stayed also. Kupp turned to Cooper, "Go ahead and say what you got. Let's get this out in the open and done with."

"Okay," Cooper said. "I like Herman, but he's new, and I think it's a bunch of crap that he's being made Damon's assistant. Stark is—and I am just about—qualified everywhere, and we've been on board a long time. We should be given that job."

"I don't owe you or Stark an explanation," Kupp replied, "but will give you one because I respect you two. This deployment will be the last for a lot of us, and, when we leave, all the knowledge and experience goes with us. Hell, I'm going to give credit where credit is due and let Damon explain to you what he told me and Lt. Martin. Go ahead, Damon."

Damon didn't look comfortable, then started, "I figure after this

Med cruise, the only two experienced radiomen left on board will be you, Cooper, and Stark. You can't run this division by yourselves. I, personally, want to leave the ship in good hands and want to train someone to replace me and join you guys in charge. The XO put Herman up for advancement a year early; he passed, and his score on the exam was the highest on the ship. I watched him closely during refresher training, and not only does he learn fast, he's well liked by everyone already. Anyway, I went to Kupp and told him what I thought, and here we are."

"Thanks, Damon," Kupp said. "Answer your question, Cooper?"

"I think it's great," Stark blurted out.

"You would," Cooper said. "Yeah, I get it. Still don't like it. He hasn't paid his dues."

"My arm says I'm off to a good start," I said, rubbing my left arm and wincing. Chesney snickered, and soon everyone joined in, even Cooper. I felt a lot better.

"Okay, enough on that," Kupp said. "Let's get to work." We went our separate ways.

"Hey, Herman," I heard Cooper say, and I headed his way. "Nothing personal, you know. Just seems you're getting a lot of special treatment, that's all. And looks like you're getting chummy with Hill and Stark. I hope we can still hit the beach together when we hit Toulon."

"Sounds good to me," I said. "I'm trying to learn all I can so asking you and Stark and all the senior guys a lot of questions. Trying to get along with everyone." Now wasn't the time to talk about his comments on Hill and Stark. I figured that conversation would come soon enough.

We anchored off the coast of Sardinia, an island west of Italy and just south of Corsica, for ten days and conducted our scheduled war games exercises. The first day, when General Quarters sounded, I experienced conducting communications under wartime conditions. No longer could we afford mistakes or time for teaching. We had a thousand Marines, about one hundred men in each landing craft, heading toward the beach relying on being able to talk to their commanders for direction. I stayed close to Damon, watched, and learned.

The pressure didn't seem to bother him, and he handled all the problems thrown at him by the watch supervisors. One of the highlights came our third day.

"Damon," Ferraro called. "I've lost comms on circuits 101 and 105. They're both high priority, and I need them now!"

"Got it," Damon said. "Give Cooper 101, and I'll take 105." He looked up circuit 105 and motioned for me to follow him. After about two minutes, he shook his head. "Circuit is fried. I'm going to have to get a new transmitter online. Go see how Cooper is doing."

"I can't get any power out of it," Cooper said when I walked up. "Man, Damon and Ferraro are going to have my ass. I can't figure it out."

Looking over his shoulder, I said, "Mind if I take a look?" I didn't wait for an answer and started to troubleshoot. I saw a knob out of place, turned it to a new position, and stepped back. "Try it now."

"I'll be damned," Cooper said as the transmitter came to life. "Thanks, Herman, you saved my butt." He ran off yelling, "Circuit 101 back online."

I went back to join Damon just as he was finishing. "Circuit 105 back online," he yelled to Ferraro. He looked at me. "You can learn a lot from Cooper too."

"I noticed," I said with a smile. When we returned to radio central, Ferraro was all smiles and talking to Cooper about getting the circuit back just in time. I heard Cooper agree and say that was a close one. He then saw me, and I said, "Good job."

At the end of the exercises, we headed for our first liberty port. We heard over the 1MC, "This is the Commanding Officer speaking. You just completed the first major exercises, and on behalf of the Commodore, Marine Commandant, and myself, well done. We are now headed to Toulon, France, for some time off, and as I promised you all: work hard, play hard." You could hear the cheers throughout the ship.

I lay in my rack that night, excited about pulling into port. Today, the XO had each section muster on the mess decks, and he, the ship's doctor, and the shore patrol officer held training on conduct ashore, a warning not to drink the water, and the seriousness of getting a venereal disease. I didn't know about the others, but the doctor got my attention. Cooper and I were in section two and would be off the first day in port. We planned to hit the beach together, get a meal, and try some French wine. France … and then Italy.

CHAPTER 20

May 1967, Toulon, France

REQUEST PERMISSION TO LEAVE THE SHIP," I SAID, saluting the officer of the deck.

"Permission granted." He saluted back.

I saluted the American flag hanging off the fantail and followed Cooper down the brow. At the bottom, I slowly placed my foot down and stepped off. France. Except for that short visit to the beach in Cuba, this was my first visit to a foreign country.

"Remember what I told you, Herman," Cooper said. "We're not stopping at the first bar we see. It's too close to the ship so will be crowded with sailors and Marines. Plus, the prices will be higher. Stick with me." After walking several blocks, we stopped at a little bar that only had a couple of customers. I sat outside while Cooper went in to get us two beers.

"Problem?" I said once he finally got to the table.

"Nah, just took a while to haggle the price and see how many francs I could get for my ten dollars. Did pretty good, got five for a dollar, and beers were only ten, so about a dollar each."

"Sounds good to me. Next round on me. I'll do the same thing, and we'll have some francs on us." I picked up the Kronenbourg, clinked Cooper's bottle, and toasted, "My first foreign beer, with many more to come." We took a long swig. It was warm and bitter. "Yuk, this is bad."

Cooper laughed. "Better get used to it. Unless we're on an American base, you'll find the beer room temperature. It's the way Europeans drink it. They don't like it cold and think we're nuts to drink it that way. So, who's right?" He shrugged. I agreed and decided to go native.

On our second beer, he said, "I wanted to thank you for covering me on that transmitter I couldn't get up. I know I should have told Ferraro and Damon you were the one who saved our asses, but I was embarrassed. You're as good as they say, and I won't forget it."

"I enjoy all my learning experiences so don't know what you're referring to." I winked at him, and we clinked beers. I knew we now had each other's back.

We walked around town, and each place we went, Cooper—and later I—would get into a conversation with the locals. We didn't speak French and didn't meet anyone who spoke good English, but through hand signals, we got our point across. Street vendors abounded, and it looked like they set up anywhere they could find room. We found one serving fried ham-and-cheese sandwiches— very flat and delicious.

That evening, we made it back to the ship on time, but when we got there, we had a little problem getting onboard. I wasn't sure who was drunker, or whose white uniform looked worse, as we tried to figure who should board first. We walked up together.

"Look," Cooper said, "all we have to do is be able to salute the OOD and step aboard." He fell down. I picked him up, sort of, and put his cover back on his head. "Thank me," he slurred, laughing.

"Come on, Cooper," I said. "Up we go, a few more steps." I guided him a bit, and we finally made it to the quarterdeck. I braced him in front of me and raised his right arm to salute. "Request permission to come aboard," I said, "for both of us." Cooper grunted.

"Permission granted," the OOD said before he started chuckling. "Herman, is that you?" He came closer. "You kidding me? You look as bad as Cooper. Get your butts below and keep the noise down. Messenger of the watch, help these two idiots." I didn't argue and eventually made it to our compartment and got us both into our racks.

The second day in port, we had the duty, which was probably a good thing. I needed to recover from the night before, and Cooper wasn't doing much better. That morning, he asked how he made it across the quarterdeck and to his rack. I told him the CO would be proud … work hard, play hard. He thanked me and left it at that.

I was getting another uniform ready for liberty the next day when Cooper told me that he was going to swap duty with someone else for a day later in another port. He would be paid, and he said he was going to try and take some extra duty days and make some money. It wasn't allowed to sell duty days, but most LPOs looked the other way. I told Cooper to have fun, and since no one was supposed to go on liberty alone, I went looking for someone to go with.

I saw Stark coming down the ladder. "Hey, Stark, want to hit the beach?

"I'm joining up with RM1 Hill," he said. "Any problem with that?"

"Sounds great, long as you don't mind a new guy tagging along."

Hill was already on the pier when Stark and I stepped off the brow. I couldn't help noticing that, although I take pride in my appearance, Stark's uniform looked a little better than mine and Hill's looked better than his.

"Okay, guys," I said. "Why do I feel like the only one who can't pass inspection?"

"It's an art," Stark said. "A little secret. Before deploying, I get six uniforms cleaned and pressed out in town. I keep the best two for inspections and wear the other four on liberty."

"Me too," Hill said. "Sort of. My wife does all my uniforms. She's big on having me look good."

"Wife?" I said. "I didn't know you were married. So you guys are telling me I either need to get married or find a good civilian cleaner. Hmm, which is cheaper?"

They laughed, and we headed down the pier toward town. We walked a few blocks and stopped at what looked like a nice restaurant. I knew they both had been to the Med before, so let them take the lead. We found a table inside, got three beers, and ordered steaks.

"How long you been married?" Stark asked Hill.

"Eight years," Hill said. "Best eight years of my life. I have three kids too, two boys and a girl."

"I want to get married someday," Stark went on, "not while I'm in the Navy. How about you, Herman?"

"Never even thought about it. Just being a sailor is keeping me busy. I think a toast to the daddy is appropriate though." We clinked beer bottles.

Our dinners arrived, and I had my first steak (at least they called it that) European style—thin meat, cooked well done. I took a bite and was surprised how tasty it was. Someone tapped on the window beside us, and we looked out to see Lt. Vargas, a stunning blonde holding his hand, waving. They continued walking.

"Before you go thinking the wrong thing," Hill said, "that's his wife with him. She is going to join him in the next couple ports we visit. They're great people and even had my whole family over for dinner."

"Were you thinking anything, Stark?" I asked with a smile. Stark shook his head and took a bite of steak. "I do have one thing I have to ask though," I said. "He seems kind of old. He has a ton of ribbons, and the other day, at the briefing, he seemed to know more than anyone in the room. How come he's only a lieutenant?"

"You are new, aren't you?" Hill said. "He was a chief radioman, had thirteen years in the Navy, and then went officer. He's a limited duty officer, LDO. That alone means he's in the top three percent of the Navy. So, yeah, he's older, a lieutenant, and like a god among communicators."

Feeling like an idiot, I sat there staring at Hill. "Damn." Former enlisted. I thought back to what Petty Officer Sabin said in boot camp about my becoming an officer. He must have been talking about my becoming an LDO. Suddenly, I felt honored he thought of me as someone in the same company as Lt. Vargas.

Leaving the restaurant, Hill said he didn't want to be a party pooper, but he'd like to have a coffee and maybe a nightcap, then head back. That sounded fine to Stark and me, and when we stopped at a small café, Hill ordered us all a coffee and liqueur called Drambuie.

As we sipped our drinks, Hill said, "You know, Herman, I was surprised to see you walking down the brow with Stark."

"You weren't alone," Stark told him. "He asked if he could join us, and I said, sure, if he didn't have a problem out here with the two of us."

"Why should there be a problem?" I asked, knowing full well where this was going. "Because you guys are senior to me? Or because you're older?"

"Smart ass," Hill said. "I'm sure you've noticed Stark and I aren't exactly part of the good old boy network in radio. I don't know about Stark, but my whole career, I'm the guy everyone wants in their watch section 'cause I'm a good radioman, they just don't want to be seen with me in public. You could take a lot of flak hanging out with us."

"Exactly how it is," Stark added. "I'm everybody's good buddy in radio, and they treat me like I have the plague when off watch."

"Yeah," I said. "I see how two-faced many of them are every day. I don't get it, because they all seem like good guys. I'll admit that I grew up in a white neighborhood, and the only colored person in my high school was the biology teacher, who I accidentally cut pretty badly when dissecting a cat." They both chuckled. "I wrestled against a few colored and met quite a few in college, but never gave it a second thought about skin color."

"I hope you don't change, Herman," Hill said. "Back at home, you're in the South now, and the Civil War is still being fought. I grew up with it and have learned to adjust so that my family and I can live a good life. The Navy helps."

"I've been lucky," Stark said. "My dad was a semi-pro boxer and made a good living. This gives him status, and my family are treated pretty good back home in Massachusetts. I'll give you an example of how stupid people can be with their discrimination. My folks were turned down for a loan to buy a home on Cape Cod. The bank gave some excuse. Then, the people in the area of the house found out who my dad was. Magically, the loan all of a sudden got approved, and we became the first black family to move there."

"Happens all the time," Hill said. "And I noticed you called us black, not colored. You on that bandwagon?"

Stark looked serious. "My folks are. They no longer use the term 'colored' at home. I think it's just a matter of time before that adjective goes away and black is the norm."

I didn't say a word. This seemed like a discussion for the two of them.

"You're probably right," Hill finally added. "I totally agree we should be called black or African-American. Just not sure if I want to take it on while in uniform and stationed in Norfolk." He looked at me. "Any opinion, Herman?"

"Not my place to have a vote here," I said. "I'll support you guys on whatever you decide. I also want you to know I appreciate all the help you've given me in radio, and I hope you'll let me hit the beach with you again. Just let me know what color you are so I don't make you mad or embarrass myself."

They both laughed, and I joined in, relieved I hadn't crossed the line. Hill slapped me on the back and took the toothpick out of his mouth. "You ever thought about politics, Herman? You could probably get a few black votes." After more laughter, he continued, "Stark is right, though. You could get a lot of flak when everyone knows you went on liberty with us. We'll have your back, but it could get ugly."

"If someone has a problem with my being with you guys, two fellow sailors on the beach in a foreign country, or anywhere in fact," I said, "then I don't think much of them or their opinion. I learned a long time ago, pick your battles, and, guys, this one is a no-brainer. I'll stand by the man for who he is, not what someone thinks he is."

On that note, we boarded the ship and called it a day. A great day, in my book.

We left Toulon and spent the next week playing war games off the Sardinian coast before heading for our second port visit in Naples, Italy. In the second night of a three-day transit to Naples, we were called to an all-hands quarters. When the hatch opened, Martin, Vargas, Kupp, and Hill came out.

"We have just learned," Martin said, "that tomorrow morning Sixth Fleet, our big boss, will board with his staff to conduct a graded communications exercise for CR Division. Normally, we are given a week's advance notice, but this will be with just a twelve-hour notification. The CO and the commodore have agreed to let Lt. Vargas and RM1 Hill augment ship's company for the conduct of this exercise. I will be the officer-in-charge, and RM2 Kupp will still be the LPO. "There will be twenty of us assigned specific watch stations for the entire exercise," Martin went on. "Once the exercise starts, if you're not part of it, stay away from all radio spaces. RM2 Kupp, read off the names and job assignments."

"If your name is called, stand fast, and if it isn't, you're dismissed," Kupp said. He called off all twenty names. At the end I heard, "RM3 Herman." *Huh? Me?* When everyone had left but the exercise team, Kupp explained each person's job. The exercise would start at 0700, so we were told to get a good night's sleep and be in radio, at our watch position, at 0630.

"Hey, Kupp," I said as we were leaving. "Are you sure you want me as the message typist? I've never been in an operational exercise before and would hate to blow it for the ship."

"I've been told you're the best typist we have, and speed and accuracy count," he said. "We can't have someone making a lot of mistakes and losing time making corrections. Just do your best, okay?" I nodded and was about to leave when he continued. "And don't let the fact that a three-star admiral will be reading those messages bother you." I stopped, turned, and saw him shrug and laugh.

May 20, 1967

Hi folks,

Today we had a big communications exercise and I was the typist for all the messages that were sent to an Admiral and his staff. I was so nervous when we started, I thought I was going to be sick. In the end though, I did really good and got a perfect score for typing. Everyone did great and our overall grade was high enough that the ship could win an important award. Our CO even came into radio tonight to congratulate us all and he told the XO to let our division get off the ship one hour early on our first day of liberty in Naples. Oh yeah, we'll be in Naples, Italy, soon.

Before I forget. We got mail in Toulon and I enjoyed all the letters. One thing, Mom. RM3 stands for radioman third class, not Room 3. Guys got a kick out of you thinking I now have my own stateroom. Besides yours, I got a nice letter from Mar and Jim. And I got an invite to Jim's graduation from Michigan Tech. Mar said they were hoping he would find a job somewhere not far from home. I also got a letter from Jackie and Gary. I don't think I know anyone who does more or works harder than Gary.

I had my first liberty in Europe when we visited Toulon. It sure was different. The people were friendly and liked Americans. All the stores are little and the streets are narrow. Cars are small and everywhere. I don't think there are any rules as drivers go through red lights, honk horns and do what they want. But it seems to work and I didn't see any accidents. And yes, Dad, I saw a lot of French girls but not Brigitte Bardot. I went with Jeff Cooper. I told you about him. He's from a small town outside Philadelphia and has been to the Med before. He's a good guy and we get along great. I had my first French beer, Kronenbourg, and it was nasty. It's bitter and they drink beer warm over here. It didn't stop me from drinking a lot of them though. Got back to the ship on time so that's all that counts.

I'm doing good at my job. I've been picked to be trained for a supervisor position already. A couple guys, even Cooper, weren't too happy about it at first but everything going good now. I'm just trying to learn as much as I can and get along with everybody, which isn't so easy. I get along with the colored guys and that doesn't sit too well with a lot of whites. It seems everyone works well together; they just don't play well. I've always heard about prejudice and now I'm seeing it first-hand. Don't worry, I'm fine and will deal with it.

Well, I just wanted to catch you up. Be Good and Take Care.

Love, Rich

I went to my locker, got my letter ready for mailing, and checked my uniforms. Our special requests were approved, and Cooper and I would be going on the three-day Rome tour May 23–25. He'd also convinced me to hit the beach the day we'd arrive in Naples by saying to just trust him.

CHAPTER 21

May 21, 1967, Naples, Italy

SHORTLY AFTER DOCKING IN NAPLES, THE announcement came over the 1MC. "This is the Commanding Officer. For their outstanding performance of duty, Liberty Call, Liberty Call for CR Division only." True to his word, the radiomen walked down the brow one hour earlier than the rest of the liberty section. We heard hoots and hollers from sailors in dress whites and Marines in their khaki and green, waiting to hit the beach.

Naples had a large American presence with thousands of military personnel and their families. We took a taxi to the Flamingo Club, an American facility located on one of the NATO bases. Cooper told me not to exchange money on the ship where we would get 500 lire to the dollar. Here, we got 600 lire to the dollar and exchanged enough money to cover our trip to Rome. We found a table and enjoyed a cold American Budweiser.

"There sure are a lot of different uniforms here," I said, looking around the club.

"It's a NATO base," Cooper said. "What did you expect? All twenty-nine countries have military here. You know, for someone so smart you can say the dumbest things." I looked at him and realized he was laughing.

I looked across the room and saw a couple of our guys at the bar. "Hey, there's Nash and Morton at the bar. And Stark and Reddy over there at that table. Want to go say hi?"

Cooper said, "Sure." He got up, walked right past where Stark and Reddy were sitting without saying a word, and stood next to

Nash at the bar. I walked up, after stopping for a couple minutes to say hello to Stark and Reddy, and stood next to Cooper. He had already ordered us a beer and was busy talking when I got there. "Took your time," he said.

"Just being friendly." I decided to let it go. I waited for a lull in the conversation before asking, "So, what's everyone want to do?"

"Nash and I are going to get a good old American meal here and then do some shopping," Morton said. "You guys?"

"I can get American food on the ship," I said. "I want to go out on the town and get some real Italian food at a real Italian restaurant. You can join us."

"Thanks, but I'm looking forward to a thick juicy T-bone, and, honestly, Nash and I aren't much on drinking."

Cooper rolled his eyes and grabbed me by the arm. "Let's get going." When we were far enough away, he continued, "Why'd you invite those guys? Damn, Herman, you have to be friends with everybody?"

We saw a sign saying Ristorante Ciao and sat at a table outside. A waiter came right out and handed us two menus. "*Buon giorno*," he said. "*Come stai?*" Then he added, "If you prefer, English? Welcome, how are you?"

"Doing good," Cooper said. "Can we get some red wine, please?"

"*Si*, I will bring you our best house wine." He left.

"He's great," I said. "Wish I spoke Italian." Recognizing spaghetti Bolognese on the menu, I ordered that when the waiter returned with our wine and a basket of bread. Cooper ordered the same. "To our first of, I hope, many fine meals in Italy and everywhere we visit." We clinked glasses and enjoyed watching people-watching until our meal came—without a doubt, the best pasta I ever had. We paid our bill, only 4,000 lire or about three dollars each, thanked the waiter and left stuffed.

On the streets, I noticed how dirty the city was. There was garbage everywhere, and no one seemed to care. And I'd thought the driving was bad in Toulon, but, compared to what I saw in Italy, the French were great drivers. Cars flew past, everyone honked their horns continuously, and it was first come, first served in intersections.

Cooper said we'd bar-hop but hit only a few places on our way back to the ship, as we were planning on saving our money. I'm not sure where we lost control of that concept. Maybe we didn't think there would be that many bars. Maybe we didn't think we would stop for an Italian beer, Peroni, at every bar we saw. It didn't matter. What mattered was we lost track of time and got back to the ship an hour late. Once again, we helped each other up the brow, stumbling badly, and finally made it to the quarterdeck. We stood as erect as we could, saluted, and asked permission to come aboard. I knew we were in trouble but didn't realize how much until I saw Lt. Cmdr. Fortune standing there.

"Permission granted," the OOD, Lt. Martin, said. "Cooper, Herman, do you know you're listed as UA, unauthorized absence? I was getting ready to send the Shore Patrol out looking for you. What do you have to say for yourselves?" he said. Lt. Cmdr. Fortune was now beside him.

Cooper was having a hard time standing, and I didn't want him to say anything to make things worse, so I tried to act sober. "My fault, sir. I told Cooper I'd get us back before end of liberty, and I lost track of time."

"No excuses, Herman," Fortune said. "You're not going to whine your way out of this—"

"Lt. Cmdr. Fortune," Lt. Martin said, cutting him off, "I am the OOD and in charge. I'm also their division officer and will decide any punishment. Please leave the quarterdeck." Fortune was fuming but left.

Martin turned to us. "You two. Get below and hit your racks. I'll deal with you tomorrow when you sober up and will remember what I say. Dismissed."

Cooper started to say something, and I quickly said, "Yes, sir." We made it below.

No one said a word to us when we entered radio in the morning. Finally, Kupp came over. "Cooper, you know better than that. You can have a good time on liberty, but you got to get back on time. Obviously, you and your twin here," he pointed at me, "are about to find out the hard way. The lieutenant said to report to his stateroom at 0830."

"Enter," Lt. Martin said when we knocked on his door.

"Reporting as ordered," Cooper and I said in unison.

"At ease, you two. Do either of you remember last night? Don't answer that. Luckily, I was the OOD when you finally decided to come back to the ship." He looked at us and couldn't help laughing. "You two were quite the sight. And Lt. Cmdr. Fortune had to be standing there. Herman, he definitely has it in for you. Listen to me and listen well. I'm not going to put you on report because, although you were UA, you didn't hurt anyone, and I can tell the XO and CO you just played hard—the CO loves that. Fortune is not going to like it, but he won't fight it because he knows he'll lose. And I'm not taking your trip to Rome away; you've already paid in advance for that.

"However," he went on, "to keep military bearing and deter others from trying the same stunt, I have to do something. The next two liberty days you have, following your Rome trip, you will volunteer for duty shore patrol. Maybe seeing and taking care of your drunk shipmates and Marines, acting like you, will make you think twice before making such fools out of yourself in the future. Question?" We stood at attention and remained silent. "Dismissed."

When we got back to radio, the Big Three and Stark were all waiting for us. Kupp had an armband with the letters SP on it and a green belt with a nightstick in it. "I just got a call from Lt. Martin telling me that you two have volunteered for shore patrol. Ferraro and I want to thank you for taking our duty day, and Chesney and Stark for their day. Here, try on the belts." All four of them burst out laughing.

I looked at Cooper, we both bowed, and together said, "Our pleasure."

May 26, 1967

Hi Folks,

I'm on a tour bus heading back to the ship in Naples. Jeff Cooper and I just spent 3 days in Rome and I want to write about it while it's still fresh in my mind. First, we had a terrific time and I'm already looking forward to going back again. Actually I know I'll be going back. I'm getting ahead of myself.

Rome is about 150 miles North of Naples. It only took our tour bus about two hours to drive there. Italy has the Autobahn and there's no speed limit. It's unbelievable how fast they drive. I know we saw cars going over 100 mph like it was nothing. Anyway, we stayed at the Hotel Nova Domus. It was terrific, had a bar and restaurant, and our room had a king-sized bed.

The first day we saw the Olympic Stadium where the 1960 Olympics were held. Outside there was a statue for every sport. Then, we went to a couple Cathedrals. I can't get over how impressive all the buildings are.

The second day we started with seeing the catacombs. We were able to enter a couple of the underground tunnels that are roped off for tourists. I almost cried walking through them because you see the actual graves built into the walls that contained Christians' bodies. The spaces are so small. Then we walked through the Colosseum and saw where the actual killings took place. Later, we visited St. Peter's Cathedral and I've never seen a place so big. Our tour guide said you actually need 3 days to properly see all of it and I believe him. We ended up at the Vatican itself and I actually saw all those paintings Michelangelo did. Did you know that it's actually Vatican City and they have their own government, police force and it's independent of Italy? I know one thing, after seeing all the gold and art here, the Catholic Church will never go broke.

You're going to love this. That night we went to a nightclub near our hotel that we heard had good entertainment. A colored guy came out on stage and started singing and I told Cooper who it was. He thought I was kidding but then we heard him stop on stage and say, "Hello to you American sailors out there," and he was pointing at us. It was Sammy Davis Jr. After his act he came over to our table and introduced us to his wife, May Britt, and friend Guy Madison. He only stayed a minute before he had to go, but he was great and bought us a drink. Made our day.

Yesterday, we went back to St. Peter's Square for a private audience with the Pope. Well, us and about 80,000 other people. I was surprised we could hear him so well and he talked to us in like 20 different languages. Definitely something I can tell my grandkids about.

I told you I'd be going back to Rome. Remember the movie, "Three Coins in a Fountain?" That was Trevi Fountain and we visited there. If you throw one coin in, it means you will return one day. Throw two in and you'll have a new romance, and three coins means you'll marry within a year. Yep, I threw one in.

Well, we're almost back to the ship. Cooper and I did get to spend a day visiting Naples before we went on the tour. We saw enough and need to save our money, so we volunteered to stand shore patrol the next few days in port and will let some of the other guys have a break from duty.

Be Good and Take Care.

Love, Rich

After our trip, I changed into my dungarees and headed to radio. "Hey, Stark," I said when I saw him at the supervisor's desk. "We're back from Rome."

"You didn't burn the city down, did you?" he said with a big smile. "Knowing you and Cooper's track record, I wouldn't be surprised."

"Very funny," I shot back. "I'll have you know, Sammy Davis Jr. bought us a drink."

"What!" Stark jumped up. "No shit? Did Cooper drink it?" I laughed and told him about the club. At first, I don't think he believed me. When I told him May Britt and Guy Madison were there, he said, "Now I know you're telling the truth. Sammy Davis just married her, and it's a big deal being an interracial marriage. I'll be damned. Can I touch you?" We both laughed. "Cooper must have been fit to be tied. Wait until I tell Hill."

"Cooper seemed a little uneasy, but I think he was impressed meeting someone that famous. I don't think he knew Sammy Davis was the one married to the gorgeous blonde. I didn't say a thing. Anything going on?" I found three letters for me in the mail.

"Not sure. I heard the Middle East is starting to act up. But they're always doing that, so who knows. Remember, you got shore patrol tomorrow."

"Yeah, looking forward to it. Not." I headed back to berthing and finally hit the rack to read my mail. I was more tired than I thought and woke up with the letters on my chest when I heard the 1MC come on. "Let us pray," said the chaplain.

"Taps, Taps, lights out." The bugle played.

CHAPTER 22

June 1967, Malta and the Tyrrhenian Sea

WE SPENT A FEW DAYS AT SEA CONDUCTING DRILLS and maneuvers, then pulled into Valletta, Malta, for another port visit. This small British island, where the people spoke Maltese and English, soon became one of our favorites. Americans were popular here, and we enjoyed the hospitality, history, and spectacular beaches. I was getting ready for my third venture ashore when all our plans changed.

The loudspeaker announced, "All hands fall into Quarters." It was 1445, and liberty was scheduled to commence at 1600. You could hear the confusion and mumbling all over the ship as everyone headed for Quarters.

Lt. Martin called us to attention. "There has been a change in the ship's schedule, and we will be getting underway at 0800 tomorrow morning. Liberty will still be granted tonight with all hands, officers and enlisted, due back onboard by 2100. The underway watch bill will go into effect at 0700 with Starboard section assuming the watch. Mail will leave the ship at 0730, and the next mail call is not known at this time. We are deployed to the Mediterranean because we are a United States Navy ship defending and supporting our country and its allies. Be ready to do it. Dismissed."

June 6, 1967

Hi Folks,
I only have a few minutes to get this in the mail so will

*make it short. We are in Valletta, Malta, a small island south of
Italy. Apparently all that talk in the papers wasn't just hype and
trouble between Israel and the Arabs is heating up. Anyway, we
are getting underway for where I don't know. Even if I did, I
couldn't tell you. I don't know when I'll be able to send another
letter but, don't worry.*

*There's also talk that we may not be going home on schedule
so don't make any travel plans until you hear from me. This is
the only letter I have time to write so please tell everyone I'm okay
and will write when I can.*

Be Good and Take Care.

Love, Rich

After leaving port, the commanding officer came on the
1MC. "This is the CO speaking. Fighting between Israel and their
neighboring Arab states has escalated, and war is imminent. Although
the United States has taken no stance in the war, we will remain
north of Africa and prepare to evacuate American citizens if called
upon. We have trained for this, and I call upon all of you to give me
your best. Set Condition Three."

The ship settled into wartime cruising, with most of the crew
going to three-section duty. In radio, the demand for additional
communication circuits required us to stand Port and Starboard duty.

Damon and I were doing final checkouts on several of my
qualification cards on June 8, when, shortly after 1500, we heard a
faint voice come over the High Command Net. "Any station this net,
any…" and it faded away. We waited for someone to reply. I manned
the circuit, and Damon went to get Ferraro.

"What is it?" Ferraro asked.

"Not sure," I said. "Someone trying to reach anyone this net. I
haven't replied yet." Then we heard the circuit activate with a faint
voice and static.

"… [static] under attack … Israeli forces …"

"Respond to unknown station," Ferraro said. He told Damon to
alert the OOD.

"Unknown station, this is ..." and I gave our call sign for USS Cambria. "You are weak and unreadable, try again."

The station came right back, identifying themselves. Damon quickly grabbed the Allied Voice Call Sign book and looked up the name. He showed it to me and Ferraro—it was USS Liberty (AGTR-5). Before I could reply, we heard the circuit activate.

"USS Liberty, this is USS Saratoga. Stand by, break, all stations this net, this is USS Saratoga, and I have Flash traffic this net. Break, Liberty, this is Saratoga, report status, over."

"Saratoga, Liberty. Air attack ... multiple cas ... cluding deaths. Torp ... direct hit starb ... amidships at waterline. Emergency destruc ... initiated. This is only comm... circ ... avail ... Over."

Capt. Haines, the CO, along with the commodore and Lt. Martin, had entered and stood in front of me, listening. He asked for an update.

"Captain," I said, "We have the USS Liberty on HICOM, sir, apparently under attack by Israel." I told him what Liberty and Saratoga said verbatim.

"Liberty, this is Saratoga, roger, help is on the way, maintain radio silence. Out."

Reddy, our ship/shore teletype operator, ran in and handed a message to Ferraro, who quickly handed it to the CO. Capt. Haines read the message and asked how he could reach the bridge. Ferraro showed him the intercom.

"Bridge, this is the CO. Give me the navigator."

"Bridge, sir, navigator here."

"Plot a course toward the Gaza Coast at flank speed. Have it ready for my review as soon as I reach the bridge. Alert the XO. CO out." He came over and sat next to me as he showed the commodore the message.

"Commodore," Capt. Haines said, "I'm going to the bridge, review and approve our transit to the Liberty, and then I think it's time we hold officers' call, including your and the Marines' staff. It appears we are under attack, and there could be a couple hundred casualties on that ship needing our help." He looked at his watch. "Sixteen hundred good for you?"

"Yes, and good job to you and your men, Lt. Martin," the commodore said as he left radio.

"Yes," Capt. Haines said. "We have no idea what those men on the Liberty are going through, but, thank goodness, help is on the way. Before I go to the bridge, how will the communications work now?" Ferraro told him we would dedicate an operator solely to the HICOM net and report all communications.

Capt. Haines looked at us and gave the thumbs-up, which we all returned. Departing, he said, "Keep me informed, Lieutenant, day and night."

"Okay, guys," Martin said. "That sure got the blood pumping. Keep monitoring, and make sure you give a good turnover to your reliefs. Great job."

We were all speculating on what was going on when we heard the 1MC come alive. "This is the CO. By now, you all have probably heard about an attack on one of our ships, and I want to stop any rumors. Earlier today, an American Navy ship was attacked and has suffered severe damage and multiple casualties. We are to provide assistance as necessary. As I speak, U.S. fighter jets have been deployed off the USS Saratoga and headed to defend the ship and her crew." You could hear the cheers from everyone onboard. "That is all for now, and may your prayers be with them."

We monitored the HICOM net, listening for any radio checks between Liberty and Saratoga, and there was silence. We assumed Saratoga was maintaining radio silence until their attacks. We listened and looked for any message traffic about attacks from the Saratoga fighter jets. Silence.

"Saratoga, this is Liberty, over," we finally heard on HICOM about 1715. Ferraro got on the intercom to the bridge and informed the OOD.

"Liberty, this is Saratoga, roger, over," we heard.

"Saratoga, this is Liberty. Hostilities have ceased. Israeli torpedo boats offering assistance. Liberty has refused. Request advise, over." Liberty's transmission was stronger and readable now.

"Commanding Officer in Radio," Ferraro called out. The CO waved off our standing and sat next to me. I quickly filled him in.

"Liberty, this is Saratoga. Air support ordered back to base. Report status, over."

Capt. Haines said, "Air support ordered back? What the hell?"

"Saratoga, this is Liberty. Ship under own power, tending to over 150 casualties. Twenty-seven known dead. Damage control and assessment in progress. Over."

"Liberty, this is Saratoga. USS Davis and USS Massey directed your location and will liaison direct. Can ship maintain present status? Over."

"Saratoga, this is Liberty. Ship in no further immediate danger. Over."

"Liberty, this is Saratoga. Roger, report changes as necessary. Out."

Reddy came running in and handed Ferraro a message. Ferraro read and handed it to the CO, who read and initialed it, asking for a copy. Capt. Haines started to leave radio, stopped and turned.

"I'm sure this goes without saying," he said. "What you just heard is extremely sensitive and is not to leave this radio shack. Our direct role of support may be over for now, but I have a feeling we haven't heard the last of it. Once again, great job, guys. I'm proud of every one of you." He left.

Ferraro looked at me. "We're being told to stand down and return to our previous orders. I'm sure the Old Man will be making an announcement. That's his style." About five minutes later, he was proven right.

"This is the CO," we heard over the 1MC. "We have just received orders to stand down. The USS America has been diverted from operations and has assumed those duties. We have received a well-done from our superiors for our outstanding response and support given. I too want to extend my well-done. That is all."

The ship returned to preparations for our next assault landing exercise off the coast of Crete. In radio, Kupp called a meeting of section supervisors to discuss communications plans. I knew that in the back of all our minds was, *How is the Liberty doing? What the heck has happened today?* I wondered if we would ever know.

The next morning, we heard over the 1MC, "This is the captain. The USS America can be seen on the horizon off the port side. All hands that can, man the rails." It didn't take long for everyone to obey, and, even at that distance, we could easily see the enormous carrier, at flank speed of over thirty-five knots, as it sailed past us.

The CO had the whistle blown and a message sent by flashing light wishing them "God speed." The America acknowledged, and the entire ship burst out in cheers. "GO USA, GO USA." Everyone seemed to share a common thought: help our shipmates and kick ass. It was a great feeling as we went back to our duties.

About 1100, Damon was reviewing my qualification cards and quizzing me when we heard HICOM activate. Chesney had passed on to us during watch relief that Commander U.S. Navy Forces Europe had taken back net control during the night.

"CINCUSNAVEUR, this is USS Liberty, over."

"Liberty, CINCUSNAVEUR, roger, over."

"CINCUSNAVEUR, this is Liberty. This remains only active communications circuit. Commanding officer requests to pass on names of the deceased for family notification, over."

"Liberty, this is CINCUSNAVEUR. Stand by." Several minutes passed. "Liberty, this is CINCUSNAVEUR, request send five names with Social Security numbers at a time. Go ahead, over."

"CINCUSNAVEUR, this is Liberty, roger, break …."

We listened as the names of the deceased crew members of USS Liberty were passed, five at a time. There wasn't a sound in radio, and I'm not sure when he arrived, but the CO was standing with us. Then the chaplain appeared and stood next to the CO.

"That is the last name, over." Liberty had finished.

We heard CINCUSNAVEUR acknowledge and sign out.

The CO and chaplain departed radio, and the ship went about its scheduled operations. In radio, we assumed our duties, and when our section was finally relieved, I was exhausted both physically and mentally.

June 9, 1967

Hi Mom and Dad,

The last letter I wrote was when we left Malta because of the Middle East problems. We are getting back to normal now so wanted to let you know it was no big deal for us. Anyway, we stood by if needed and it turned out not to be necessary. Hope you didn't worry.

On a positive note, I'm qualifying for watch supervisor. This means I could have my own section with eight other third-class and four seamen. I'm proud of myself because some guys have over two years onboard and haven't qualified and would be working for me. We are heading for some exercises off the coast of Greece and then we'll be having a port visit in Taranto, Italy. It looks like I'll have my birthday off so intend to toast everyone when I turn 21.

Will write again soon.

Be Good and Take Care.

Love, Rich

The next day we heard that hostilities had ceased, and Israel had apologized for attacking the USS Liberty by mistake. Mistake? We also heard the conflict was being called the Six-Day War. I knew my folks would definitely hear about that and worry, so I was glad mail was going out soon. And what I told them was true; it ended up being no big deal for us. I couldn't tell them anything about what role we did play.

That didn't keep it from playing over and over in my head. Hearing that voice say they were under attack and had taken casualties. Hearing the Saratoga say help was on the way, and a short time later say it wasn't. Then, seeing the America, at full speed, heading to support. How could anyone attack the Liberty, or any U.S. ship, by mistake? I wondered if we'd ever hear the real story. Then again, the

CO made it clear that what we heard goes no further. That didn't matter. Listening to all the names of the deceased being sent, while the CO and chaplain stood with us, would forever be embedded as a memory in my mind.

"Let us pray," the chaplain said. "Taps, Taps, lights out." The bugle played.

CHAPTER 23

June 1967, Taranto, Italy

WE HAD COMPLETED ANOTHER SUCCESSFUL ASSAULT landing exercise and transited from Souda Bay, Crete, to the Taranto, Italy, where a port visit would start June 21.

During our last watch underway, Damon told Ferraro that he was recommending me for watch supervisor. He said he had taught me all he could and was confident I was ready. When our section was relieved, Ferraro had me meet him in the teletype repair shop. He told me I'd been recommended by Damon and explained that the process would start with a "mini-board" by Ferraro. He spent the next half-hour grilling me, before calling for Damon to join us.

"He has a few items to work on, but he's ready," Ferraro told Damon. "I'll ask Kupp to schedule a qualification board." He looked at me. "Step two requires facing a formal board consisting of Kupp, Chesney, Stark, and myself as voting members. Damon sits on the board as a technical advisor only. Kupp will let you know the time and place. Probably next underway. Good job to you both."

He shook our hands and was departing when he turned. "Oh, yeah, understand you turn twenty-one while in port, Herman. Enjoy your birthday."

There were no piers to accommodate our size, so all the squadron ships anchored in the harbor when we arrived in Taranto. At the time, I didn't consider it a big deal that we'd need to ride liberty boats to and from shore. If only I could have seen into the future.

The first day in port, I had duty, which was fine with me because I was off the second day—when I would turn twenty-one at midnight.

The guys who returned from liberty the first day said it was a terrible port. Nothing opened until after 2000, and even then, it was a boring city. I didn't pay much attention and only cared that I could get something to eat and toast my birthday on time. Liberty was scheduled to end at 0200 for enlisted and 0300 for officers.

Cooper and I took the 1900 liberty boat, and, stepping ashore, we immediately saw what everyone was talking about. The city looked dark, with few local people in the streets. Even worse, a couple hundred sailors and Marines on liberty roamed around with very few places to go. We finally found a small café with a bar, blocks off the beaten path. After a couple of Peroni beers, we had a good pasta dinner with red wine. We managed to kill time until about 2300, when we decided to look for a place closer to the landing.

Heading to the waterfront, a little tipsy, we noticed hardly anyone still on liberty. We figured everyone got bored and went back to the ship. Cooper wanted to go back too but said he'd help me celebrate turning twenty-one at midnight and then catch the boat back a half-hour later. We found a place with about a dozen locals inside and an empty table.

The waitress, a lovely brunette, came over, and I said, "*Due Peroni?*" She smiled, nodded, and went to the bar. "I think I'm in love," I said, watching her walk away. Cooper laughed. When she brought our beers, I asked, "Speak English?"

"Little. I am Rosa. You?"

"I am Rich, and this is Jeff."

"Reech and Jeff. *Si*. You married?" She pointed to the ring on my finger.

"No, no, high school ring." I'd grown so much since I graduated that my ring only fit on my left hand. Dumb.

"No, Reech married." She giggled.

"No, look." I took the ring off and tried to show her the writing. She wagged her finger at me. Cooper roared with laughter. I realized it was a lost cause and decided to change the subject.

I pointed to myself, saying, "My birthday."

"*Buon compleanno?*" she said.

"*Si*," I said as it sounded good to me. I pointed at my watch. It was 2345. "Midnight. Twenty-one." I put my hands up and flashed my fingers to indicate my age.

"*Ventuno*? Ah, *ventuno*."

"*Si*. Me drink," I pretended putting a glass to my mouth, "legal America."

"*Si, si*."

Cooper was cracking up. I went to the bar with Rosa and pointed to some shot glasses and a bottle of Jack Daniels. "Ten," I said, pointing at myself. Then I pointed at everyone in the bar. Rosa smiled.

"*Dieci*." She had the bartender pour ten shots and put them in front of me. He then poured shots for everyone, including herself, Cooper, and the bartender. I pointed at my watch, handed my class ring to Rosa, kissed her, and at exactly midnight, she yelled, "*Buon ventuno compleanno*, Reech." Everyone toasted me, and I started drinking the shots one by one.

"Petty Officer," I heard someone saying, "are you okay?" He was shaking my shoulder. I looked up and saw several officers standing there.

"Yes, sir," I said. Where was Cooper? Where was anyone? All I saw was officers.

"Son," one of them said, "you missed the last liberty boat. Don't worry, we'll get you back on the officers' launch. Here it comes now. It's 0140, so you'll even make it back on time. Let's go." He and another officer helped me up.

"It's my birthday," I slurred as I stood. They looked familiar. "Hey, you the ship's doctor." He didn't seem amused. I also recognized the other officer. "And you the chaplain. I really enjoy your prayers."

"That's good, son," the chaplain said, laughing now. "Let's get you home." The boat pulled alongside the pier, and they helped me aboard. They were probably afraid I'd fall overboard, so they helped me below into the cabin, where I sat.

I woke up and realized I was lying on the deck of the ship. Above me, I saw the bottom of a boat. *A boat?* My head was pounding.

I looked around, didn't recognize anything, and tried to remember how I got here. *My birthday. Officers talking to me?* I looked at my watch. It was 0630. One thing I did know, besides being in a world of trouble, was this was not the Cambria. I got up, saw what looked like a quarterdeck, and headed that way. I saw the OOD, walked up, and said, "Morning, I'm RM3 Herman, and—"

"Herman?" the OOD said. "What? RM3 Herman off the Cambria?" he yelled. He looked at the ship's patch on my right sleeve and said, "Get the XO. NOW." The messenger of the watch made a phone call. "Stand there and don't say a word," the OOD said, glaring at me.

"What you got, Chief?" a lieutenant commander said as he approached the quarterdeck. The OOD filled him in. "Herman, huh? Chief, call the Cambria on your radio and tell them we found their missing sailor." He looked at me, "Do you have any idea how much trouble you've caused, Petty Officer? Your ship alerted all ships that they had a sailor unaccounted for. Last seen about 0130 on an officers' boat." He was about to continue when the OOD stopped him.

"XO, Cambria XO on the line, sir," the OOD said.

"USS Shadwell, XO here," he said into the phone. After a minute he continued, "Yes, sir. He seems to be a little worse for wear, but fine. Will have him standing by." He handed the phone back to the OOD and got into my face. "You are facing some serious charges, sailor. Don't say a word until you get back to your ship. That's an order."

"Yes, sir." My head was killing me, I had to go to the bathroom, and I was starting to remember more about last night. I was in so much trouble.

The XO sent the captain's gig to get me. As I boarded, I saw my old knife-throwing friend, Hoss, at the helm. With a big smile, he motioned a finger going across his throat. Obeying orders, I said nothing. As we approached the Cambria, I saw Cooper and a bunch of the radiomen on the weather deck outside radio, waving and cheering. I stepped off the gig and was heading up the brow when there he was, near the quarterdeck, the last person I wanted to see. Lt. Cmdr. Fortune.

"Got you this time, Herman," he yelled. Was he actually pumping his fist? "I knew you'd screw up. You can't get out of this."

Once onboard, the OOD logged me in as having returned at 0720. The MAA was prepared to escort me when Lt. Martin appeared.

"I'll escort Petty Officer Herman," he told the MAA, who saluted and handed my division officer the report chit. Lt. Cmdr. Fortune was about to say something, when Martin said, "We're going straight to XO's Mast." Fortune had a big smile and then a smirk on his face as we passed. The MAA went with us.

We were almost to the XO's stateroom when Martin stopped outside an officers' head. He handed me what he was carrying—his douche kit. "Get in there and do what you have to. Try and make yourself presentable."

I was never so glad to see a urinal. I used some of the lieutenant's toothpaste on my finger and brushed my teeth, washed my face and hands, and straightened my uniform the best I could. I wouldn't pass any inspections, but I looked and felt better anyway. "Thanks, Lieutenant," I said, handing him his kit when I came out.

"Not much I can say or do for you," he said. "The XO placed you on report himself and told me to bring you straight to him for XO's Mast. Lt. Cmdr. Fortune said he expected CO's Mast today and looked forward to you being busted and receiving brig time. All I can say is be honest, agree to non-judicial punishment—NJP—and good luck. The MAA will instruct you on Mast procedure." It took the MAA about five minutes to prepare me, and Martin knocked on the XO's stateroom door.

"Enter," the XO said.

I took three steps into the stateroom, came to attention, saluted the XO, who was standing by his desk, and said, "Petty Officer Third Class Herman, reporting as ordered, sir." The XO saluted back. Martin entered, and the MAA closed the stateroom door and stood at attention inside.

"Petty Officer Herman," the XO started. "Do you understand

why you are here and the charge against you? Do you also accept my recommendation as to disposition of this matter, even if it means referral to court-martial rather than NJP?"

"Yes, sir," I said, now scared to death. Court-martial?

"Parade rest. Before I hear from you, Herman, let you hear from me and what I know, or think I know, about the events of last night. Fact: You were aware that your liberty ended at 0200. Fact: You were discovered on the USS Shadwell at 0630, making you UA for four and a half hours, and that is the one charge, Violation of the UCMJ Article 86, you face. *For now.*" Fact: You were found on a naval vessel, not your own, at sea and in a foreign port. This disturbs me the most, and I hope you realize how serious it is. Do you realize that you could have been on a Russian ship and not even known it? You could have become a bargaining chip in an international incident. I'm sure that borders on a charge so serious, it not only could end your career, you could be imprisoned." He took a drink of water, and someone knocked on the door.

"Request permission to enter," a voice said.

"Enter," the XO said. The ship's doctor and chaplain entered. "This better be important, Doc, Chaplain."

"We believe it is, XO," the chaplain said. "Request to speak freely, sir." The XO nodded. "Well, sir, last night, or early this morning I guess, the doctor and I saw Petty Officer Herman at the boat landing. He had just missed the liberty boat back to the ship, which would have gotten him there on time, by the way, and we ordered him to accompany us on the officers' boat. We got to talking and forgot about him until we heard he was missing this morning. We knew he was, ah, very tired after celebrating his birthday turning twenty-one, and we should have made sure he made it back aboard. The mess Petty Officer Herman has gotten into shouldn't have happened. As naval officers, we should have handled our responsibility better and are equally, if not more so, accountable."

The XO didn't speak. I didn't move. It was as if all the air had been taken out of the stateroom. Finally, the XO said, "Thank you for coming forward and shedding some light. I will take your comments into consideration. Dismissed." As they were leaving, he said, "Doc, Chaplain, why don't you join me this afternoon, say, 1500, for coffee?" They nodded and left.

"Petty Officer Herman, do you care to add anything?"

I wasn't sure what to do or say. Then I remembered the lieutenant telling me just to be honest. I stood at attention. "XO, I offer no excuses. I know better and not only realize how serious this could have been, but I feel I have disappointed the faith and trust the chain of command, and especially you, put in me. I appreciate the doctor and chaplain coming forward, but it was mine, and not their responsibility. That's all, sir." He stared at me, expressionless, for several minutes.

"Very well," he said. "Attention to orders." Martin and the MAA snapped to. "It is the finding of this XO's Mast that Petty Officer Herman receive two days of extra duty, which shall be stood as shore patrol as assigned by the division and shore patrol officer." He signed the report chit and handed it to the MAA, who left. Lt. Martin and I were about to leave when the XO said, "Not so fast. Close the door, Lieutenant." He sat at his desk and motioned for Martin to sit also. I remained standing. "What do you think, Lieutenant?"

"More than fair, XO. I'm sure Petty Officer Herman knows that."

"Fair or not, it comes down to being held accountable," the XO said, leaning back. "You did that, Herman, and you were right. I had faith in you, and that is why I called for immediate XO's Mast. What you did was beyond serious, but the CO and I both believe in backing our good sailors. No one got hurt, and diplomatic relations didn't suffer. I know the CO will back me up, but you should know that his relief, Captain Wise, is onboard. He may not see it the same way." He laughed.

"I never counted on your supporters showing up. If you had tried to let the doctor and chaplain take the fall for you, I would have crucified you. You didn't, and I respect that. At our coffee this afternoon, I'm going to make sure they know that. Now, when you leave here, I expect you to let your peers know you're not some folk hero and you screwed up. Once again, I'll deal with Fortune. Now, back to work."

"Yes, sir," I said, feeling much better than when I came in. I started to leave.

"One more thing, Herman," the XO said. "About 1500 this afternoon, you may want to return the favor and say a little prayer for the chaplain."

After getting cleaned up, I headed to radio knowing I was going to get bombarded with questions. I wasn't prepared for the reception I got.

"Here comes the groom now," Cooper said. "How was your wedding night?" The Big Three, along with Damon, Stark, Reddy, and others, threw rice on me and started cheering.

"What the hell you talking about?" I asked. "And what happened to you last night, Cooper?"

"You don't remember asking Rosa to marry you?" he asked. "You gave her your ring, planted a big kiss, and I'm sure the bartender said something about *matrimonio*. We looked it up, and it means marriage ceremony." Everyone guffawed.

"Oh, give me a break. And what did happen to you?"

"I somehow caught the liberty boat and made it back on time. I thought you were with me. So tell us all the details. You going to captain's mast or straight to court-martial like Fortune was saying?"

"I'm going to tell you all one time." I recapped my evening from the time the officers found me until my XO's Mast. "I hope you all agree it's a good story that could have had a very bad ending, and let's leave it at that. I was lucky."

"Agree," Kupp said. "Old Fortune is going to go nuts when he hears this. We're just glad you're back safe. Sorry no one had your back." He looked at Cooper. "Lesson learned, guys, let's not let it happen to anyone again. Take care of each other. Back to work."

I figured that was the end of it. Then, we had a ship's party in honor of the CO's upcoming change of command. After leaving Taranto, we anchored off a small, deserted island, and Capt. Haines called for a beach party with a cookout, swim call, and sports competition. The crew must have toasted Capt. Haines a dozen times with beers. We loved him. Everyone was back onboard ship when the 1MC activated.

"All hands, man the rails port side." The crew fell in. Five minutes later we heard, "Attention to port." Wearing swimming gear, shorts, and no hats, we came to attention. "Commanding Officer, USS Cambria, arriving." We looked and here came Capt. Haines, waterskiing behind his gig with Hoss at the helm. "Hand salute." We all saluted, even without covers, and watched the CO ski by, drop his swim trunks, and point to his ass, yelling, "TAKE THAT, FORTUNE!" And he mooned him. The crew went crazy, and then we heard, "Commanding Officer, USS Cambria, departing." He skied off. "Dismissed."

I lay in my rack picturing Capt. Haines mooning Lt. Cmdr. Fortune. I knew he didn't do it for me, but deep down I took some satisfaction that I was a small part of it. *I will never forget you, Capt. Haines, and I will never forget turning twenty-one and my birthday celebration in Taranto, Italy.* My thoughts turned elsewhere. I was going to miss my class ring, and I hoped I wasn't actually married.

CHAPTER 24

July 1967, Ionian Sea and Livorno, Italy

DEPLOYED AND UNDERWAY, THE CHANGE OF command was low-key, and Capt. Wise became our new CO on July 1. When the ceremony concluded, Capt. Haines left for the USS Shadwell, where he boarded a helicopter for transport ashore. The helo flew low over the Cambria, and the crew waved their final farewell to their old CO.

We were settling into our normal routine when I got called to report to Lt. Martin's office. Now what had I done? However, when I got there, I found Kupp, Ferraro, Chesney, Stark, and Damon in the office, with a chair in a corner waiting for me.

"This is your formal qualification board for communication watch supervisor," Kupp began. "Before we begin, do you have any questions, or would you like a head break?"

"No," I said, trying not to sound nervous. "I'm good to go."

Kupp stood and removed a sheet revealing a white board with numerous circuits, frequencies, and locations, as well as watch standers on duty. "For this exam, this is your communications status."

Chesney started, "The ship just suffered a momentary power loss knocking out all circuits. Walk us through your restoration plan and how you set your priorities."

"My first priority would be determining what equipment assets I may have lost. I would direct Damon to the transmitter room and Cooper to the receiver banks while I contacted the bridge. Once all three have reported the status, I would direct reactivating circuits in the following order …"

For the next two hours, I answered their questions. Finally, Kupp told me to take a break, and I stepped outside. Cooper was standing in as supervisor while the others held my board.

"So," he said, "how was it?" He didn't seem too happy.

"Find out in a couple of minutes," I said.

"You'll do fine. Ferraro wouldn't have wasted everyone's time if you weren't ready. Besides, you're their boy, aren't you?"

"What's that supposed to mean?" I didn't like the way he said that. He stared at me and was about to say something when Damon called me back in.

"Congratulations, Herman," Kupp said, shaking my hand. "You're the first third-class and definitely the youngest to ever qualify for watch supervisor in my almost four years on board. And we all know you are now twenty-one." Everyone laughed. He left to take the qualification card to Martin.

Ferraro and Stark shook my hand, and Chesney, pretending he was going to tack on my crow again, finally extended his hand and smiled. Damon nodded his approval. "I think it's important you know what swayed the board in your favor," Ferraro said. "When you didn't know something, rather than guess, you said you would go ask someone. Realizing no one can know everything, you knew there are good people around you to help. That's a sign of a good supervisor." I looked at Damon, who now had a big smile.

"It's official," Kupp said, returning with my card. "He's qualified; now let's see if he proves us right. Back to work."

When we left the office, Chesney went to get an update from Cooper before taking over as supervisor again. I waited to talk to Cooper, but, instead of coming over, he went the other way. It was time he and I had a talk and figured out what was bothering him. Obviously, it would have to wait. Maybe on watch that night.

July 1, 1967

Hi Mom and Dad,

I go on watch soon but today was a big day and I wanted to write and let you know how things are going. Like I said in my last letter, things have calmed down over here and it never affected us much. I hope the press back home didn't make it out like we were in danger or anything. Anyway, I got some good stuff to write about.

Big news! I was able to celebrate turning 21 in style in Taranto, Italy. I had a good Italian pasta dinner with local red wine and at midnight I was able to toast my birthday with Cooper and some nice local people. I don't speak Italian and they didn't speak English but we managed using hand language to get across what was happening. On the way back to the ship I joined up with the ship's doctor and chaplain and they topped off my birthday with letting me ride with them on the officers' boat. It was a great experience.

Today was the ship's change of command. The other day we had a ship's picnic on a deserted island and the crew got to say their goodbye to Captain Haines with beer salutes. Later he gave a special goodbye to us all by skiing alongside the ship. It was very unique. Captain Wise became our CO this morning and he mentioned he would be sending letters to all our families so you can look forward to that.

More big news! I qualified as watch supervisor. I told you a little bit about the job before. Anyway, I've only been onboard six months and I'm only a third-class petty officer so I'm not sure how well others will take it. I think Cooper, who's been on board a couple years and not qualified yet, is upset. Like always, I'll work it out. Anyway, it's a big responsibility so wish me luck.

We got mail in Taranto and I received a lot of birthday cards. Mar said she was doing great and I should be an uncle in October. Also got cards from Margy and Irv and Gary and Jackie. I hope everyone realizes how much mail means to me.

Well, about time to go on watch. We have some more war games coming up and then will visit Livorno, Italy. I'm going to try and take another tour while we're in port. I also volunteered to stand shore patrol a couple days to give other guys a break. I'm getting pretty good at it.

Be Good and Take Care.
Love, Rich

I was at chow, before relieving the watch, when Kupp sat down next to me. "I wanted to let you know that I'm putting you in Chesney's section starting today. Cooper is close to being board-eligible for watch supervisor, and I want Damon to dedicate his last few weeks onboard to making that happen. Also, between you and me, Cooper has been dragging his feet long enough, and it's time he starts pulling more of his own weight. It's going to be up to you, Stark, and him after this deployment. I know Cooper isn't going to like it, but, tough. You've set the standard now, and I hope you'll help him. Any problem with that?"

"Not on my part," I answered. "How about in port duty?"

"I'll put you in the same section for liberty, for now. You've earned that." He picked up his tray and left. This meant I didn't have watch until morning. A whole evening off. I decided to catch the movie on the mess decks and get a good night's sleep.

Chesney welcomed me and had me perform his duties, under his close eye, the first day. The second day, he had me relieve Ferraro as supervisor, telling me it's easier to learn to drive the car behind the wheel. That day, the Marines' assault exercise began, and the squadron communication watch officers started standing watch and screening all message traffic. Throughout the watch, I made a point to check with them, making sure their requirements were being met.

After a week of war games, we stood down and transited to our port visit. I tried talking to Cooper during watch turnovers, but we never seemed to have enough time. We did get a chance to discuss liberty when we reached port and agreed to hit the beach together the first day in Livorno, Italy.

That turned out to be a memorable day. "Hey, Stark," I called out. I was following Cooper up the ladder from our berthing compartment when I saw him and Reddy putting their whites on. "You guys want to join us?"

"Sure," Stark said. "We'll meet you on the pier in a couple minutes. Thanks."

Cooper stopped at the top of the ladder, turned, and glared at me. "What do you mean, join us?" he said. "I'm not going on the beach with those two."

It was time to put an end to this. I couldn't go up another rung, so, looking up, I said, "Well, have a good time then, because I'm going with them."

Instantly, I was kicked in the head and fell backwards. I lay dazed at the bottom of the ladder, thinking my face was broken.

"Are you okay?" I heard. It was Stark. "Reddy, get a towel. Damn, help me get him to sick bay."

"What have you gotten into now, Herman?" It was my friend, the doctor, talking to me.

Sitting on a table, I noticed blood, a lot of it, on my uniform. "I guess I fell going up the ladder, Doc."

"I see. Well, your nose isn't broken, and your eye socket seems okay. Fortunately, your broken glasses didn't cause any damage. We can stitch up that nasty cut above your eye. You're going to have one nasty bruise, though. I'd say you were one lucky guy, considering. For the record then, you fell down the ladder?"

"Yeah, trying to go up too fast to get on liberty."

"Okay," he said and started writing. "I won't mention anything about what looks like a shoe print." He turned and smiled. "Usually, I treat guys who are drunk and fall down, not sober and fall up the ladder. I'll have the corpsman come stitch you up. You can leave when you're up to it. Always interesting with you, Herman."

Stark was waiting for me outside sick bay. "The doc said you'll mend." He looked closer at me. "Ouch. Thought you might like company back to the compartment."

"Thanks," I said. "Appreciate it. Wow, hit a nerve, I guess."

"I think it was a long time coming," Stark said. "Sorry it had to be you. You don't have to fight our battles, you know. It should have been one of us."

"Your battles? And one of us? It shouldn't be a you or us, Stark.

And I didn't fight your battle, it was mine. I chose this. No one is going to tell me who to and who not to like, and who I can and can't go on liberty with. Doesn't work that way. If Cooper or anyone else feels that way, then I'm going to be seeing the doc a lot, because it's got to stop. We need each other and need to take care of each other. Damn!"

"You're right. For what it's worth, I'm proud to be called your friend. Can I buy you a beer?" I smiled and nodded. I changed uniforms, got my spare pair of glasses, and we went ashore. I truly enjoyed that beer.

News of the encounter between Cooper and me traveled fast. The next day, Martin had us report to his office, along with Kupp and Stark. "I understand that there was an incident yesterday, which has officially been reported as RM3 Herman having suffered an accidental fall." He looked at me for a few seconds. "I'm hoping there is nothing more to it than that; however, let me make this clear, if there is another underlying reason, then I want it dealt with and resolved quickly. We cannot have dissension in this division. Understood?"

"Yes, sir," we replied in unison.

I left radio and was walking down the weather deck when Cooper called out, "Herman, got a minute?"

"Sure," I said. We both leaned over the railing.

"Sorry, Herman," he started. "I mean that. It's just that you made me so mad when you asked those guys to join us. You put me in a bad spot, and I took it out on you. Don't you get it?"

"Asking those guys?" I said. "You mean Stark and Reddy, two of our shipmates who stand watch with us? Stark, who is a qualified supervisor and a great guy? And Reddy, who gets seasick as soon as the ship moves but never complains or misses a watch? Those guys who never flinch when it comes time to help with field day or make a supply run? You mean those guys? It's those guys I want to hang out with, Cooper. Just like you. Good guys.

"It's hard to explain," he said. "My whole life I've been told to stay away from colored people. I was taught they couldn't be trusted.

It's just the way it is. I like Stark and Reddy, but I can't be seen on the beach with them. Do you understand?"

"No, I don't understand, but I can try to see why you do. I wasn't raised that way. I'm not going to try and tell you how wrong you are or how you should be. And you shouldn't judge me. I feel sorry that you can't accept a person for who they are, not what you've been taught they are. I'll tell you what. I won't try to change you, and you don't try to change me. If along the way, one of us does, then so be it. I haven't met anyone in radio I don't want to see or be seen with having a beer on the beach. And I'm going to. I hope we can still be good friends and associate on and off the ship. Deal?"

Cooper looked down, then at my face. "You're something else. While we're at it, I may as well tell you this too. I was kind of the guy everyone looked to around here until you showed up. All of a sudden, you were getting all the attention. Now, you qualified watch supervisor ahead of me and could be my boss. It just pisses me off. Anyway, I feel better. And, yeah, I want to be friends. Do you want to hit me or something to make things even?"

I thought about how my dad met Harry Newsom. I smiled. "If you haven't noticed, I'm not much of a fighter, and I don't intend to start now. How about we get your lazy butt qualified watch supervisor next underway?" He laughed and shook my hand, and I felt we had overcome a tremendous hurdle between us and could now move on.

We spent ten days in Livorno, and I took a bus tour to Pisa with Cooper. The Leaning Tower turned out to be something you write home about, but we were disappointed. All it did was lean.

Back from the tour, I turned in early. Our section had the watch in the morning, and it would be my first time as supervisor with the ship getting underway. Our deployment was more than half over, and I couldn't imagine the next two months being as challenging as what I had experienced since leaving Norfolk. One thing I did feel good about; I may not have taken the easiest route or handled it the best way, but I was sailing tomorrow with two new friends for life.

CHAPTER 25

August 1967, Mediterranean and crossing the Atlantic

WE SPENT THE NEXT TWENTY-SEVEN DAYS AT SEA conducting two major Marine assault landing war games and participated in a five-country, twenty-three-ship NATO exercise. The pace was nonstop, and every watch presented new challenges. In our third week of being underway, we got the word that Cooper would have his formal qualification board the next day.

It seemed strange to be part of the voting board, but Kupp got me right into the flow of things by having me set up the exercise communication status board. After two hours, Cooper was told to take a break, and I found out how the voting worked. "Just a yes or a no," Kupp said and polled each of us. After all said yes, he looked at Ferraro. "Charlie, you voted yes, but you don't look that confident." Wow, I thought, he called him by his first name.

Ferraro sat for a moment before answering. "Cooper has the knowledge and ability—it's just that everything seems to be a game to him, and I'm a little concerned, if a crisis hits, he won't handle the pressure. Hopefully, I'm wrong."

"Anyone else?" Kupp said.

I waited and, when no one else spoke, decided to add my two cents. "I know I'm the new guy, but here's my take. Cooper deals with his nerves by making a joke out of it. It's how he copes with a crisis. In the end, I think he'll relax his section and solve any problem thrown at him."

"I agree," Stark said, startling us; usually he didn't voice his opinions. "If you've noticed, since he and Herman had that up close and personal discussion, Cooper is dealing with everyone a lot better. He's more relaxed, and, tell you the truth—and I wouldn't have said this before—I would welcome him as my section leader. I think you all have relaxed more."

There was absolute silence as everyone stared at him. Damon, wearing a big smile, winked at me. Ferraro nodded, and Chesney shrugged. Kupp said, "Well, now, that's a statement, and about the biggest vote of confidence I have ever heard. Thanks for being so honest, John." *First name again?*

Kupp opened the door and called Cooper in. After congratulating him, Kupp went to get Martin's approval, making it official. One by one, we congratulated the new watch supervisor. "Cooper, I want you to know how proud we are of you," Kupp said when he returned. "This underway, you buckled down and worked hard to get to where you are now. And it's about time." We all chuckled. "Seriously, we want you to know we have noticed a change in you, and it's a very positive one. Good job."

"You know," Ferraro said, "before we all start crying, I'd like to add that this means we now have three solid supervisors to take over, and the Big Three can retire and leave knowing the division is in good hands at the end of this deployment. And a lot of that credit goes to RM3 Dave Damon. I think we all owe him a drink our next port before he leaves us."

Before anyone could respond, Cooper said, "I'd like to buy that first round if I could. I appreciate you guys putting up with me, and it'd be my way to say thanks." He walked over to Stark and extended his hand. "And that includes you. Friends?" They shook.

The next day, Chesney told me Lt. Martin wanted us both in his office; Vargas, Hill, Ferraro, and Kupp were already there. Martin announced that he wanted us to hear about a proposal Vargas had brought to him.

Vargas began, "During major exercises, as you know, we have a communication watch officer augment your watch sections to personally screen message traffic for the commodore. First, let me say that you all have done a great job. That said, all three of these CWOs have come to the same conclusion, and briefed the commodore on it, that their job is always made easier when the ship's watch supervisor screens their messages with them and helps them prioritize." He paused, and I thought, oh, oh. Chesney told me I was spoiling them, and it could come back and bite us.

"That's not our job though," Kupp said. He glared at me. "It's also not our responsibility."

"I know that," Vargas said, "but it has benefitted the staff on doing their job. The commodore has asked that I look at it and see if maybe we should make it a permanent watch position."

"Before we get all worked up," Martin said, looking at Kupp and knowing he was going to fight this, "I think we should remember that one of our major jobs is to support the commodore. Let's hear Lt. Vargas out before working up a lather." Kupp looked at Ferraro, then Chesney, and all three looked at me. If looks could kill.

"Thank you," Vargas said. He looked around, then said with a laugh, "Okay, let's state the obvious. RM3 Herman has created this dilemma, but before you all decide to throw him overboard," everyone now chuckled, "let's look at it this way. The commodore wants his watch officers to have an assistant. So, instead of looking at reasons why it can't be done, let's look at how it can. We have reviewed this in depth, and RM1 Hill has come up with a plan. RM1 Hill."

Hill, toothpick in mouth, stood, taking a position so everyone could see him. I glanced at the Big Three and immediately thought of the day he was introduced to us and the negative comments including, "I'll never take orders from him." I didn't envy him, but he seemed confident.

Removing the toothpick, he said, "One thing I have noticed is how good CR Division is at doing their jobs. When we deployed, you had only a few well-qualified radiomen and a lot of new eager ones. It has been a pleasure watching you senior guys, I think they call you the Big Three," nodding at them, "and that exceptionally talented RM3 Damon train your personnel. And just how effective have you been? You now have two more qualified watch supervisors and can sustain a three-section watch bill underway. So why am I telling you all this? Because *you* are the reason you *can* support the additional watch stander."

He stopped, put the toothpick back in his mouth, and let everyone think about what he had said. There was no immediate rejection or even grumbling. Hill had stroked their ego and put them in a position of having to accept another challenge and not fail.

"And how do we do that?" Kupp asked, looking at the others, who had no choice but to listen.

Hill threw away his toothpick and said, "We will add an assistant communications watch officer to squadron's staff. On a trial basis, RM3 Herman, who started this, will be assigned temporary duty to squadron during operations when the staff is stood up. All three CWOs already have confidence in him. He and I will stand port and starboard duty as the assistant CWO. At the end of operations, RM3 Herman will return to ship's company."

Martin spoke up. "I agree with squadron on giving it a try, and like RM1 Hill said, you guys have worked hard and through your qualification program can support letting Herman go TAD and still remain in three-section."

Vargas added, "This is another challenge for you guys, and if you can pull it off, it will be the icing on the cake for a very successful deployment." Once again, he and Hill knew just how to get the division to respond positively and with enthusiasm.

"Comments," Martin said.

"Yes, sir," Kupp said. "Can someone explain to me how Herman always gets into the shits and comes out smelling like a rose?"

"What you talking about," I quickly said. "I'm the one who's going to be spending twelve on, twelve off duty." All the guys started booing and pretending to beat on me.

"With that, you're dismissed," Martin said. Laughter continued as we left in a good mood.

Aug 18, 1967

Hey Mom and Dad,

I know it's been a while since writing but since we left Livorno, Italy, we've been at sea and I've been so busy I just never seem to have the time to write. Tomorrow we pull into Valencia, Spain, and I'll be visiting another country for the first time.

I'm not sure what's the most important thing that's happened since I last wrote. I did have one experience that will be a memory for life. Remember how you and Harry Newsom met, Dad? Before becoming best friends, you stood up to him and actually had a fight? Well, I sort of had the same thing happen. I've told you about my friend Cooper. Well, we were going on liberty and had a disagreement on who we should be seen with. I'm not much of a fighter, sorry, Dad, and took a couple stitches but stood my ground. Later we talked about it and now I think Cooper will be a good friend for life. I'm finding out that, in the Navy anyway, everyone is expected to work together but maybe not play together.

I did go on a bus tour to Pisa and saw the Leaning Tower. I took pictures to show when I come home. Let's just say I can say I've been there and leave it at that.

Remember my telling you I qualified as a watch supervisor? Well, I actually got to stand the watch the last couple weeks at sea and I loved it. The problem is, I may have stood the watch too well. Although not part of my job, I took it upon myself to help the squadron watch officers sort their messages into what was the most important and what priority it should be given to the chain of command. It turned out the commodore was so impressed he wants this all the time. Yep, our next underway I will be working for the squadron instead of the ship. At first the other guys were pretty upset with me but now have seen it as a good thing. I hope. I'll let you know.

I don't know much about Valencia, other than it's on the east coast about mid-country. We were told some of the best bull fighting in the world is here so we may try and do that. We've been at sea a long time so I'm just looking forward to getting off ship for a while. Hard to believe, we have one more at sea period and then go to Rota, Spain, for turnover. Then, head for home. Do you think you guys may meet the ship? That's be great if you could.

Well, want to get this ready for mail and check on my liberty uniforms. Looking forward to getting mail tomorrow. Hope I get lots of letters.

Be Good and Take Care.

Love, Rich

Our port visit to Valencia provided a nice break, after almost a month of fast-paced operations at sea. Our big day out was a get-together to say goodbye to Damon, who would leave the ship in Rota. I made it to a bullfight and managed for the first time not to get into any trouble. Whether the crew was getting burned out or everyone was just looking for the deployment to end, we were actually anxious to leave port to conduct our final scheduled exercises and final port stop before beginning our Atlantic transit home.

I was on duty the night before leaving port when Kupp stopped by. "I'm about to post the underway watch bill," he said, "and I wanted to let you know that you're not on it. I decided, since you're going to be standing watches with squadron when the exercises start in two days, that you may as well report to RM1 Hill early. This way, you guys can figure out how to run this new assistant CWO watch position and hopefully make it work. I know we give you a hard time for this happening, but if it works and makes things better for the ship and squadron, then I'm all for it. You know, Herman, you have a way of making things better, and you could have a great future in the Navy. If you can manage to stay out of trouble." He laughed and started to leave. He turned and added, "But you never heard any of that from me."

"Heard what?" I said.

Aug 31, 1967

Hi Folks,

I'm in Rota, Spain, right now, and our ship is in the process of being relieved by the USS Chilton and Amphibious Squadron Eight. We get underway soon and will be on our way home. Mail is going off the ship tomorrow so I wanted to write one last letter before I get home. I got your letters and you said you may try and meet the ship. That would be great. Just in case, I've already asked to have the first day in Norfolk off.

I did get to a bullfight in Valencia. It wasn't anything like I thought it would be. Cooper and I went and we had seats near the top of a big stadium of about 25,000 people. When we got there, I decided I was going to pull for the bull because from what I've ever seen they are slaughtered. Well, about ten minutes after the first bull came out, I changed my mind. I always thought it was a matador and bull. Actually, the bull fights three guys first, and they stick all sorts of little swords in his back. In the first minute, two of the guys got gored and had to be carried out. The matador came out and I thought he was going to get killed at first but then he pulled through. I was definitely on his side at end. Anyway, like the Leaning Tower of Pisa, I can say I saw it. I would never go again.

Remember my telling you about Cooper and I becoming friends and the issue I had to deal with the colored and whites? Well, since I wrote you, Cooper got qualified as watch supervisor, and he was so happy he said he'd buy everyone a drink next port. Long story short, we had a little farewell for the guy who helped qualify most of us and not only did Cooper buy a round, he sat between Stark and Hill who are both colored. I loved it and he seemed to have a good time. Cooper has invited me to go home with him for a weekend when we get back and he asked me not to tell any of his friends or family. I don't think I will ever understand. I do feel good that we all are getting along better though.

This last underway I stood watch with squadron, and it went

185

great so I was worried about nothing. When it was over, the job I sort of helped make turned out to be so successful, the commodore wants it to be permanent. They're calling it the "Herman billet."

Have you ever heard of Jeane Dixon? She's some psychic who got famous for predicting J.F. Kennedy's assassination. Anyway, she's predicted only three of our six ships will return to Norfolk. How weird is that? Some guys on the ship are actually worried but I'm not going to. At least, I don't think I am. Only kidding.

Want to get this in the mail. Hope to see you on the pier.

Be Good and Take Care.

Love, Rich

We were halfway through our transit home when we started getting messages about Hurricane Doria. Six days from our scheduled arrival date, we were getting tailored weather alerts about possible tracks the storm could take. Some had her making landfall on Florida's west coast; some had her going as far north as New York. I had never been in or even cared about a hurricane, so all I knew for sure was everyone agreed they were unpredictable. Four days from our arrival, three of our six ships were diverted away from the storm, and the other three, including Cambria, stayed on the original course. *I'll be damned, Jeane Dixon was right.*

On September 14, Doria had weakened and was off the coast of Florida. We pulled into Cherry Point, North Carolina, and offloaded all Marine personnel. That night, we transited to Norfolk and prepared for a noon arrival. I had always heard about channel fever, and now I got to experience it. The whole crew was too keyed up to sleep. Movies ran all night, and the chow hall served sandwiches and bug juice. At 1100, we heard over the 1MC, "Man the rails, prepare to moor alongside."

When we tied up, I was with all the other radiomen not on watch, along the rail on our weather deck. I scanned the crowd on the pier, but didn't see Mom and Dad. I continued looking for them even after we were secured. I couldn't believe how disappointed I was.

Finally, realizing they weren't coming, I left the ship to at least enjoy being on American soil again.

"The club will close in ten minutes," the bartender said. I was at the enlisted club having some food and a few beers. I figured the folks were at home working, and I planned to call them soon, when Mom would be lighting a cigarette and she and Dad getting comfortable after dinner.

"Excuse me," I said. "Closing? Why?"

"Haven't you been watching TV? Hurricane Doria took a sharp turn and is headed this way. The base is going into lockdown, and all personnel are being recalled to their ships. The smaller ones have been getting underway all afternoon. You need to pay up and get going, son."

Shaken, I paid my bill and stepped outside, only to realize the winds were getting stronger. I made my way to the piers and found a phone booth. Mom answered on the first ring.

"Oh, Rich, are you all right?" she said. "We've been so worried about you."

"I'm fine, Mom. What happened to you guys? I thought you were going to be on the pier."

"Oh, honey, we're so sorry. We decided at the last minute not to come. You know Marlys is due soon, and I thought it best I be nearby since it's her first baby and all. Then we saw all the weather reports on Hurricane Doria, and we weren't even sure you would be returning for a while. We talked to Mark Newsom, and he said he would meet the ship and explain. He wasn't there?"

"I understand, Mom. Mark didn't meet ship, but I think he may be under orders to stay where he is." The wind shook the phone booth. "I've been called back to my ship, and the base is going into lockdown. Well, I better get going. I'm fine and will—"

A gust of wind blew the phone booth, and me, over. Lying on my side on the door inside the phone booth, I was trapped. The receiver was dead.

"Hey," someone yelled. "You okay in there?" Two shore patrols were kneeling and looking in at me.

"I think so. Just stuck." Water was streaming in and soaking me.

"Hang on," one of them said. "We're going to try and roll you ninety degrees to free the door. If that doesn't work, we'll break the glass. Ready? One, two, three." The phone booth rolled, and they were able to push the door in and open. I scrambled out. I thanked them, and they headed off as if they did this every day.

I made it to the ship and, after a quick explanation as to why my uniform was such a mess, was informed by the OOD to get inside and help secure the ship for heavy winds. We were riding out Hurricane Doria in port. As I left the quarterdeck, he said, "I've heard about you, Herman. Never a dull moment."

Doria weakened and moved out to sea that weekend. On Monday, Lt. Martin told me the squadron would be moving off the ship until next year's deployment and asked that I make myself available to help.

"Petty Officer Herman," Lt. Vargas said as he and Hill entered radio. "I understand you volunteered to help us move ashore."

"Yes, sir," I said. "Always at your service."

"I already did inventory, Lieutenant," Hill said, his trademark toothpick in his mouth. "Just need to load and carry."

The lieutenant worked as hard as Hill and I did, and we were done in a couple hours. We loaded the last crate on their truck when Vargas pulled out a cooler and handed us each a cold beer. "Well deserved," he said. We enjoyed our beer and made small talk.

"I'm going to miss you guys," I said.

"We'll be on the next Med deployment before you know it," Vargas said. "And the RM1 and I both figure you'll be running the division by then." He threw the cooler in the truck, and we all shook hands before they drove off.

CHAPTER 26

New Year's Eve, 1967, Norfolk

HARD TO BELIEVE—YESTERDAY HAD BEEN MY ONE-year anniversary onboard Cambria. Not long ago, Lt. Vargas had told me the next deployment would come sooner than I thought. In a way, I guess he was right. In a couple of days, we'd head for the Caribbean for refresher training, preparing for our next Mediterranean deployment. On watch and waiting for midnight, I thought about all that had happened, not only this year but since September.

Kupp, Ferraro, Chesney, and Damon—the backbone of the division—were gone. We had seen new men report aboard—RMSN Janos, RMSN Bonds, and RMSN Brinda—but they lacked experience. We'd been promised a chief and a first-class soon. Stark, Cooper, and I were in charge for now. I had taken over as the division training petty officer from Kupp and implemented an aggressive program. We'd find out how effective it had been when we got to Cuba.

I'd finished my advancement courses and passed the leadership test. In February, I would take the E-5 exam. I owed this to the XO, who once again had supported my early advancement. In late October, the XO had me and Lt. Martin report to his stateroom, and he introduced his relief.

"Lt. Martin, Petty Officer Herman, this is Cmdr. Gordon," he said. "He wanted to meet all the division officers and their top performers personally, so he could put a face to a name in the future. I have provided him a brief background on you already, RM3

Herman. We've had some experiences, but don't worry, I've assured Cmdr. Gordon that you are my poster boy for a good reason."

"Thank you, sir," I said, "I think." Luckily, this brought laughs. "I am going to miss you, XO." I meant that and shook his hand before leaving.

⚜

I lived on the ship but was fortunate to have somewhere to go to get away from time to time. Most of my liberty time was with Mark and Patti. On some nights when Mark was working at the club, bowling, or playing softball, Patti would pick me up, and I spent time with her and her four children from a previous marriage. Mark told me he hadn't figured out a way to tell his parents that he was dating a woman with children. He said his mom and dad would never accept her because she was divorced, which was against the Catholic religion.

I also went away several weekends with Jeff Cooper to Chesterfield, Pennsylvania, to visit his family. I would never forget how I was welcomed and accepted by his mom and dad. To say their family was different from mine would be a major understatement. I'd certainly not forget that first meeting.

"You mean you never rode on a commuter train before?" Jeff asked. We had taken the bus that morning from Norfolk to Philadelphia and boarded the Reading Railroad heading to Norristown, with a stop near his home.

"In grade school, we rode the train," I said. "It went about five miles to St. Paul and then back again to Minneapolis. I hardly remember it."

"I've taken the Reading all my life," he said. "My dad commutes to work every day on it. He says it's the only time he gets to read the paper in peace."

"Chesterfield," a voice said over the speaker.

"That's us," Jeff said. I followed him onto the boarding platform with a sign saying Chesterfield, Pop. 1037. We walked about four blocks to a narrow, three-story house. Jeff walked up, went in, and yelled, "Hey, Babs, I'm home."

"Oh, Jeffie," I heard a voice say, "don't call me that. Welcome home, son." A short lady with gray hair came into the room, hugged Jeff, and then saw me. "Oh, this must be your friend. Herman, isn't it? My, my, you do look a lot like Jeffie."

"Yes, ma'am," I said. "Nice to meet you, Mrs. Cooper. And I'm Rich." She seemed older and looked more like my grandma than my mom.

"Call her Babs," Jeff said. I couldn't believe he called his mother by her first name.

"Jeffie, don't call me that," she scolded him. Then she said to me, "Please, call me Babs. And welcome. Jeffie, I put Rich in the room on the third floor. Why don't you guys get settled, and then would you run to Red's before your dad gets home?"

Red's turned out to be the local liquor store. Jeff drove us there in the family's 1967 Buick Riviera, which was about the finest car I'd ever been in. "Nice car," I said.

"Yeah, my dad thought the mayor should be seen in a nice vehicle," Jeff said. He must have seen the look on my face. "No, he's not the mayor. Long story." We got three cases of Rolling Rock— a local beer, I figured—two quarts of Jack Daniels, and a gallon of Mogen David wine. "Put it on my dad's tab, Red." The guy behind the counter waved and asked that Jeff give his best to his folks.

"Babs," Jeff yelled, "we're back. Want a shot and a beer?"

"Oh, Jeffie," she blushed, "stop that, you know I don't drink. And don't call me that."

"So I should return the Mogen David then?" He laughed.

"That's wine, Jeffie. That's different."

The front door slammed. "Damn idiots," I heard a male voice say. "Anyone here? Bring me a beer."

Jeff grabbed a beer and motioned for me to follow. "Hey, Dad, this is Herman, my friend I told you about." He handed his dad a beer and turned to me. "This is my dad, Jeff Senior."

"Nice to meet you, sir," I said, extending my hand. Mr. Cooper, a big guy with wavy white hair, didn't look happy.

"Herman," he said, shaking my hand. "Where's your beer? Babs, get our guest a beer, for Christ's sake." Mrs. Cooper ran to the kitchen and brought me a beer without saying a word. Mr. Cooper didn't even acknowledge her being there.

"What you pissed about, Dad?" I was startled that he could use that language in front of his parents.

"Your damn aunt and uncle are trying to sell the property out from under me." The phone rang, and Mr. Cooper answered it. He listened for a minute, his face turned scarlet, and he yelled into the phone, "Over my dead body." He slammed the phone down, then picked it up, ripped the cord out of the wall, and threw it across the room.

"Jeff, Jeff," Mrs. Cooper said, jumping up. "Calm down. You're going to have a coronary."

"I won't calm down. That was our lawyer, and he said there was nothing I can do about it, the property will be sold, and the profits split three ways. My parents left that place to the family to enjoy, not sell for profit. Damn leeches." He stormed out of the room. Mrs. Cooper followed him.

"My grandparents have a home in Wildwood, New Jersey, on the oceanfront," Jeff said. "We go down there weekends every summer. Anyway, my mom and dad took care of them the last couple of years. and everyone figured the property would go to Dad when they died. Turns out, Grandpa Cooper died last year and Grandma Cooper a couple months later, and apparently there is no will. My aunt and uncle, who had nothing to do with and didn't even visit their own parents the last few years, sued for a fair share and apparently have won. You just saw what Dad thinks about it."

An hour later, Mrs. Cooper called us to dinner. I was surprised to find Mr. Cooper already sitting at the table, looking like nothing happened. We sat down, and his mom brought in a platter of pork chops and placed it on the table. "Can I help you?" I asked.

"Just sit," Mr. Cooper said. "She can get it." I could tell it was not a good time to argue. "So, Rich, isn't it? Damn, you do look a lot like Jeff. Sorry about that." He looked at his son and started laughing. Then we all joined in. We enjoyed a delicious meal and talked about our families with an occasional interruption asking Mrs. Cooper for something.

"Babs," Jeff Jr. said, "any more pork chops?"

"I'll get them," she replied. "And don't call me that." She went to the kitchen.

"Don't call your mother that," Jeff Sr. said.

After dinner, I asked, "Can I help clear the dishes?"

"No, no," she quickly answered before Jeff Sr. could say anything. "Jeffie, why don't you and your dad take Rich down to McGuire's and introduce him around."

"Good idea, Babs," Jeff said. "Come on, Dad."

"Don't call me that," his mom said.

"Don't call your mother that," Mr. Cooper said. "Let's go. My treat." We headed out the door.

McGuire's turned out to be a pub within walking distance. About twenty people were inside, mostly standing at the bar drinking beer with shots. The bartender yelled, "Hey, the mayor is here." Everyone started cheering. Would I ever find out this mayor story?

"I'm not the mayor, damn it," Jeff Sr. yelled. The crowd roared. "Get me, my son, and his friend Rich a beer and a shot, Pete," he shouted.

"Yes, sir, Mayor." The bartender poured three beers with shots of Jack Daniels and placed them at the end of the bar. "On the house, Mister Mayor, I mean Jeff, sir. Hey, everyone," he yelled. "To Jeff, Jeffie, and his friend, which makes him our friend, Rich." Everyone toasted us. I loved this place.

The next morning, I came down to the kitchen, and Mrs. Cooper gave me a cup of coffee. Jeff and his dad were still asleep. After some small talk, she said, "You have to be the politest person I've ever met. And definitely the only one to call me ma'am. I take it you don't call your mother by her first name?"

"No, ma'am," I said. "I call her Mom. It's just the way I was taught. One thing I've learned since joining the Navy is, it seems to be a cultural thing depending on what part of the country you're from. There's not a right or wrong way; it's just what is accepted."

"How nice," she said. "I want you to know we are very happy Jeffie brought you home to meet us. He's never done that before and sometimes we worry about him."

"I think you've done great raising him, Mrs. Cooper," I said honestly. "Jeff is a great guy and well-liked by everyone on the ship. He's also very good at what he does and is a big reason I've done as well as I have this past year. I couldn't ask for a better friend."

"Thank you," she said. "You don't know how happy that makes me feel. How about a good old Pennsylvania breakfast?" I realized she had tears in her eyes.

"Yes, ma'am," I said, "whatever that is." She stood up and got busy.

"Hey, Babs," Jeff said, entering the kitchen. "What's for breakfast?" He walked over and saw what his mom was making. "You don't expect Rich to eat that, do you?"

"He may like it, and don't call me that."

After finishing a plate of scrambled eggs, some kind of tasty sausage, and toast, I said, "Delicious. What kind of meat was that?"

"What?" Jeff said. "You actually liked that? I'll be damned. Good job, Babs."

"It's called scrapple, and it's a Pennsylvania special sausage," she said.

"It's what's left over after the pigs have eaten, you mean," Jeff said, grinning.

"Don't tell him that, Jeffie. Are you going to give Cindy a call?"

That afternoon, Jeff and his girlfriend, Cindy, showed me around. They made plans for the evening and invited me, but I told them to go ahead and I'd take it easy for one night. After dinner, I made myself at home on the living room couch and was content to watch TV.

"Hey, Rich," Jeff Sr. said. "I'm going to run over to another one of my hangouts. How about keeping me company?"

We entered a bar called Rooney's, and it was like last night all over again. "Hey, the mayor is here with Jeffie," the bartender yelled. "First drink is on me."

"No, everyone," Mr. Cooper said, "this isn't Jeffie, it's his Navy friend Rich. And I'm not the mayor, damn it."

"Well," someone at the bar yelled, "he looks like Jeffie. And you're the mayor to most of us." Cheers went up. I don't think we ever bought a drink, and everyone had a story to tell me about the Coopers. Everything except the mayor story, and I didn't ask. Another amazing place.

"Herman," I heard Jeff saying as he was shaking me. "Come on, man, we got a train to catch." Morning already? My head was killing me.

"Thank you for everything," I said to the Coopers. "I had a great time."

"Anytime, Rich," Mr. Cooper said. "You helped me enjoy this weekend when I needed to get my mind off things. I hope you come again. And," he hugged Jeff, "try and keep this one out of trouble, huh?"

"You bet," I said.

"That goes for me, too," Mrs. Cooper said. She came over and hugged me.

"Ah, Babs," Jeff said. "Don't cry now." He gave her a big hug, and we walked out the door. We were walking down the sidewalk when I heard one it more time.

"Don't call me that."

On the bus back, I finally asked, "Okay, what's the mayor story?"

Jeff laughed. "You may have noticed my dad is very popular and well-liked in town. Last year, a bunch of people convinced him to run for mayor. He got banners and buttons and all that stuff. Even bought the Riviera. He would go to the local businesses and shake hands, kiss babies, whatever. On the day of the election, he and my mom stood outside the polling place all day long waving and all that. Anyway, you may have noticed the town population isn't much over a thousand. When the polls closed and the votes were counted, my dad lost by one vote. They did a recount, and it was the same, he lost by one vote. It was that night when Dad realized they spent all day outside the poll campaigning, and they forgot to vote themselves. He should have won by one vote. Now, the town won't let him forget it, and they call him the mayor, sort of."

I visited the Coopers two more weekends and had become like another son. I had an open invitation to visit even if Jeffie couldn't make it. With each visit, some things would never change. I called his mom ma'am, and Jeff called her Babs. She'd tell me to call her Babs and for Jeff not to call her that. I absolutely loved this family.

Now, it was closing in on midnight New Year's Eve. Against all rules, I had smuggled a pint of Jack Daniels aboard and saved it for tonight. Cooper was home in Chesterfield and Stark in Boston, so I'd have to toast them from a distance. It was time. "Hawkins and Janos, come in here," I called out.

"Yes, Petty Officer Herman," they said, entering radio.

"You never saw this," I said. I poured us each a small glass of Tennessee's finest whiskey, and we watched the clock tick down.

"Happy New Year," we all shouted and clinked our glasses. "Welcome, 1968."

CHAPTER 27

Spring 1968, Norfolk

YOU SURE YOU DON'T KNOW WHAT THIS IS ABOUT?"
Lt. Martin asked.

"I really don't, sir," I said defensively. The XO's yeoman had called
Martin, saying the XO wanted to see him at 0900 and to bring me
along. We'd been standing outside his stateroom for ten minutes.

When invited to enter, we stood at attention before Commander
Gordon. I'd been here before. Martin looked scared to death.

"At ease," Gordon said. "Lt. Martin, I've asked you here because
I think it's important for junior officers to witness, firsthand, how to
help career development of our men. While sometimes necessary, too
often young officers think they only need to counsel their men when
they've done something wrong. I believe it's equally as important to
do so when our men do something right. Fortunately, or unfortunately,
RM3 Herman has seen both ends." He laughed. "So, Lieutenant,"
the XO added, "during my relief, the last XO told me about RM3
Herman; what can you add?"

"Well, sir," Martin said. "On the positive, although young and
only a third class, he is probably my saving grace for making the
division run. On the negative, he likes to have a good time and drives
me nuts trying to keep him out of trouble, especially with Lt. Cmdr.
Fortune."

Gordon looked at him and then me. "Sounds about right. This
will help. Lt. Cmdr. Fortune is being transferred before we deploy.
Now, let me tell you why you're here. When Herman checked
onboard, the XO looked over his record, thought he showed potential,

and recommended him for advancement a year early. Guess what? Herman proved him right and succeeded in making third class in just one year. Well, he's done it again, and I wanted to be the one to let him know. He is the first sailor I have ever seen make second class in only two years. Congratulations, Petty Officer Second Class Herman." He stood and shook my hand.

Speechless, I shook his hand. Finally, I said, "Thank you, XO. For everything." Then I realized Lt. Martin was also shaking my hand and congratulating me.

"What I want you to take away from this, Lieutenant," the XO added, "is that if you think someone is worth it, then go to bat for them. Your men will usually come through for you. Now, I'm going to have the yeoman post all the exam results outside the admin office. Several other radiomen are also advancing. Your date of actual advancement is the day we deploy for the Med, by the way, RM3 Herman."

Walking back to radio, Martin said, "Well, that makes it a lot easier making you the LPO."

"What?" I wasn't expecting that.

"I found out we're not getting a chief or even a first class before we deploy. I know RM2 Stark is senior to you, but I think he'd agree that you should have the job. Don't say anything yet. I want a chance to talk to him, and I'll make it official after that. Okay?"

"Yes, sir," I said. What a day. I made second class, I was going to be LPO, and Fortune was leaving. I wondered who else was on the advancement list and how Cooper did. I couldn't wait to tell Mom and Dad. I needed to get my uniforms done with the new insignias. *Guess I'll be getting another sore arm the day we get underway. At least there aren't that many E-5 and above who can tack it on. Actually, who cares?* I felt great.

Word got out quickly why Martin and I saw the XO, and everyone was aware I would be making second class the day we deployed. Stark seemed thrilled—and relieved—that I was going to be the LPO. Cooper, who didn't pass the E-5 exam, said he was happy for me and was glad I was going to be the LPO and not Stark.

I hated to admit it, but it probably was for the best. As the lieutenant said, we weren't getting any senior radiomen onboard, and it would be up to the new Big Three to carry the load. We still had good men, like Reddy and Nash, with us. Stark, Cooper, and I spent a lot of time training and had seen some positive potential in some of the new men. RM3 Hawkins was a real go-getter and never got tired. He also was one of the few who enjoyed doing equipment maintenance, including radio antennas on all the masts. He had no fear of heights. Janos, Bonds, and Brinda were eager to learn so, hopefully, would qualify quickly.

I didn't get a chance to get home on leave before this deployment, but I did get back to visit the Coopers with Jeff. Not only was I considered a second son now, but the townspeople at both McGuire's and Rooney's had made me an honorary citizen of Chesterfield. These were hard-working, religious, and patriotic Americans. I didn't agree with some of their opinions, but I accepted them as genuine and didn't judge. In turn, they accepted me for who I was. I loved that town, differences and all.

"Attention to quarters," Lt. Martin announced. "Okay, guys, we have over one hundred supply chits to be processed to complete our loadout before deploying. Stand fast after quarters for Petty Officer Cooper's direction. We deploy in six days."

Here we go again, I thought. Cooper organized the supply runs, and everyone moved out smartly without question. Like last year, he hoped to get done in one day, although we thought this was not realistic because we didn't have anyone senior who could pull strings with the other divisions the way Kupp and Chesney did. Then, about thirty minutes after we started, the first boxes started to arrive; within an hour, things were running top speed. Cooper saw Bonds and asked, "How did you guys get this stuff so fast?"

Bonds, stopping to take a breath, said, "All I know is when we showed up down below, the leading storekeeper told us to go to the head of the line, and the other divisions are waiting for us to finish. I did see Hawkins talking to him earlier."

Cooper looked at him, then me, and shrugged. He didn't have a clue. The supply run was nearly complete after only six hours. Near the end, Hawkins showed up, whistling, with a bunch of filled requisitions, and asked, "What's next?" He hadn't even broken a sweat.

"I think that's everything," Cooper said. "You know how we got to the head of the line?"

"Amazing what a couple bottles of good vodka can get you," Hawkins said, laughing. Cooper, Stark, and I cracked up. We had a new go-to guy.

While Cooper finished logging everything in, the guys hung around on the weather deck; he then went into radio and returned with Martin. "I understand you just set a record for quickest supply run," the lieutenant said, smiling. "Great job, and you can secure for the day to conduct personal business. Dismissed." Walking toward the hatch, he stopped and whispered to me, "Think the XO would agree with that?" He winked and entered radio. I was gaining more and more respect for him.

A few days later, Martin called us to attention again. "Amphibious Squadron Six will be embarking today," he said. "I expect all of you to make them feel welcome." The hatch opened, and Vargas and Hill came out. Wait, another guy in khakis was with them. Martin welcomed them and invited Vargas to speak.

Vargas looked out over the division, nodding at a few of us. "I see some familiar faces. With me are RM1 Hill, who many of you will remember, and our new addition, RMCS Brewer. We look forward to another deployment, and, like always, will try and stay out of your way. I believe you will be helping us, Petty Officer Herman?"

It was like old times. I shook hands with Vargas and Hill, and they formally introduced me to Brewer. "Petty Officer Herman is the reason you're here, Senior Chief," Vargas said. "He's the one you heard about being responsible for your billet being created."

"Good job, Petty Officer," the senior chief said. "I understand that you will be the new division LPO." Vargas and Hill were nodding in agreement.

"News travels fast," I said, wondering how they knew that. "Now, what would you like to do first?" Quickly, I learned that he might be a senior chief, but, like the lieutenant, Brewer worked just as hard carrying boxes aboard from the pier and getting their office organized. I was surprised when the senior chief asked if I would attend the underway mission brief for new personnel with him. I remembered doing that last year with Hill.

Later, with input from Stark and Cooper, I made out my first underway watch bill as the LPO. Not that long ago I was the new guy; now I would be the top guy. The leading petty officer. Damon would be proud, I thought.

April 15, 1968

Hey Folks,

I just tried calling to say goodbye for a while. Sorry I missed you. We leave in the morning. There is going to be an advancement ceremony on the mess decks before we go so I'll be a second class when we leave. In a way I am looking forward to going to the Med again and I enjoy being at sea. I'm a little nervous though. I told you I was made the Leading Petty Officer, LPO, so it'll be up to me to get everyone trained and I'll be responsible for how well we perform. I'll let you know how I do.

I did spend yesterday with Mark Newsom and his girlfriend Patti. I think I told you Mark calls me his cousin and they do treat me like family. I understand Harry and Gladys are visiting this summer. Patti is divorced with four kids so you can probably expect to hear a lot about that when they return. Mark is worried they will say the church won't let them get married and won't accept her. Patti is a great lady, and good for Mark, so I hope it goes well.

Something new I learned this year though was our deployment is going to be shortened from six to four months because we need to train the Marines faster so they can go to Vietnam. Our CO said the conflict, war, over there has gotten worse and more and more men are needed. Doesn't seem fair to rush these guys through training but what do I know? That reminds me, do you ever hear anything about Tom Gilmore? I think he's on his second tour in Vietnam. Hope he's okay.

Well, this is short but, I wanted you to know I tried calling. Will write to you soon.

Be Good and Take Care.

Love, Rich

CHAPTER 28

May 1968, Malta and the Mediterranean

PETTY OFFICER HERMAN," HILL SAID. "I THOUGHT you might be here."

"My favorite spot," I answered. I was on the fantail enjoying the view of the ocean under the moon. We would pass through the Strait of Gibraltar during the early morning hours, and the ship and I would be entering the Mediterranean Sea for my second time. "Didn't know you knew about it."

"RM2 Stark told me," he said. "You've been so busy during the transit over, we haven't had a chance to talk much. The senior chief and I think you've done a good job, considering how new your people are and having to stand twelve-hour watches, plus support the ship's intense training schedule. How you holding up?"

"Time flies when you're having a good time." I laughed. "By the way, Lt. Vargas told me you passed the chief exam and are board eligible. What does that mean exactly?"

"There's a separate selection process for chiefs. First you have to pass the exam, then that score is added to your performance evaluations overall score, and if high enough, you become what is called board eligible. The board meets only once a year in August, and they go through and rank every record. It's determined how many new chiefs are needed for your rating, and if your ranking makes the cut, you get selected. It's a tedious process but also very fair, and it is what separates the Navy from all the other services, where you just pass a test and put your time in. Anyway, I won't find out until the end of August if I make it. It's my first time eligible, so I don't expect to make it this year."

"Wow," I said. "I always wondered why the Navy made such a big deal about those who make chief. Now I know. I'm betting on you, Hill, and pulling for you. You'd make a great chief. Can I ask you something personal?"

"You can ask, Herman; I may not answer. What is it?"

"Why do you always have a toothpick in your mouth?"

Hill chuckled, somehow keeping the toothpick in place. "You are the first person to ever ask me that. After all the time we've been together, Lt. Vargas has never asked, and RMCS Brewer hasn't yet either. I'm going to tell you because I think you will understand." He looked at me seriously.

"Since I joined the Navy, going on eleven years now, I have been looked at and treated differently. Every day following boot camp, I could feel the tension around me, and at times I thought I would explode in retaliation at how I was sometimes treated. My grandfather told me to put a toothpick in my mouth, and any time I thought I may lose my temper, to concentrate on chewing it until the feeling subsided. It has worked so far, and I still carry a toothpick wherever I go." He looked over the fantail, and we remained silent.

"Thank you," I finally said. "It's your story to tell, and it's safe with me." We shook hands.

"Now," he added. "The real reason I came out here is to give you a heads-up. After we complete turnover in Rota tomorrow, the commodore is going to hold our first war game briefings, and Lt. Vargas wanted me to tell you that you are going to be invited to attend with Lt. Martin to discuss communications. Basically, he wants you to keep the lieutenant out of trouble. Remember, your CO and the Marine commandant will be there too, but no pressure. Anyway, look surprised when you find out and come prepared." He put a fresh toothpick in his mouth and left.

May 18, 1968

Hi Folks,

First, I apologize for not writing for a month. Since we left Norfolk, I have been so busy I barely have time to eat and sleep, let alone write. I'm not really complaining, just hoping you understand. Today, we finally got to stand down from operations and I have some time to myself.

I did get promoted the day we left so you can address my letters to RM2 now. It feels good to have made second class in two years. And being the Leading Petty Officer is quite an achievement even if I say so myself. I think I am doing okay but, there has been times I wished I wasn't in charge. Anyway, we are headed for Valletta, Malta, and will pull in for rest and relaxation tomorrow. You may remember we stopped here last year and left early to go help the USS Liberty. What a mess that ended up being.

Like I said, we've been busy. We made our transit over without too much trouble. Things did change though once we got to the Med and had our first Marine war games.

Our mission is to train Marines on how to make amphibious assaults from sea and then infiltrate and fight ashore. To do this we need to be able to be in communications with them at all times. Well, we had a hard time the whole exercise. Weather was horrible, equipment kept failing and I didn't have enough guys qualified to handle everything. I think Stark, Cooper and I have been getting two to three hours sleep a day. It's over now though, and today I attended the debriefing with my boss, LT Martin. The Commodore, my CO and the Marine Commander overall were pleased with the exercise, although my division got our fair share and a long list of lessons learned to be addressed and corrected.

I know this is short, just wanted you to know I'm okay. I'm headed for a hot shower and some much-needed sleep before I, hopefully, enjoy liberty in Malta.

Be Good and Take Care.

Love, Rich

After tying up pierside in Valletta, the ship held division quarters as this would be the first time our new sailors went on liberty in a foreign land, and the commanding officer wanted division officers to make sure everyone was aware of his policies. The next day, Lt. Martin addressed us in a follow-up about conduct. "I want to make sure each of you understands that you represent the United States when you are on liberty and that we are here as guests of the people of Malta," he said. "I hope you paid particularly close attention to the doctor and the consequences of getting too friendly with the local ladies. I think you all know what I mean. That said, enjoy your time off. You deserve it. Dismissed."

I remembered from last year, and was reminded by the XO during his briefing, that most Maltese people spoke English and loved Americans. They also thought highly of the Turkish, and I found that strange, because I didn't think relations between the U.S. and Turkey were that good right then. I decided that was politics and not my worry. I found Cooper, and we left the ship.

"I'm not getting in that thing," Cooper said. The pier was at the base of a 100-foot-high mountain. To get to the city of Valletta, you could walk up the steep staircase, walk the winding road, or ride what they called the lift. "It doesn't look safe to me," he added.

"Come on," I said. Looking at the wooden cage that was called the lift, I had my doubts too, but I didn't feel like walking in the heat. "I'm taking it. Either come with me, or I'll meet you at the top after you make that long, hot walk." I stepped onto the lift and gave the operator the fare.

"Oh, all right, but if we die, I'll never forgive you, Herman." Cooper got on, and after about a four-minute, somewhat shaky ride, we made it to the top. Getting off, he smiled. "See, that wasn't so bad, was it?" I burst out laughing, and we headed to the first bar we could find.

We had a great ten-day visit, enjoying some of the most amazing beaches in the Mediterranean. At night, it was easy to find a good place for a fabulous meal and then a club with decent entertainment at good prices. It was one of our most successful port visits—until our last night.

Cooper and I had spent the day at the beach and joined Nash, Hawkins, and a few others for dinner. Next, we all visited a club, had a few drinks, and managed to get in some dancing with the local ladies. Everyone in town knew we were leaving in the morning, and folks were saying goodbye with toasts and trading addresses to write. It was about 2300 when, somewhat sloshed, we decided to head back to the ship. About six of us were in a group walking toward the waterfront when a taxi pulled alongside.

"Americano," the driver said, "you want ride back to ship."

"Nah, we're good," Cooper answered. We kept walking.

"No," the driver insisted, "you take my taxi. Cheap. Get in."

"We don't want to ride, jerk," Cooper said. "Go away." We walked on, and the taxi took off. We'd gone about a hundred yards when Cooper yelled, "Watch out!" The taxi was headed right at us.

I was on the ground looking up when I saw the taxi hit Cooper and push him back against a building. Cooper, bent at the waist, fell onto the hood with his legs trapped against the wall. It was then that I realized he had pushed me out of the way. The taxi backed up and started to drive away. Cooper collapsed on the ground with blood gushing out below his knees.

As the taxi moved away, I jumped up and grabbed the door handle, trying to run alongside. I broke off the car antenna and started hitting the driver. "You ran over my friend, you son of a bitch," I yelled, swinging the antenna at him. The driver lost control, and we hit a curb, sending me flying down the sidewalk. The next thing I knew, my feet were off the ground, and a gigantic sailor had me by the collar.

"Settle down," the shore patrol guy said. I was hanging there in mid-air, dazed. "I'm going to put you down. Just stand there." When he put me down, I realized there was a Marine with him, and they were talking to four Maltese policemen. I saw the taxi but no driver. The shore patrol guy said, "They have agreed to let us escort you to the police station. Stay between us and don't say a word. These people want to string you up." A large crowd had gathered.

"A taxi driver ran over my friend," I said defensively. He looked at me, and I didn't say another word. What mess had I gotten into now? I didn't care. Cooper might have saved my life.

I was locked in a small room at the police station for about an hour until the door opened and a Navy lieutenant entered. I recognized the ship's JAG officer, who gave our conduct ashore briefing. After the door was shut, he had me tell him what happened.

"I fully understand what, and why, you did what you did," he said. "Now, let me tell you the reality. We, you, are in the nation of Malta. You committed an offense on their territory, against one of their citizens, and are being charged under their law. It is only a courtesy that I have been allowed to speak to you. You may be justified in what you did. They don't care. This judge does not even have to see you. He can decide, all on his own, based on what is presented before him tonight, what your punishment will be. Sure, we can appeal, and maybe in two years, if you're lucky, you may be tried before a jury, and the U.S. may be able to represent you. Maybe not. Do you understand how serious this is, Petty Officer Herman?"

"I'm beginning to. Doesn't seem right. That taxi driver ran right over Cooper for no reason at all."

"In your eyes," the JAG said. "Let me find out about Cooper and see what this judge has in mind." He left the room and returned in about thirty minutes.

"Cooper is okay," he started. "Lacerations on his shins and bad bone bruise but nothing broken. He's back on ship." I took a deep breath, relieved. "Now, here are our … your choices. You can go to prison and await trial in a couple years, or you can apologize to the court, pay a fine equivalent to about a hundred forty dollars, and go back to the ship. What do you want to do?"

"Okay," I said. "You got my attention. Problem is, I don't have any money."

"Let me worry about that." He led me into a small room, which I quickly figured out was the courtroom. A guy wearing a white wig sat behind a bench, and a cop stood next to him. "My client wishes to apologize, Your Honor," my lawyer said.

"Very well," the judge said. "Good choice." A door opened from the side, and the taxi driver entered and stood next to the bench. He had bandages on his head and neck. "Go ahead, young man."

"I'm sorry for my actions, Your Honor," I said. "They were uncalled for and will never happen again."

"Accepted," he ruled. "Now, pay your fine."

"Right here, Your Honor," a voice behind me said. I turned, and Lt. Vargas walked up to the bench with the money. He handed it to the judge, who counted it, filled out what I figured was a receipt, and said, "Court proceedings are over," hitting a gavel three times.

Walking up the brow to the quarterdeck, I saw the XO standing there with Lt. Martin. At least Lt. Cmdr. Fortune wasn't here anymore to gloat. The XO motioned to us all, including the JAG and Vargas, to follow him. Everyone got settled in the XO's stateroom, and I stood at attention. "Here we are again, Herman," the XO said. "What is it with you and international incidents? No, don't answer that. For all our benefit, tell us exactly what happened."

"Well, XO," I started, "we were returning …" I left out nothing, and no one interrupted.

"Anyone dispute what RM2 Herman just said?" the XO asked.

"If I may, sir?" Vargas said. The XO nodded, and he continued. "I was nearby when all this took place, and, seeing Herman involved, I followed to the police station. I overheard a couple of the locals say that the taxi driver was sympathetic to the Turkish government anti-democracy protesters, and earlier this evening he boasted that he was going to mess up a couple of Americans. I believe Herman and his guys were just in the wrong place at the wrong time. I didn't have time to tell the JAG and decided to be quiet so as not to cause, like you said, an international incident. I think the judge may have known too. It could have been very ugly if that taxi driver had gotten away and bragged about bullying Americans. As it turned out, Herman scared the shit out of him, and he didn't say a word."

The XO started laughing. "Thanks, Lieutenant, you've made my day. Now, here's what we're going to do. Lt. Vargas and I, with the JAG, are going to brief the CO and commodore on exactly what happened. However, what you heard in this room about the taxi driver and his reasons for the attack will stay in this room. Understood?" He looked at each person, making sure they nodded yes.

"It turns out you not only dodged a bullet again, Herman, but you may have saved the U.S. an embarrassing situation. I don't want to hear about it being anything other than you're lucky to be back on the ship. And how about no future antics involving other countries?"

"No problem," I said. "I just want to make sure Cooper is okay and put it all behind me. And thank you too, Lt. Vargas, for being there. I'll pay you back the money. A couple of years in a Malta prison wouldn't be a good career move."

Visiting Cooper in sick bay, I learned his injuries turned out to be minor and he would be released later in the day. He'd be hobbling around for a while but could stand his watches. I managed a couple of hours sleep before assuming the watch and received a big round of applause when I entered radio. We had been underway a few hours when Lt. Martin appeared.

"Quite a night," he said, smiling. "I guess we've seen both sides of you again. I'd like to add, you sure have a strange way to demonstrate leadership. This was just the first month of our deployment—got anything exciting planned for the next three?"

"I seriously hope not," I said. "I seriously hope not."

CHAPTER 29

June 1968, Aegean Sea

IT HAD BEEN ALMOST THREE WEEKS SINCE WE LEFT Malta. "On the positive side," Lt. Vargas said, "communications performed better this past exercise period, and there were no significant issues that resulted in the Marines not being able to meet their mission."

I was sitting in the squadron comm office after the debrief given to my CO, the commodore, and the Marine commander. Martin, Brewer, Hill, and I were now holding our own debrief to identify where we still had weaknesses. As usual, Vargas was upbeat and positive.

"Still," Martin said, "lots of room for improvement. I think Petty Officer Herman is moving in the right direction, and we'll be even better the next time. Am I right?" He was looking right at me.

"Yes, sir," I said. "I'll modify my training to include what I've learned here, and we'll just get better and better." In truth, I had taken the lessons learned from the Atlantic transit and the last exercise and implemented an intensive training program; we came up only a bit short. I was still proud of my division's performance but didn't want to be too defensive.

"I've seen big improvement since we deployed," Brewer said. "If there's one thing I've learned in twenty-two years in the Navy is, you can always get better. Good job, Lt. Martin and RM2 Herman."

On the way back to radio, Martin said, "Well, it could have been worse, I guess. Anything I can do to help, RM2 Herman?"

"Yes, sir," I said. "At quarters tomorrow, tell the guys they're doing a good job. They could use a positive stroke right now." What I wanted to tell him was to get us a chief, a couple of first-class, and about eight more radiomen. This pace was killing us. Thank goodness we were pulling into Izmir, Turkey, soon for a short port visit.

June 15, 1968

Hi Folks,

I'm in Izmir, Turkey. We just finished another big war game exercise off the coast of Crete and are getting a few day's rest. Yep, I get to see another country. I haven't been on liberty yet so don't know what it is like but, apparently, it's not the friendliest place in the world. I'll let you know.

I had a great time in Valletta, Malta. The Maltese people are friendly and love Americans. The beaches' sand is white and raked every night so when you arrive in the morning, they are smooth and clean. I meant to write before I left but the last night there we ended being out late and I didn't have time. One of the reasons we were out late was Cooper got hurt and needed some medical help. It wasn't serious and he is okay but by the time we got him taken care of, it involved a taxi driver, from Turkey by the way, a couple shore patrol and local policemen. I even got to witness an actual court case, they're held at night, and see how their laws work. Really interesting and I'll tell you all about it when I get home.

I did receive all your letters and loved it. Oh, I finally got a letter from Todd and Pam. Anyway, he's getting out soon and they will be coming home. Guess that leaves me and Tom Gilmore the only ones I know still on active duty. I worry about him in Vietnam and hope he is doing okay.

Be Good and Take Care.

Love, Rich

The word passed quickly, after the first day of liberty, that the Turkish people weren't too friendly. Although there were no confrontations, our guys said they felt uneasy walking on the streets.

There was a U.S. Air Force base here, and it was highly recommended that this be the place you went once leaving the ship. With my history of adventures, or misadventures, I told Cooper and the other guys that's where I was going. No one disagreed, and about ten of us left together.

After several hours at the club, Cooper said, "I'm going to try the slot machines."

"Sounds good," I said. This place had several eating areas and a dozen bars, plus entertainment stages and gambling everywhere. The guys broke up into groups, and Cooper and I headed to a country-western place first. After visiting several more bars, we had porterhouse steaks at one of the restaurants. I'm not much of a gambler but tagged along as Cooper played roulette and blackjack. Now he was on the move again.

"Tell you what," he said. Maybe my boredom was beginning to show. "Let's play the nickel and dime slot machines. That way you can play instead of just watching me."

I got two dollars in nickels and started to play. My biggest problem was I didn't understand what was a winner. Unless I spun and cherries showed up, I wasn't sure I won until I heard coins drop in my tray. Cooper thought it was hilarious. I was having a good time so didn't care. And a waitress kept bringing me rum and Cokes. After about an hour, I heard bells go off, and it turned out I won ten dollars in nickels. Half smashed by now, I cashed in my nickels for dimes and found a new machine.

"I'm about broke," Cooper said as he stood by me. "Wow, you're twenty dollars ahead, Herman."

"Yeah, I'm on a roll." I was in my own little world. Drop a coin, pull the handle, sip on a drink, and wait to see if coins fell into my tray. Now, it was Cooper who was bored, so I decided to call it a night. "I've had enough, Jeff—let's head back to the ship early for a change, and come back another day." This was a fine idea, if we would only stick to it. I cashed in my coins for paper currency, and we left.

On the way to the ship, Cooper stopped and looked inside a

window of a local club. "Hey, Herman, I see belly dancers in there. Let's check it out."

"I don't think that's such a good idea." I kept walking. After a few steps, I realized he was gone. I looked back, saw him entering the club, and decided I'd better stay with him. Inside, I could hardly see for all the smoke. Cooper was waving for me to join him by a small table. I could see a bunch of round stages surrounded by guys sitting on pillows smoking out of giant water pipes. "You do realize we stand out like sore thumbs in our uniforms?" I didn't like the looks we were getting.

A young man came up to us smiling. "You sit and watch dance? Only 1,000 lira." Cooper nodded, and we were shown to two pillows to sit on by a stage, which was a circle about two feet high and eight feet in diameter. The waiter took our lira, about three American dollars, and put a water pipe in front of us. "Show starts soon." He walked away.

"We've got to be nuts," I said, laughing. A waitress came over, and Cooper ordered two beers. Three other guys were sitting on pillows at our stage, talking, and puffing on water pipes. I saw Cooper holding the water pipe tube, looking as if he was going to try it. "Don't even think about it, Jeff. You have no idea what the hell you're smoking, and I'm sure it's illegal. We're probably in deep trouble just being here."

"Hookah," the waitress said bringing us our beers, called Efes. She pointed at the water pipe. "Very good to smoke. Make you happy." Luckily, the lights dimmed; she grabbed some money from Cooper and hurried off. Cooper pushed the hookah aside. A spotlight shone on our stage, and wild music started.

Suddenly a woman who looked like a genie with bare feet and a veil on her face was moving around in circles and shaking her entire body. I had heard about belly dancers, but I never in my life expected what I was watching. How could anyone make their body move like that, especially the belly? I couldn't take my eyes off of her. Then, all hell broke loose.

"*Kilij, kilij*," or something like that, the man next to me yelled.

He stood up and glared at me. Then he raised his fist, jumped on stage, grabbed the dancer, and started screaming in what I assumed was Turkish. The lights came on in the club, and men everywhere started yelling and gathering in groups.

"Get out of here." Our waiter came running over. He pushed Cooper toward the door and pulled me along. "Quickly."

We ran, but I wasn't sure why. "What's going on?" I asked. "Why's he so mad?"

"The dancer is his wife, and you stared at her. That is disrespectful, and he wants to duel. *Kilij* is Turkish for sword." The waiter came out into the street with us. "Get back to your ship. It'll take him a minute to calm down, and then he'll come after you with friends. It's an honor thing. Now, go."

"You did it again, Herman," Cooper said, and we headed for the ship. We heard some yelling behind us and realized the husband and several of his friends were following us. We went into a sprint. They did too.

I was never so happy to see the brow, and we were at top speed when we got to it. The small mob wasn't far behind and was pretty vocal, so it got the attention of the quarterdeck watch. Out of breath, Cooper and I walked up the brow and heard over the 1MC, "Security to the quarterdeck." By the time we reached the top and asked permission to come aboard, armed security personnel were standing by. The Turks stopped and didn't try boarding. They remained at the bottom of the brow a few minutes, then walked away. Cooper and I breathed a sigh of relief, and then I realized who was standing with us.

"I just knew it," the XO said. "As soon as I heard the call for security, I said I bet this will involve Herman. And here you are. I thought you promised me no more international incidents." I was about to say something when he raised his hand. "No, no. Not a word. I'll send for you when I'm ready and you're sober. Hit your racks."

At 0900 the next morning, Cooper and I were standing at attention before the XO in his stateroom. Martin, the JAG, and the ship's supply officer were also there. "I have here, RM2 Herman and

RM3 Cooper," the XO said, holding up a piece of paper, "an incident report filed by last night's shore patrol officer. It states that two unknown sailors were believed to have caused a disturbance at a nightclub and were seen running through the streets with some local men in pursuit." He looked at Cooper, then me. "Would either of you know anything about this?"

Before Cooper could answer, I said, "It is possible, XO. Could there have been more than one incident?" I saw the JAG smile, but I could tell the XO didn't want to hear and was about to say something. I quickly added, "Yes, I think it may have involved us, sir."

"Right answer," the XO said and shook his head at me. "This report is short on details, so why don't you tell me exactly what happened."

I had told Cooper earlier this morning to shoot straight with the XO and let me take the lead, and I followed my own advice saying, "I always wanted to see a belly dancer, XO, and on the way back to the ship last night, I asked RM3 Cooper to join me at a local club." I could sense the tension leave Cooper as he realized I was taking the blame. I told the story of what happened, at least what I thought happened, and ended by saying, "I really didn't think I did anything wrong at the time, XO."

The XO stared at me. Finally, he said to the supply officer, "Supply, you're our expert on protocol and customs. Where did Herman go wrong?"

"Well, sir," he said, "belly dancing is an art form and highly respected in Turkey. The dancers are considered performers of fine art and held in high esteem. I think what happened here is Herman admired the dancer so much that he was probably infatuated, and his facial expression may have been construed as lust, not admiration."

"Christ," the XO said, "you sound more like the JAG than the protocol officer." Whether he meant to be funny or not, everyone started laughing. "Okay. JAG, look at this incident report." He handed it over. "Bottom line, what do I have to do with it legally?"

"Well, sir," the JAG said, "this is pretty vague, and I think the shore patrol officer was just covering his butt by filing it. No names are given, and no one from the club wanted to make a statement."

"If I may," the supply officer jumped in, "the dancer's husband felt his wife was disrespected last night and wanted to save face in front of his friends. He did that by chasing RM2 Herman back to the ship. As far as he is concerned, he has restored honor, and the incident is over."

"I agree, XO," the JAG added. "No statements were given because now the Turks have bragging rights. If we pursue this, matters could get much worse."

"Unless you feel like fighting a duel, Petty Officer Herman," the XO said, standing only inches away from my face, "this matter is over. Lt. Martin and RM2 Herman, remain; the rest of you are dismissed." When just the three of us remained, he said, "Herman, you are like a magnet to trouble. Our relations here in Turkey are shaky at best, and I want you to cool your heels onboard the rest of this port visit. Will you volunteer to do that?"

"Absolutely," I said. "I have a lot of work to do and was thinking of the same thing."

Martin laughed, and the XO joined in. Then, the 1MC announced, "Security to the quarterdeck." The XO ran out.

I decided to go back to radio using the pierside weather decks. When I came out on the main deck, I saw a small group of people near the brow holding a burning American flag. They were carrying signs saying, "Americans Go Home." I saw the CO and XO on the quarterdeck, and then several armed Marines walked down the brow. One of the protesters met with the senior Marine, exchanged a few words, and then walked away motioning for the others to follow. Two Marines went onto the pier, put the fire out, folded the flag, and brought it aboard. An hour later, the announcement was made that the ship would be getting underway at 1600. I prepared the watch bill and hoped it wasn't my incident at the club that caused this protest. Maybe I hadn't heard the last of it after all.

The crew was called to division quarters at 1530. CR division mustered on our weather deck at 1520, and all the talk was about our port visit being cut short. Cooper knew I was worried that our incident may have caused this rapid departure, and I could be facing a major discipline issue. Lt. Martin came out the hatch, and I yelled, "Attention to quarters."

"Parade rest," Martin said. "The captain just held officers' call to address our getting underway on short notice. First of all, any incident you may have heard about that did, or didn't, occur is nothing but a rumor and has nothing to do with our departure." I could breathe again. "The fact is, U.S. and Turkish relations have been tenuous for a long time. Over the past several months, tensions have been strained, and a few Turkish anti-democratic government groups are starting to stir the pot. This is what took place this morning with the burning of the American flag. It has been decided that it would be best to get all American ships out of harm's way and let the diplomats handle it. We will conduct some independent training underway and pick up normal operations next week. One more thing. I want you to know that I appreciate all the efforts you have put in, and your progress is not going unnoticed. Keep up the good work."

I couldn't wait to get away from Turkey. First, my run-in with the taxi driver in Malta, who turned out to be from Turkey, and now my run-in with a Turkish husband of a belly dancer who didn't like me admiring his wife's talents. Farewell and good riddance. Of course, my liberty days were over anyway, so it was fine with me to be at sea.

July 17, 1968

Hi folks,

Been a while since I wrote, sorry. We just pulled into Toulon, France, which if you remember was the first port I ever visited in Europe.

Since I last wrote, we left Izmir, Turkey, and have been at sea over three weeks conducting exercises. You may have read about us not getting along so well with the Turkish government. Well, this resulted in us leaving early so we wouldn't be involved in any anti-government incidents. Some protesters actually burned an American flag on our pier while we were there. I only got one night of liberty so didn't see much. I did get to have some fun at an Air Force club there and even won a few bucks playing the slot machines. I'm still not much of a gambler. Also, Jeff Cooper and I did get to see a belly dancer and she was great. We met her husband and learned that in their culture, his wife is a fine artist and adored. It was an exciting evening actually.

We just finished a major Marine assault landing exercise and my guys did great. At the debrief with my commanding officer, the commodore and the Marine commander, it was pointed out that communications were superb. I'm proud of my guys and all the hard work they put in. The squadron communication guys even said they were springing for the first beers this port visit. That will be a first.

Received all your letters. It's hard to imagine Louie even married, let alone a father. So, I now have a baby niece, Joline, to meet when I come home. You asked about any reaction we had to the killing of Robert Kennedy. It was a shock for sure. Most of the guys, if they said anything at all, thought he was even a better guy than JFK. Many on the ship say it was in retaliation for the killing of Martin Luther King, Jr. I've gotten close to both RM1 Hill and RM2 Stark and they just think both deaths were a waste. They also think Martin Luther King was a real gift to his race and his death will have lasting effects for years to come. Time will tell. Looks to me like it is going to be Nixon vs. Humphrey now for president. I asked for an absentee ballot from Minnesota.

From here we go to Livorno, Italy, and this deployment starts to wind down. Time flies when having fun.

Be Good and Take Care.

Love, Rich

The final weeks of our deployment passed without any major problems or, in my case, liberty incidents. We visited Livorno, Italy, and Athens, Greece, enjoying sightseeing and magnificent beaches. For once, the only times I saw the XO were in passing, and I only needed to salute and move on. By mid-August, we had finished our last scheduled operations, and I wrote home the night before we were to conduct turnover and be relieved by the USS Chilton.

Aug 15, 1968

Hi Mom and Dad,

I just learned that a special mail call is being held tomorrow so wanted to drop you a quick note before we head for home.

The biggest thing is I decided not to take leave right away when we get back. As much as I want to come home, I think I'll save my money and try and come at Christmas for a longer time.

The last weeks have been good ones. We visited Livorno, Italy, and I always enjoy the beaches and food there. And, we went to Athens, Greece, and I took a couple tours to see the sights. I saw the Acropolis, Parthenon and even where the first Olympics were held. Between us, I know it is historical and all that but it's a bunch of rocks and stones. Anyway, I can say I've been there.

My division has performed very well and the commanding officer even visited both my sections to personally thank the guys. Boy, was that a hit, and our division officer was so happy with us. We are still under manned but, holding our own. As soon as we get back, squadron moves ashore so LT Vargas, RMCS Brewer and RM1 Hill will be leaving. I like working with them. Oh well, that's the Navy.

Be Good and Take Care.

Love, Rich

"Hey, guys," I said to Stark and Cooper. We were a week away from offloading the Marines at Cherry Point, North Carolina, and I wanted to discuss the division's qualification status. "We got a lot of guys qualified this deployment but no one as watch supervisor, which leaves just the three of us. Do you think anyone is ready?"

"Reddy and Hawkins might be ready," Stark said.

"Hawkins maybe," Cooper said, "but—and no offense, Stark— Reddy is a good operator and can easily handle a section in port. I don't think he'll ever have what it takes to lead a section at sea. Just my opinion."

"He's right," Stark agreed. "Janos and Bonds will probably be next."

"That's what I thought," I added. "Just wanted to get your input. Now, let's go see why Lt. Vargas wants to talk to the division."

I called out, "Attention to quarters." The hatch opened, and Martin, Brewer, and Hill came out. They stood facing the division. I wondered where Vargas was.

"Attention on deck," we heard Vargas yell, as he came out holding the hatch open. "Amphibious Squadron Six, arriving." The commodore and his chief of staff, followed by our CO and XO, stepped out on the weather deck and stood before us.

"At ease, men," the commodore said. "I don't get to do this very often; in fact, I have never done this onboard USS Cambria." He chuckled, so everyone else did. "I am here for not one but two occasions today. First, Chief of Staff, if you please."

"RM1 Hill," the chief of staff said. "Front and center." Hill, quickly taking out his toothpick, stepped forward. The chief of staff handed the commodore something. "It is with great pleasure that we inform you that you have been selected for promotion to chief petty officer, U.S. Navy."

The commodore handed Hill what turned out to be chief collar devices and shook his hand. We all cheered, then got silent. "Congratulations, Chief," the commodore said. "It will be official September 16, but we wanted to inform you in front of all these men." I could tell Hill had tears in his eyes.

"Now, Lt. Vargas will tell you the second reason we are here."

"Thank you, Commodore," Vargas said. "Capt. Wise, Lt. Martin." Our CO and division officer looked surprised as they stepped forward.

"It is with great pleasure that I present the Green C award to the USS Cambria for fiscal year 1968. The citation reads that this is awarded to the top-rated ship, in its class, in the U.S. Navy for performance of communications duties. Captain, I'd like to add, this is the first time the Cambria has ever won this award in its history. Well done."

Capt. Wise stepped forward. "Thank you, Lieutenant, I accept on behalf of my ship and crew, but let me be honest. The commodore and all of us know the true winners of this award are Lt. Martin and his communications division. Great job, guys." Our whole division exploded in cheers and back-slapping.

"Attention on deck," Vargas yelled. "Amphibious Squadron Six departing." The awards party was over. "With your permission," the lieutenant continued, "CR Division, dismissed."

Before leaving, the XO came over for a second. Smiling, he said, "Work hard, play hard. You are a walking poster boy for that, Herman." He left with the others. Was that a compliment?

We offloaded the Marines the following week, and I thought, *Another deployment over, and time for a little rest and relaxation.* We would return home to Norfolk the next day.

CHAPTER 30

September 1968, Norfolk

"ATTENTION TO QUARTERS," I YELLED. "YES, THE rumor is true. We are getting a chief. Lt. Martin told me last night that he should be reporting this morning. While we wait, let me cover a few things. At ease." This was the first time we were all back together for quarters since returning from deployment. Now, all the leave periods were over, a few guys transferred out, and a few in. A lot had happened this last month.

I was finishing up my comments when the hatch opened, and Martin and our new chief walked out. What? Could it be who I thought? Yes, the toothpick was a dead giveaway; it was RMC Hill. He looked sharp in khakis. We must have been in shock when he walked over, and we all came to attention without being told.

"As you can see," Martin said, "RMC Hill has returned to us as ship's company and is your new division chief. RM2 Herman remains LPO. Chief Hill."

"Thank you, sir," he said. "I know most of you know me from being with squadron. I look forward to being your chief. We have a busy operational schedule coming up and a lot of work to do. Let's get to work. RM2 Herman, RM2 Stark, and RM3 Cooper, come to my office when done here." He and Martin left.

"Okay," Chief Hill said. Stark, Cooper, and I were now in his office. "The reason I wanted to talk to you separately is simple. You're the Big Three. You have known me a long time as a first class. I am now a chief, your chief. When you see me, you see anchors on my collar, which signifies my level of leadership. Nothing more, nothing less. I don't expect, and definitely won't accept, a problem with that. Understood?"

"Yes, Chief," we said almost in unison.

"Good. Now, let's clear up one more similar point. RM2 Stark, are you comfortable with RM2 Herman staying as LPO? You are technically senior, and I will give you the job based on seniority if you ask."

"No, Chief," Stark said. "Things have worked well with Herman as LPO, so why change now. We get along great, and, hell, we even won the Green C."

"I just wanted to make sure from day one," the chief said, "that we are all on the same page. Hope you didn't take offense that I asked, Herman."

"Would it have mattered if I did?" I said, laughing.

"No. All that behind us, tell me where we stand and what your plans are for divisional qualifications. I see you're leaving us in December, Cooper, and that is going to be a big loss. Care to extend?"

"No," Cooper said. "I've thought about it, but I'm anxious to give civilian life a try. I'm looking at going to computer school. I think there's a real future there."

The chief nodded. "Well, good luck. Let me know if I can help you make the transition to civilian life. Now, where's that training plan?"

It was obvious that Cooper was glad he had made up his mind and shared his decision. I could also tell he admired and respected Chief Hill, although he would never admit that back home. I grabbed my training folder, and we spent the next several hours doing an in-depth analysis of our training program and making adjustments.

"I think we have a good foundation laid out," Chief Hill said. "Of course, it is what I call a work in progress, so it will be modified as we go. Now, Stark, Cooper, I'd like to talk to Herman about a few things." They left.

Hill said, "Surprised to see me? Lt. Vargas says hi, by the way."

"I think it's great," I said honestly. "How did you end up with orders to Cambria?"

"Turns out, when you make chief, the Navy likes to transfer you to a new command. Apparently, it makes going from dungarees to khakis an easier transition. Anyway, I talked it over with the lieutenant and RMCS Brewer, and they both thought this would be a good career move for me, as well as I'd still be a big asset to the squadron when deployed. The commodore loved the idea, made a phone call, and here I am."

"How are the wife and kids adjusting?"

"You can call her Sami, Herman. She liked you immediately when she and the kids met you. She's doing well and kept busy with her teaching job. With her teacher's pay and three growing kids, the extra money from making chief is helping. Sami also tutors on the side for spending money. So life is good right now. How about you. Other than Cooper going to leave us, anything else I need to know right now?"

"Honestly, Chief," I said, "the division is still strong, but, as always, we lost a couple of guys and, as you saw, we need to qualify underway radio supervisors between now and our January Med deployment. Lt. Martin is a good division officer, and I think you'll find him a strong supporter. You're familiar with our layout and, of course, operational requirements, so that's about it."

He took the toothpick out of his mouth. "Thanks, Herman. We get underway October 1 for a least a month, if not six weeks, so let's make the most of that time. Now, let me go down and get settled into the chief's quarters. I know Chief Hawkins and Chief Porter will be glad to see me." He could tell I had a confused look on my face. "I'll be the third colored chief in ship's company," he added, smiling. "I think a new toothpick will be required," and he took out a fresh one and placed it in his mouth. "Step at a time, Herman, step at a time."

CHAPTER 31

October 1968, Western Atlantic

ON OCTOBER 1, WE LEFT NORFOLK FOR A ONE-month deployment in support of Apollo 7, the first U.S. manned mission into space. Cambria had a space capsule, identical in size to the actual mission one, and a NASA technical and recovery specialist onboard.

We steered a straight course for an area approximately 100 miles northwest of the Canary Islands. Our mission was to serve as the backup recovery vessel for Apollo 7 when they returned to earth. The aircraft carrier USS Essex was the primary recovery vessel off the East Coast. Communications played a vital role in the success of the mission, so Martin, Hill, and I attended the initial briefing our first day at sea.

Cmdr. Gordon introduced the NASA representative, who briefed us on the operational plan and the ship's requirements. Probably the most significant thing I heard, other than maintaining constant communications with mission control, was that once the space capsule reentered the earth's atmosphere, it was scheduled to splash down off the East Coast, and the Essex would do the recovery. But if that reentry was more than several seconds late, Cambria would do the recovery, a couple of thousand miles away. *Several seconds. Wow.*

The communications plan assigned two primary and two secondary frequencies for voice circuits that Cambria was to maintain with mission control at Kennedy Space Center. All four circuits would be activated and have communication checks on a strict schedule. Hill and I selected six transceivers and assigned them as dedicated to Apollo 7. We oversaw maintenance checks on each piece of equipment, double-checked our work, and then tuned the equipment and placed it in standby.

Quarters began at 1600, and Lt. Martin addressed us. "Tomorrow morning, we will start communicating directly with NASA mission control at Cape Kennedy. Chief Hill and I just briefed the CO, XO, and senior watch officer on the circuits that are dedicated to the Apollo 7 mission. Between now and tomorrow morning, I want every radioman, whether you will personally be involved or not, briefed on these circuits. I cannot stress enough how important it is that we have constant communications. Until this mission is over, either RMC Hill, RM2 Herman, or RM2 Stark will be in radio at all times. Any, and I mean any, loss of communications will be reported to the OOD immediately. You're taking part in history, gentlemen; let's enjoy it."

The CO and the NASA rep were in radio. It was almost time for our first voice radio check with mission control. The plan called for us to maintain the circuits in radio at the supervisor's desk. A monitor would be available on the bridge for the OOD to listen to. If we became the actual recovery platform, the circuits would be transferred to the bridge for the CO, OOD, and NASA representative to use. I was given the honor to conduct the first radio check, because most agreed I had the easiest voice to understand.

"NASA mission control, this is USS Cambria, radio check over," I said, my heart pounding.

"Cambria, this is mission control, got you loud and clear, how me, over?"

"Mission control, Cambria, read you the same. Standing by for instructions, over."

"Cambria, mission control, roger, nothing at this time, out."

There weren't any cheers, but there were a lot of smiles. My heart stopped pounding. The CO and NASA rep shook hands, and Lt. Martin escorted them out of radio. Operations had officially begun.

Every day during our transit, the ship would train recovering the mission module. The simulated capsule would be dropped overboard, and the ship would steam off. The capsule had a sound beacon that transmitted a steady three-second tone, fifteen times a minute. Search planes deployed to pick up the beacon would direct our ship to the capsule's location, and we would do the recovery. During this time, we maintained communications with mission control on our radio circuits, and weather conditions and coordination instructions were passed. October 10 was our last day of practice, and on October 11, radio was crowded as we, and millions of other Americans, listened to the countdown and blast off of Apollo 7. Astronauts Schirra, Eisele, and Cunningham were headed to space.

The Apollo 7 mission was conducted as planned and deemed a tremendous success. We remained on station in the secondary recovery area. The night before reentry, we were alerted that Hurricane Gladys could become a factor, and Cambria was readied to effect recovery. By morning, October 22, the weather was clear, and Apollo 7 splashed down exactly on schedule, ten days, twenty hours and nine minutes after launch. The USS Essex recovered the capsule, and the USS Cambria was relieved of duties.

"Mission control, Cambria, standing by for instruction," I said.

"Cambria, mission control, thank you for all your help. Good job from the mission control commander, Cape Kennedy. Secure this net. Out."

I contacted the OOD on the bridge, notifying him we were secured from all voice circuits by mission control and that their commander passed on a well-done.

It was over. Radio was packed as everyone listened to splashdown. No one said anything, and then we heard the 1MC activate.

"This is the CO. We have been secured from operations in support of the Apollo 7 mission. Although not called on, Cambria was well prepared, and I am proud of you all. This was a mission vital to the United States. It was successful, and, remember, you were still a part of its history. Now, I have been informed that our request has been approved and we are headed for a liberty stop in the Canary Islands. That is all." You could hear the cheers around the ship.

We pulled into Las Palmas, Canary Islands, two days later for our unexpected port visit. The CO couldn't have been any more popular than after his announcement we were going here. The crew attended the usual mandatory briefing on the culture and customs of any new port. We learned the Canary Islands, about sixty miles west of Morocco, were a Spanish community, and most people spoke English. One thing stood out about this brief: there was a Russian destroyer here on a port visit, and we were warned not to initiate contact with its sailors.

This would be the last time that Cooper would visit a foreign port in uniform, so I talked to Hill about an idea I had to organize a party where the old-timers could get together one more time and say farewell. He totally supported this and approved my duty sections. Stark also liked the idea, and it was easy to get others to sign up. Now, all I had to do was get Cooper to attend.

"Hey, Jeff," I said as we were getting ready for liberty. "Anything special you want to do when we get ashore?"

"Just want to go to lie on the beach, have a couple beers, enjoy the view, and stay out of trouble. Oh, and how could I forget? Attend my farewell party you're trying to keep secret."

"How did you find out?"

"You may be surprised, Herman." He looked like he wasn't going to tell me, then said, "One of the new guys told me. He thought I should know because Stark and Reddy would be there." He quickly added, "Don't worry, I set him straight. I told him I would be disappointed if they weren't, seeing as they are good friends of mine. I then told him he will be lucky if he gets assigned to one of their sections, because they're great teachers and role models. How about that?"

I put my hand over my heart and pretended to stagger. "I feel faint." I started laughing.

"Yeah, yeah," he said. "You know, between us, it feels good to say that. Now, let's go."

After beach time, we joined everyone at a restaurant, where a waiter put several tables together as there were about twelve of us. Drinks and food were ordered, and we all shared stories about Cooper—with the young guys not sure which tales were true.

We had been there well over an hour when some Russian sailors showed up. I got everyone's attention and told them to ignore them. For about five minutes anyway.

"You," a Russian sailor said, walking over and pointing at Stark. "We know you, yes?" We ignored him. "You, dark skin, I talk to you." He then called over two of his friends, and he pointed at Stark and talked to them in most likely Russian. "Yes, you Olympics. No?"

"You recognize him?" Cooper said. "Yes, he is Bob Hayes. Olympic runner." He patted Stark on the back. "Fastest man in the world." I was appalled. I couldn't be involved in another international incident and tried to get Cooper's attention.

"*Nyet*," the Russian said. He called over another of his shipmates and pointed at him. "Fastest Russian. We race."

"Great," Cooper said, standing up. "Come on, Mr. Hayes." He pulled Stark up. "Race for drinks." He started outside, pulling a reluctant Stark with him.

"For drinks," the Russian said, and everyone headed outside.

"What the hell you doing, Cooper?" Stark pleaded.

"This is not a good idea," I said.

"Hawkins," Cooper said, ignoring us. He then turned to the Russian standing there. "He'll mark off a hundred meters. Race for beer."

"*Nyet*," the Russian said. "Vodka." He told one of his guys something, and he and Hawkins marked off what might have been 100 meters and indicated an imaginary starting line. The Russian had his runner take his shirt off and stand on the line.

"You got this, Stark," Cooper said. Stark shook his head, took off his shirt, and got on the starting line.

The Russian yelled something, and his guy and Hawkins grasped hands and stood at arm's length like a finishing tape.

Probably 100 people had gathered now, talking about what was happening. Suddenly you could hear shouts of "USA, USA" and "SSR, SSR." It was getting exciting, and, at this point, I gave up and let Cooper and the guys have their fun. After several more words were exchanged, a local citizen stepped forward and started the countdown. "On your mark, get set, go!"

Stark got off to a slow start and was behind by several yards about halfway. Then, he took off like he was shot out of a cannon, and he beat the Russian by at least five yards. The crowd went crazy, and I noticed several policemen had gathered and watched too. They were smiling and applauding, so I figured all was good. Everyone headed back to the restaurant.

"Hawkins, Reddy," I shouted. They saw me and came over. "Get our guys back to the ship. I'll stick with Stark and Cooper, have one drink, and get them back. We don't want any trouble. Now, go." They nodded and got everyone away. Stark and Cooper were already in the restaurant with their Russian friends.

"Vodka for my friends," the Russian leader said. Shots of vodka were passed around, and he slapped Stark on the back and shouted, "Bob Hayes, very fast."

"Stark, Cooper," I said. "Let's get out of here while we can." We waited for the right time and slipped out. To our surprise, only the quarterdeck watch was present when we came back aboard, and we went straight to our berthing compartment.

The next morning, at quarters, we filled Chief Hill in on what happened. I thought he was going to swallow his toothpick, he chewed it so hard. Lt. Martin joined us. "At ease," he said. "Well, I just came from an interesting officers' call. All the talk is about Bob Hayes, the American gold medal winner in the 1964 Olympics at 100 meters, being in town. Rumor has it, he actually ran against a Russian sailor yesterday. Any of you know anything about that?"

"No, sir," Hill said. "If true, that would have been fun to see, and I know we'd all like to meet him. Do you know if he won, sir?" We were all ready to burst out laughing.

"No, Chief," Martin said, looking at him strangely. "You don't believe that story, do you? Bob Hayes here, come on. Get serious." He left, shaking his head.

We departed Las Palmas October 29 for what we thought would

be an easy transit back to Norfolk. All that changed our second day at sea when a message was received, and the section on watch realized they couldn't decrypt it.

"Herman," Janos said, panting. "You're wanted in radio ASAP!" I could tell from his face this was for real.

When I got to radio, Chief Hill told me to join Lt. Martin in the crypto vault. By regulations, it takes two members from a designated Crypto Team, one being an officer, to decrypt sensitive information. Martin and I decrypted the message and asked for the CO to join us. The captain read the decrypted message. "Who all will see this?" he asked.

"Only RM2 Herman and I in radio," Martin said. "We will make no copies and will remain here with all the crypto equipment required for this classification message standing by for your direction."

The CO wrote out a reply and asked that we get it encrypted and sent as soon as possible. He then asked about the voice circuit we were to guard. I told him it would be activated and given a top priority. As he was leaving the vault, he turned and said, "I'd like one of you to personally come see me when that message is receipted for, and if we hear from USNS Mizar. Me, only me." He departed. I stayed in the vault while Martin went to brief Hill about the voice circuit and the CO's orders.

When Hill sent me to tell the CO that the message was receipted for, I found the CO on the bridge with the navigator and OOD. The CO came over, and I told him the message was successfully transmitted. He thanked me and took the 1MC handset.

"This is the commanding officer, set Condition Three." He replaced the handset and announced on the bridge, "OOD, recommend we make course for the Azores."

About seven hours later, "This is the captain," came over the 1MC. "We have been diverted from our transit home and are currently in an area in the Mid-Atlantic about 450 miles southwest of Azores. Earlier today, a possible discovery was made on the ocean floor which is of vital interest to the United States of America. We will rendezvous with a research ship, USNS Mizar. USS Cambria is here to deter any nation, other than our own, from interfering in recovery efforts. That is all for now."

There, it was out. Without giving details, the CO let his crew know what was going on; rumors could stop. Of course, what was found was still a mystery, and from what Martin and I saw, I hoped it stayed that way. Also, the CO didn't tell the crew that a Russian destroyer had been seen lingering in the area.

"USS Cambria, this is USNS Mizar, over." Chief Hill ran out to get the captain.

"USNS Mizar, Cambria, roger, loud and clear," I replied.

"Cambria, Mizar. Message for commanding officer, over."

"Mizar, stand by." Hill and the captain entered radio. I gave an update and gave the handset to the CO, who then asked for everyone, except Martin and me, to leave. Chief Hill hurried everyone out, including himself.

"Mizar, Cambria, commanding officer here with properly cleared personnel only. Over."

"Cambria, Mizar, roger." The individual on the other end then gave a detailed report on what was happening and his requirements. Both Martin and I copied down what was said so there would be no mistakes on what was heard. After several exchanges, the CO and his counterpart on the Mizar agreed on what was to happen next.

"Mizar, Cambria, understood, out." The CO called to the bridge, asking the XO and operations officer to join him in radio. While waiting, he reread both Martin's and my copies of the conversation he just had. When all the players were present, the CO briefed on what operations were needed. Finishing, he looked at me and the lieutenant. "I got that right, didn't I?" he said.

"Yes, sir," we said in unison.

"XO, ops," the CO continued. "We have to do this right. For all of you, I know you understand the importance of what is about to take place and that there cannot be a leak of this information. Ever."

At 0200 the next morning, in complete darkness, a small boat pulled alongside Cambria, a man boarded by himself, and the small boat pulled away. The deck and passageway had been cleared. The

CO and XO escorted the man, who looked to be wrapped in a straitjacket, to the CO's quarters; he entered and had the door shut behind him. Not a single word was exchanged. For the next twenty-eight hours, Cambria made best speed to another rendezvous point, and the only person to go in and out of the CO's cabin was the CO himself. At 0600 the following day, the man was escorted, once again by the CO and XO, and he boarded another small boat that pulled alongside. They disappeared in the darkness.

"USNS Mizar, USS Cambria, over."

"Cambria, Mizar, over."

"Mizar, Cambria. Package delivered, over."

"Cambria, Mizar, roger, thank you, Captain, Mizar, out!"

The CO put the handset back. He keyed the bridge and said, "OOD, set Condition Four and recommend you make best course for home." With only Martin and me present, the CO said, "One more thing we three must do." And we did.

Nov 13, 1968

Hi Folks,

You probably weren't expecting this letter, were you. We pull into port tomorrow and I'll be calling but if you look at the outside of this envelope you will see something special and I thought I'd write a short note to get it postmarked and you can keep it as a souvenir. Yes, it has the Apollo 7 stamp on it. Hope you didn't damage it opening the letter. Make sure you save it.

Anyway, we didn't get to recover the actual space capsule with the astronauts, the USS Essex did. We were the backup. It was still exciting and I got to talk to NASA mission control at Cape Kennedy every day when we practiced. Something I can tell my grandchildren, right?

We did get liberty in the Canary Islands and that was fun. We met some Russian sailors and they thought John Stark was Bob Hayes, the Olympian and fastest man in the world. Stark said that it proves all people think colored people look alike. He laughed when he said it. Anyway, we played along and they said that one of their guys was faster and wanted a race. Cooper convinced Stark to do it and he won. It was hilarious. The Russians then bought us vodka drinks. You know, we had a great time with them and it makes me wonder why our countries are enemies. Makes no sense sometimes.

On the way back home, we took a detour and helped a sailor lost at sea get home safe. A humanitarian deed by the Navy you'll never read about.

Be Good and Take Care.

Love, Rich

I finished my letter home that night and crawled into my rack. Everything I wrote was the truth, sort of. About Apollo 7 anyway. I doubted I would ever be able to talk about why we actually stopped to pick that man up, in the middle of the Atlantic, and get him home safe. I wondered if the world would ever know the real truth. The USNS Mizar believed they had found the wreckage of a U.S. submarine lost at sea. Hopefully, the man we picked up with thousands of photos strapped to his body would be able to provide the answers.

I wondered if I would ever be able to tell my grandchildren about the night of October 31, 1968, when a Navy captain, a lieutenant, and I shared a prayer and tears for the ninety-nine crew members and families of the USS Scorpion (SSN-589), lost at sea May 22, 1968.

"Taps, Taps, lights out." The bugle played.

CHAPTER 32

December 1968, Norfolk

IT WAS THE FIRST DAY OF LEAVE FOR THOSE TAKING the Christmas period December 13-27. I hadn't been home to celebrate bringing in the new year since I joined the Navy, so I opted for the second leave period, starting December 30. This also gave me a chance to update personnel records with last-minute changes before the end of the year. One thing that can always be counted on in the military is constant change, and that was on my mind as I watched guys depart the ship.

We'd had a change of command, and Capt. Wise was relieved by Capt. House as commanding officer. Several new radiomen reported to the ship when we got back last month and checked into the division. The first two, both RMSAs just out of boot camp, were nervous, listened to every word Hill said, and seemed happy to have someone to lead them around and get checked in. The third, an RM3, came into radio like he owned the place. He bounced on his feet as he walked, had long, wavy blond hair and a big smile, and went right up to Chief Hill like they were old friends.

"Hi, Chief, I'm RM3 Terry Hoffman reporting in as ordered. Great to meet you, and I think we'll get along just fine."

"You do, do you?" Hill said, toothpick going into his mouth. "Whatever gave you that idea, Petty Officer?" I could tell the chief was not ready for this guy.

"Because I'm happy to be here, my wife is happy to be here, and I am a very good radioman, Chief. You're lucky to have me."

I decided it was time to intervene. "Welcome aboard, RM3

Hoffman," I said, "I'm RM2 Herman, your LPO." Before I could get another word out, he was shaking my hand.

"Nice to meet you," he said. "Wow, you're young. I like that." He kept smiling and pushed his hair back out of his eyes. Might have to talk to him about that hair. It was so light I wasn't even sure you would call it blond.

Hill stayed silent, and I had Hoffman sit down and tell us a little bit about himself. We learned he was from Atlanta, had attended the University of Georgia until joining the Navy, his wife's name was Jill, they had an apartment in town, and he had been on shore duty at the communication station here in Norfolk. He had two years left on active duty and then planned on being a professional radio and TV sportscaster. He definitely had the looks and talking part down. Cocky as he was, I liked this guy.

I knew who I wanted checking him in and called for Nash. They hit it off and marched away to get Hoffman settled. I turned to Chief Hill. "Let's hope he performs as well as he talks." He laughed.

We had qualified Hawkins to replace Cooper as underway radio supervisor while at sea last month, and Bonds and Janos should be ready before our next deployment to the Mediterranean. We trained hard in port and had seen major advances made among all the guys in the division using the training plan we made when Chief Hill arrived.

I had planned to go to Chesterfield with Cooper for Thanksgiving but came down with a case of tonsillitis and had to cancel. I did call and talked to his parents. Mrs. Cooper cried and couldn't thank me enough for thinking of them. I told them I hoped to visit sometime before getting out of the Navy next year. They said my room would be ready, and the town would throw a party.

As Stark entered radio one day, I said, "Hey, John, I've got a great idea." We had been spending a lot of time together, helping Chief Hill get the division organized and running the way he wanted. At quarters recently, we'd heard guys comparing us to the TV characters on *I Spy*, where Robert Culp and Bill Cosby played a mixed-race pair of detective partners. We didn't mind, and Martin and Hill thought it was a sign that there was good morale throughout the division.

"Will this idea get us in trouble?" Stark replied.

"No. You're going on leave to Milwaukee, right?" He nodded. "You'll be close to Minneapolis—why don't you think about coming to see me and my family the last couple of days, and then we'll fly back together? I think you'd have a great time."

"You're kidding. No, you're not kidding, are you? May work. Sounds like fun. Let me check on flights and let you know."

My leave started on schedule. I landed December 30 on time, even with a snowstorm in progress, and I was looking for my folks when I entered the terminal. Usually, Mom gets up front, but I didn't see her.

"Hey, sailor," a familiar voice shouted.

"Darrell," I said, embracing him and beaming. "What're you doing here?"

"Your dad called about you coming home, and I volunteered to pick you up in this storm. Hell, I haven't seen you since you went patriotic on me. Come on, let's go."

Once we got on the road, I said, "So, what's the real deal with you gone all the time?"

He laughed and didn't answer at first. Finally, he said, "I got the best job in the world. People from all over the country are buying Winnebago RVs built here in Minnesota. What I do is deliver them to people wherever they are in the country. Then, I get paid to fly back. Simple as that."

"Sounds too simple to me," I said, looking at him skeptically. He had a smile on his face that only he could show. I knew there was more to the story but let it go. "So, to my folks, and we'll catch up on the last three years."

Mom and Dad loved having Darrell and me in the house together again that afternoon. Louie dropped by, and I got to meet my sister-in-law, Bonnie, and niece, Joline. Even seeing him, it was hard accepting Louie as a father. Mom told me Tom Gilmore was out of the Army and home, and I definitely intended to see him.

Darrell took me to a New Year's Eve party that turned out to be a little more than I was ready for. It was at a house near the university campus and attended by mostly students. Having fun, I struck up a conversation with a senior named Dianne, a pretty brunette who planned to teach in elementary school. I heard voices getting louder and realized Vietnam was being discussed and that the majority were against the war, as they called it. For some unknown reason, Darrell let it be known I was in the Navy, and all eyes turned on me. I decided to leave before it got ugly and headed for the door.

"Hey, buddy," Darrell said. "I'm sorry. I didn't think people would be that serious. Here, I'll take you home."

"Don't bother," a female voice said. "I'll take him." Dianne grabbed her coat and my arm, and we left. Darrell, speechless, managed to smile and give me the thumbs-up.

Dianne drove me, in her new Mustang hatchback, to a secluded spot overlooking the Mississippi River. "In case you're wondering, the car is a pre-graduation gift from my parents. I'm sorry about how you were treated back there. Not everyone is anti-government, and those that are just look for trouble."

"I'm used to it," I said. I told her about the date Todd and I had where the girls refused to go out with baby-killers and slammed the door in our face. She laughed, and I began to realize she was special. We talked about our families, about her future in teaching, and about my having one more year left and hoping to return to school right here. It was almost midnight.

"Hang on a second," she said. She reached under the seat and pulled out a bottle of Gallo and some plastic cups. "Hope you can handle cheap."

"Looks like fine wine to me." I opened the bottle and poured us each a glass, and we looked over the river. "Three, two, one. Happy New Year, Dianne." We toasted, kissed, and ushered in 1969.

When she dropped me off about 2:30, I explained New Year's Day was a special family affair, which I hadn't been to in three years, and I'd call in a few days. She said she understood and would be waiting. Wow, what a night.

After spending New Year's Day with the family at Margy and Irving's house, I kept up tradition and picked Dad up at work Friday. I wore my dress blues, now with my second-class crow, and arrived early to see everyone. Being Friday, most of the guys joined us for shots and a beer across the street before going home. The owner of the bar even bought a round and gave me my drinks for free. I behaved myself and drove Dad home. I could tell he loved this day.

Darrell called Saturday to say he was leaving to deliver a Winnebago to New Mexico and wasn't sure when he'd be back. He said that if I was already gone, he would make a point to call Dad soon to make the ice fishing trip we had talked about. I told him I was counting on him to make it happen and to have a safe trip. It was hard to ever get or stay mad at him.

Dianne and I got together a few times and had a lot of fun. Mom and Dad took us out to dinner one evening, and Mom and Dianne hit it off immediately. Mom even gave Dianne her work number and told her to call her Angie, and they planned to get together for lunch sometime. When I dropped her off that night, Dianne said she had never been so impressed by a woman. "She's brilliant," she said. "And an executive assistant to the director of social services for the city? Wow."

"Yep," I said. "That's Mom." I liked Dianne but wasn't sure I wanted her to be getting close to my family. I was leaving and probably not coming home for quite a while, so I wasn't ready to get serious about anything. Besides, she was also leaving, going to her student teaching job in Rochester. When we parted, we had each other's numbers and addresses and agreed to keep in touch. I would leave it at that.

Tom Gilmore came over one day, and Dad, who always liked him, stayed home from work to see him. I met Tom at the door, noticing he was thinner but looked good, and took him into the kitchen.

Dad shook his hand and handed him a beer. "I'm just glad you're home safe, Tom. I know your mom is. You did two tours in Vietnam, right?"

"Yes," he said quietly, sipping his beer. "I don't really like to talk about it. How you doing, Rich?"

Before I could answer, my dad accidentally knocked over his beer, and it crashed on the floor. Tom dove under the table, grabbed his knees to his chest, and started shaking. I bent down and knelt next to him. "It's okay, Tom. It's okay."

He stared at me and rocked back and forth. I could tell Dad didn't know what to do. Hell, I didn't know what to do. Finally, Tom stood and said, "I think I should go home. Thanks for the beer." He seemed to have regained his composure, and I walked him to his car, shook his hand, and watched him drive away.

I picked up the phone and called his mom. I told her what happened, and she said Tom was having a hard time since his last tour in Vietnam and was getting seen at the VA. She said he was pulling up and seemed okay. She thanked me for caring and said she was calling the VA right away. "If there is anything I or my family can do, just call," I said. "And we mean that, Mrs. Gilmore. Tom is like family to us too."

A few days later, I had a call from John Stark, saying it looked like he wouldn't be able to visit after all. "There's another bad snowstorm," I told Mom and Dad, "and he's afraid he might get stuck and not be able to get back to the ship. I looked at the weather, and I may have trouble making my own connecting flight."

As it turned out, Stark's flight from Milwaukee wasn't canceled, but he gave his seat to another sailor who needed to get back to his ship that was getting underway. He caught the next available flight and got back to Cambria sixteen hours late. My flight was delayed in Minneapolis, and I missed my connecting flight in Chicago, had to wait twelve hours, and ended up getting back two hours late. Not exactly the examples you want to set for the young sailors in the division.

Jan 17, 1969

Hi folks,

Just a quick note to let you know I made it back okay. I was a little late but so many guys missed flights because of the weather the XO excused everyone. John Stark did want to tell you something though.

"Mr. and Mrs. Herman,

I wanted to personally apologize for not making it to your home. I was looking forward to meeting you and talking to the parents who have raised a son I now call my friend. Maybe, if the offer still stands, we can try again in the future. All the best to you both. I'll look after Rich.

John Stark"

As you can tell, he's a great guy. He got back to the ship late too. He's serious about trying to come home with me next time and he's invited me to go with him to his folks' place on Cape Cod.

It was a terrific leave and I appreciate everything you did. You're great parents and I'm glad you're mine.

Be Good and Take Care.

Love, Rich

CHAPTER 33

January 1969, Norfolk

COME IN, HERMAN," CHIEF HILL SAID. "LET ME introduce you to RM1 Berglund."

Apparently, the XO had listened when Lt. Martin talked about CR Division having to go over a year without a chief or senior radioman for the leading petty officer. We'd gotten Chief Hill and now an RM1. I extended my hand and welcomed him aboard. Berglund seemed older than Hill. His dress blues looked good and had quite a few ribbons. He was sober, but he looked like he might be a big drinker.

Hill said, "I was telling Petty Officer Berglund that you have been serving as our division LPO for a long time and would look forward to having someone help carry the load. Why don't you get him settled in and his paperwork processed?"

Berglund and I went to the Enlisted Club that night. I figured he would be taking over as LPO, and a good way to start the turnover would be over dinner and away from the ship. I learned he had been in the Navy seventeen years, was divorced, and had no children. We talked a little about my background and about the guys in the division.

"I'll let you form your own opinion about everyone," I said. "I can only tell you my experiences of the last couple of years. I will say that Chief Hill and Lt. Martin have always backed me. I think it's because I'm straight with them, good or bad."

"Appreciate the input," he said. "Now, I'll be honest with you. I know I'll never make chief. Hell, I can't even pass the test. I'm old-school radioman and have never been able to keep up with all the new equipment and electronic advances. I've also had a few problems after drinking too much. But I'm not a quitter and think I'll be a good LPO if I have strong support in handling the communications stuff. I've always been a pretty good leader. From what I hear, I think we can become a good team. For the record, I'm only thirty-five, just had some tough duty." He smiled, then laughed.

"Sounds like a plan." I joined him in laughing.

The next morning, Hill introduced Berglund to the division and said that he would be taking over as LPO. I could tell that Stark, Reddy, Nash, and others who had been onboard a long time were glad to see an RM1. After quarters, Hill asked me to join him. "Well," he said, "what's your first impression?"

"Good. We had dinner last night, and I got to know him a little. I think he will be an asset to the division."

"I hear a *but* in there." He removed his toothpick. "Between us, Herman. I reviewed RM1 Berglund's service record, and from what I see, he can be a fairly good leader, but he may have let drinking hurt his career. And he has been left behind in the new communications world. He's very weak in electronics and systems. And, you didn't hear this from me, he's never been able to pass the chief's exam and will retire as a first class. Nothing wrong with that, mind you, just a fact. So he may become LPO, but I'm still going to need you to fill in to cover his weak areas. Problem with that?"

"Isn't that why we're a team, Chief?" Berglund had told me almost those exact words the night before. At least I knew he was honest. I respected him for that. "Why don't I give the best turnover I can, and we'll go from there."

Having several week-long periods at sea, we put them to good use with training. Bonds and Janos would be boarded for underway radio supervisors before we deployed; Brinda was close. As a pleasant surprise, Hoffman not only proved he could back up his cocky attitude, but he surpassed it. His friendliness was infectious, and the bounce in his step and long blond hair were getting to be as recognizable as Chief Hill's toothpick. I figured he'd qualify for supervisor soon.

"Hey, Herman," Hoffman said. "Don't mean to eavesdrop but I may be able to help."

I had been talking to Berglund and Stark about a letter I'd gotten from Dianne. Her student teaching was ending, and she had a week off before her final classes started. She asked me about coming down to Norfolk to visit, and I was saying it wouldn't work because I worked all day. And where would she stay? "Help how?" I asked Hoffman.

"Look, Jill and I have an apartment on Military Highway," he said. "I've been looking for a time that I could move her back home while I'm deployed. How about I give notice to my landlord that I'll pay rent until the end of the month?" He looked at Berglund. "If you and the chief approve leave for me to move Jill home the last week of February, Herman can have my apartment for his girlfriend to stay at. We kill two birds with one stone."

"I can make that happen," Berglund said. "I can't give you the whole week off though, Herman."

I thought for a second. "Let's do it." I figured Patti and the kids would like to have Dianne around during the day. "Only if I can give one week's portion of the rent though, Hoffman."

Before picking Dianne up at the airport, I stopped by Hoffman's apartment to get the keys. Jill Hoffman, an attractive redhead with freckles, seemed to be a perfect fit with Terry. Where he was outgoing and flamboyant, she was quiet and rolled her eyes as he talked and smiled. She told me about things to do in the local area and where to drop off the key for the landlord at the end of the month. Finally, they drove off to get Jill settled for the six-month separation.

"Not as fancy as your Mustang," I said as I opened the door of the 1962 Thunderbird and helped Dianne in at the airport. Mark had loaned me his car while she was here.

"Looks like a classic to me," she said. Dianne looked great, and I was happy to see her. "Before I forget." She handed me an envelope. Inside were five twenty-dollar bills with a note from my mom telling me to treat her right. "Your mom and I have had lunch a few times, and she thought it was wonderful that I was making this trip. Needless to say, honey, I like your mom."

Honey? Did she call me honey? Oh boy. "That's nice. Let me show you where we'll be staying, and then Mark and Patti have invited us over for dinner."

Stark took one of my duty days and Bonds another; Chief Hill let me off early every day. I dropped Dianne off at Patti's each morning, and they had no problem finding things to keep occupied. I picked her up at night, and we toured the sights and spent some quiet time at the apartment. I began to sense that Dianne was getting a lot more serious than me.

"When you get back in the fall, will you come stay with me?" she asked.

"I don't know, Dianne. That's a long way off. You don't even know where you'll get a job teaching yet. It could be Alaska." That didn't sit well. "I'm just saying. Let's just see what happens and go from there. I'm not ready to settle down yet. You know I want to get out and go back to the U."

"You could probably find a good college wherever I am. At least think about it. Your mom thinks we're good together."

"Like I said, let's see what happens."

I took her to the airport and returned Mark's car. I'd enjoyed the week with Dianne but was glad she was heading back.

"So when is the wedding?" Mark asked when I handed him his keys. He must have seen the shock on my face. "Hey, that's what Patti told me. She said Dianne and your mom already had you guys married."

"Obviously, I need to talk to Mom." Mark and Patti cracked up, and he took me back to the ship.

"Attention to quarters," Berglund said, standing next to Hill. He had officially relieved me as LPO, and I now stood in ranks with the rest of the division. The hatch opened and Martin came out followed by some familiar figures. .

"At ease," Martin said. "First of all, I'd like to say congratulations to RM3 Hawkins. You will be advanced to Radioman Second Class April 16." Cheers went up. "Now, Amphibious Squadron Six will be embarking his staff today, and I've invited Lt. Vargas and RMCS Brewer, many of you know, to say a few words."

"I'm not big on speeches," Vargas said, "and just wanted to say hello once again. We look forward to working with you again, and we'll try and stay out of your way." He waved, RMCS Brewer smiled, and they left, as did Martin.

"Listen up," RMC Hill said. "It's loadout day. RM3 Bonds, as supply petty officer, has all the supply chits and will coordinate, and RM1 Berglund will supervise this evolution."

The day went smoothly, and when we mustered that afternoon, Hill came out with our LPO. "Another record-setting day loading supplies," the chief said. "I guess we say thank you to RM3 Hawkins?"

"Vodka is a wonderful thing, Chief Hill," Hawkins called out. Everyone laughed and clapped.

"I didn't hear that," Hill said, smiling. "We deploy soon, guys. Make sure you have all your paperwork in order and uniforms ready to go. The lieutenant passes along his well-done today, and early liberty for all those not in the duty section. RM1 Berglund, RM2 Herman, and RM2 Stark in my office. Dismissed." Stark and I looked at each other, confused, and joined our LPO in Hill's office. The chief said, "RM1 Berglund asked for this meeting. Go ahead."

"I have made up my first underway watch bill as LPO. I wanted to go over it with all of you and explain how and why I assigned personnel the way I did. I would rather do this now, and, if I've made any glaring errors, let's talk about it before the rest of the division sees it." Berglund handed us each a copy of the watch bill he would be submitting to the chief.

I noticed right away that he and I weren't listed in a section. He had us getting underway in two sections, Port and Starboard, with RM2 Stark and RM2 (a little early but a nice touch) Hawkins as supervisors. Berglund was listed only as LPO; I was listed as a floater and one-on-one trainer. I looked at the personnel assigned to each section and thought he'd done a good job. I stayed silent.

"Looks good to me," Stark said. He was always positive and supportive of whatever was best for the division. He didn't look at me or make any mention of my assignment.

"At first," Hill said, "I questioned your section supervisors. Stark, obviously, but not Herman. Now, I think I know what you're trying to do. Hawkins has qualified and deserves a chance, and this way Herman is always available if needed. I like that. Wish I would have thought about it."

"Thanks, Chief," Berglund said, sounding relieved. "As a floater, Herman will be on call and can be of benefit to both sections when needed. Also, as I understand it, during Marine assault exercises and anytime squadron activates the CWO watch, he supplements their watch bill and is a loss anyway. All other times, he will be assigned an individual to give one-on-one intense training to. I've heard stories about an RM3 Damon and how he was some kind of guru of all trainers. That will now be Herman."

"He's nailed that," Stark blurted out. "All the good ones are Damon-trained."

"I like it," Hill said. "Submit it."

Mar 17, 1969

Hi folks,

I always like to write you a little something just before going to sea. Also, I can say Happy Birthday, Dad.

I feel comfortable leaving this time. One thing, Mom, I like Dianne and will be keeping in touch but don't have us married yet, okay? I'm a long way from that commitment so don't let her make you think otherwise. Thanks. I'll be giving her a call shortly and hope to get that across to her. I also had a nice dinner with Mark and Patti yesterday.

This deployment will be a little different. I have Chief Hill now and a first-class radioman has reported aboard and taken over at the Leading Petty Officer. I'm not even going to be standing watches. Nope, I'm going to be used as a trouble-shooter and qualification trainer. Should be fun.

Well, will get this in mail. Next letter from the Med.

Be Good and Take Care.

Love, Rich

CHAPTER 34

April 1969, Mediterranean Sea

SOME THINGS DON'T CHANGE," HILL SAID, PUTTING
a new toothpick in his mouth.

"Hey, Chief," I said. "No, this will always be my favorite spot."
We looked out over the fantail at an almost full moon illuminating
the calm Atlantic. During the night, we would pass through the Strait
of Gibraltar, and I would start my third Mediterranean deployment.
"I guess it would be fair to say it is now our favorite spot?"

"It is beautiful and peaceful," he said. "That was a pretty rough
crossing though. And poor Reddy, after all this time he still gets
seasick."

"And never misses a watch," I added. We'd hit two significant
storms during our transit across. About half the ship's crew and almost
all the 700 Marines we embarked at Cherry Point were still trying to
recover. For a few days. it was difficult to walk the passageways with
all the sick guys sitting and throwing up in bags. "So, Chief, think
we're ready for this?"

"I think things went well, considering we have a lot of new guys.
RM1 Berglund seems to be working out, and that watch bill he put
us in proved to be right on. How're you feeling? I know you've been
putting in twenty-hour days."

"Yeah, I'm good. I'm going to recommend we board Bonds,
Brinda, and Janos for underway supervisor the day we're in Rota
doing turnover. I think Hoffman will be ready by the time we hit
Naples. I'm going to board Reddy too. He's a great operator, and I
think he deserves to do it just to have it in his record."

"Do it," Chief Hill said smiling. "That Hoffman is something else. I don't think I have ever seen anyone with an attitude like his. Does anything bother him? And that hair. You didn't hear this from me but, I wish we had another ten just like him." We both chuckled. "Well, Herman, I'm calling it a night. Get some rest, you hear?"

A few days later in Rota, Lt. Martin addressed us at quarters.

"First, I want to congratulate RM3 Bonds, RM3 Brinda, and RM3 Janos on qualifying as radio supervisors underway," he said. "I had RMC Hill do a little research, and as far as we can tell, this is the first time we have ever had six qualified at one time. I also understand this is due largely in part to a legend from the past, RM3 Damon, and now to RM2 Herman. Great job."

Martin gave us a moment to celebrate with cheers, back slaps and handshakes. At my recommendation, we had boarded all three together the day before. It took over three hours and left everyone exhausted. In the end, it was well worth it, and all three had solid performances. I let them back each other up fielding questions because I thought that was real-world.

"Okay, settle down," the lieutenant said. "A little surprise for you all. At turnover yesterday, we learned that, when we get to the island of Crete, we are going to be involved in making a movie called *Patton*. Before the war games begin, several of the actors will board, and they'll film Marines going over the side, getting into our landing craft, and making beach assaults. They may want to use some of our communication circuits, so we need to be ready to assist. We'll learn more when we get there."

On April 8, we anchored in the Sea of Crete, offshore from Iraklion. Shortly after arrival, a small boat with several Navy officers escorted the movie actors aboard. Standing on the weather deck outside radio, we had a good view of everyone as they climbed the ladder. I wasn't a big movie buff, but even I couldn't help noticing George C. Scott and Karl Malden. Capt. House and Cmdr. Gordon greeted them, and everyone disappeared, probably heading to the wardroom.

Word spread fast about the actors being onboard. Scott, after the briefings concluded in the wardroom, demanded he be taken back immediately to his hotel in town. Malden, on the other hand, accepted the CO's invitation and spent the night on Cambria. He had dinner in the wardroom with the officers, then asked to meet with the crew.

Malden spent hours that night talking to the enlisted personnel on the mess decks, and I was able to attend for a while. He said he worked hard but was still lucky to have made it as an actor. He talked about having a Czech background, growing up in Chicago, and not speaking English until he started school. He asked everyone questions about their families and seemed genuinely interested in the jobs we did and life onboard a ship. He signed autographs and posed for pictures. It was after midnight when he finally said he had to get some sleep before filming started in the morning. He left to a standing ovation.

Filming started at daybreak. The star, Scott, was already on the main deck, in uniform and screaming at everyone. He had a little whip—a rider's crop?—in his right hand and kept banging it on his leg. One guy—the director, I guessed—was trying to organize the first shoot and getting actors where they belonged. I was impressed with two cameras that were extended outboard of the ship, about ten feet above the deck, ready to film men as they went over the side and down the cargo nets into the landing craft below. Easily a hundred extras in World War II uniforms were standing by. Finally, they appeared to be ready.

"Let's do this in one shoot, people," the director shouted. "Ready, action!" About twenty guys went over the rail and started down the nets. Another twenty followed, and eventually all the extras were over and gone. "Cut!" The director got into a discussion with several others, and then Scott screamed something and stormed off. "Okay, people. We're going to go with that. A couple of the guys got stuck or fell, but my video guy said he can work around that. Let's get all actors leading the landing in the boats, and let's hit the beach. Find Mr. Scott and Mr. Malden, and have them join me in the officers' boat to head ashore. Make it look real, people."

Our two most qualified ship's coxswains were driving the landing craft. Fifty extras dressed as World War II Marines boarded each boat. Three times, the boats landed and lowered the fronts so the Marines could charge out and run through the water onto the beach. All three times, the extras playing the Marines were too sick to leave the boat, and when the front came down, most were sitting and throwing up. I didn't see it, but rumor had it that Scott went berserk, while Malden thought it was funny.

After much discussion, it was decided that actual Marines would be used, and fifty were selected from those onboard for each boat. They got into the movie uniforms, and the boats once again hit the beach, dropped the fronts, and every Marine charged out onto the beach. Done perfectly in one shoot. Although we were standing by, our communication circuits were never used.

"This is the captain," we heard over the 1MC. "I want to pass along a well-done to all hands from Mr. Franklin Schaffner, director of the movie *Patton* for the support given him the last two days. And, to the Marines who showed those actors what real men are made of, I personally give a special well-done." You could hear all the Marines on board cheering. "Now, it's time to get back to the real world. Set Condition Three."

We lifted anchor and rejoined the other squadron ships, who were already in the second day of a scheduled ten-day exercise on a nearby deserted island. Operations went well until the fourth day, when a severe storm hit. Winds gusted over seventy miles an hour, making it difficult to maintain contact with the Marines on the beach.

"Herman," I heard someone saying. "You're needed in radio."

I had been in the rack about two hours after having been up for over thirty. I was used to it. As soon as I entered radio, I knew something serious was happening. Chief Hill and a Marine officer were at the supervisor's desk, and Hawkins was trying to raise someone on a voice circuit. "Chief?" I said.

Hill said, "We got a call that there is a Marine needing immediate medical evacuation to the hospital in Iraklion, Crete. We've lost comms."

The Marine major said, "The Marine commandant has approved a helo to go get him, even in this weather, but not if we don't have comms. Any ideas?"

I had Hawkins try again and listened. I looked at the map of where the Marine was located and made sure the equipment assigned was good for that location with the best antenna for coverage. It was not only the best we had, but it was the only one that would work for that area. Hawkins had the setup perfect. I was pretty sure what the problem was.

"I need to go check this antenna." I pointed out which one it was. "Reddy, get me a pair of rubber gloves, a crescent wrench, and some duct tape." I put a safety harness on, then told Hawkins to make sure all active circuits on that mast were shut off. I told Reddy to double-check and make sure the circuits were secure. This was going to be hard enough, and I didn't need to worry about getting shocked or, worse yet, electrocuted.

"Can you climb that mast in this weather?" the major asked.

"Do we have a choice?" I replied.

"I'm coming with you," Chief Hill said. I saw he was putting on a safety harness. He grabbed a portable radio and gave one to Hawkins and another to the major. "Channel three, be ready for my call."

We got to the bottom of the mast, and I looked up at the antenna. In the rain, my visual inspection told me nothing. I climbed the seventy-five-foot mast, and Hill came right behind me. I had been up here many times but never in winds like this. Reaching the yardarm, I managed to get into a sitting position and check the antenna base. As I thought, the stress from the wind had caused a small crack at the base, allowing water to build up inside.

I pointed it out to Chief Hill and yelled, "It's flooded. I need to take this plate off, drain the water, and reattach. Then I'll duct-tape it. Should hold until we get to port."

"How heavy is that plate?"

"Going to find out." A gust of wind nearly blew both of us off the mast, and we could do nothing but hang on. Finally, it subsided, and I loosened the bolts. One by one, I handed the eight bolts to the chief and, with his help, lifted the heavy plate free.

Water gushed out. I dried the insulators and inside the best I could, and we reattached the plate. I covered the crack and then wrapped the entire base in duct tape. We headed down. As soon as I felt far enough away from the antenna, I told Chief Hill to go for it.

"RM3 Hawkins, Chief Hill, over," he said into the portable radio.

"Roger, chief."

"Activate the circuit and hold a radio check with the beach, over."

"Roger, stand by."

We continued our climb down the mast. I was in no hurry and realized my knees were a little shaky. It seemed to take forever.

"Chief?" We could hear the excitement in Hawkins' voice. "Radio check good, and I've turned the circuit over to the major and Marines, over."

"Roger, Herman and I on the way back." We high-fived.

"You guys were crazy to go up there," Martin said when we entered radio. He and Vargas, standing next to him, apparently had been called to radio.

"Not as crazy as that helo pilot and his crew," I said. "They're trying to airlift that Marine in these winds between mountains."

"The ship's doctor and surgical corpsman went too," Vargas added.

"Attention on deck!" Hawkins shouted. "The CO and XO entering radio."

"At ease," the CO said. "Lt. Martin, did you authorize these two men going up the aft mast in this storm to work on that antenna?" We could see he wasn't happy.

"It was my decision, Captain," Hill said before Martin could say a word. "Everything was happening quickly, and I thought it was the best course of action to take. RM2 Herman knew exactly what needed to be done, and I provided his backup. We just did it."

I didn't think the CO was expecting that. He shook his head and seemed to relax a bit. "Well, Chief, I can't argue with the results, but, if there is ever a next time, I do not want to see my two best communicators put in harm's way." Before he could continue, the intercom activated.

"Radio, OOD. Is the captain there?"

"Listening, OOD."

"Captain, we just heard from the helo, and they have the patient onboard and are transporting to Iraklion. Pilot said weather improving. Doctor says he believes it is ruptured appendix, patient stable."

"OOD, radio. CO acknowledges."

"Well, all's well that ends well," the CO said. As he and the XO started to leave, he turned at the hatch. "Chief, next time send someone else up there with Herman. Good job, men." They departed.

April 23, 1969

Hi folks,

We pull into Iraklion, Crete, tomorrow for a short port visit and I want to get a letter off to you letting you know all is good. We just finished another lengthy exercise and it'll be nice to get off the ship and stretch our legs. One of our guys, Hawkins, was advanced to second class so we'll try and celebrate that with a beer toast for sure. Also, April 14 was my third anniversary of going to boot camp. One to go. We had our standard briefing today on the local customs and how we are ambassadors of the United States and need to act accordingly. There doesn't seem to be too much to do here so may just take it easy and save my money.

We had some excitement as soon as we got here. Our ship was selected to be used for the filming of Marine landings during World War II for the movie Patton. George C. Scott is playing Patton and he and Karl Malden were onboard for two days. I'll just say, from what I saw first-hand, George C. Scott is a spoiled jerk and had nothing good to say while here. Karl Malden was just the opposite. He spent the night onboard and talked for hours to us enlisted guys on the mess decks. He's a great guy. One highlight of filming was the actors playing Marines got so sick riding in our landing boats that actual Marines had to replace them. It was hilarious.

We also had an exciting night during the exercise. A bad storm, winds up to 70 mph, hit and a Marine on shore needed to be evacuated off the deserted island to a hospital here in Crete. A Marine helicopter pilot and his crew volunteered to fly in between some mountains and they were able to airlift him out. Our ship's doctor and corpsman also volunteered. Long story short, the Marine's appendix burst and he probably would have died if not gotten to the hospital when he did. Anyway, he survived thanks to the heroics of that flight team.

I'm looking forward to mail call tomorrow. You probably know how Dianne's student teaching went. I forgot to ask before I left if you got that three acres of river property up north. It sounded like a wonderful place to build a home for when you retire. I'm also hoping to hear if Jackie had her baby and if Sonya has a brother or sister.

Well, all for now. Will write again after I get your letters.

Be Good and Take Care.

Love, Rich

CHAPTER 35

May 1969, Sea of Crete

STILL OUR SECRET, I SEE," CHIEF HILL SAID AS HE SAT down next to me on the fantail.

"Yeah," I answered. "Not many guys are roaming the decks at 0200. What're you doing up at this hour, Chief?"

"Believe it or not, Herman, you're not the only one who keeps crazy hours." He smiled and put in a new toothpick. "I figured you might be out here and thought I'd stop by. There's something I want to talk to you about."

He sounded serious. "Sure, Chief, fire away."

"We've never discussed what you were planning to do with your career. When we get back, you'll be looking at only seven months to go before your enlistment is up. You could probably get a nice bonus, about six thousand dollars to re-up. I'm sure we could get you any school you want and duty in an area of your choice. With your record, I think the XO would even consider recommending you for the first-class advancement exam. You could actually be a four-year E-6. I've never met one but do know they exist. Or do you plan to get out?"

"Wow, you recruiting me, Chief?" I said, laughing. "No, I plan to get out. The ship doesn't deploy again until next March, and my enlistment is up in April so they won't take me. When I enlisted, I was a sophomore at the University of Minnesota. I'd like to apply for a ninety-day early out and start school in January. I plan to pre-register this fall and apply for the GI Bill. I'm hoping you and Lt. Martin will recommend approval of that."

"I see no reason not to support your wishes," the chief said. "As much as I'd like to see you stick around, I feel it's important that good sailors be rewarded for performance. Glad we had this talk. I'm still going to work on you though." He smiled and started to leave. "I think you'd make a great master chief or officer. You should know, so does Lt. Vargas."

Now that gave me something to think about. A four-year first-class? Master chief or even LDO? Master Chief Herman, Lieutenant Herman. Nice ring to it. Or not.

May 4, 1969

Hi Mom and Dad,

I decided to take the opportunity and answer your letters. First of all, I can't tell you how much it means to get all the mail and I hope you tell everyone else that too. I just don't have the time to answer everyone individually.

So, Sonya has a brother. I loved the birth announcement and letter I got from Jackie. Punky, I know I'm the only one who calls her that, sure did good when she married Gary and I can't wait to see them.

Mar said she and Jim were looking at moving to the Upper Peninsula of Michigan. Sounded like a good job offer for Jim and Mar said she would have no problem getting a teaching job in a small town. She seems happy and that's all I care about.

I'm glad you got that property up north and your plans for building on it sound great. I would never have thought of taking down the garage in town, section by section, and hauling it up to the river and put it back together again. Lots of work, Dad, good luck. Of course, like you said, there is no rush.

In Dianne's letter she said student teaching was fun and she'd be done soon and ready to take her finals for graduation. Apparently, you hear more from her than I do.

Going to stop here and will add to it before next mail call.

May 22, 1969

Just going to add a bit to this letter and get it ready for the mail. Kind of like two letters in one. Our war games finished and this time there wasn't much excitement and we performed really well. We pull into Naples, Italy, tomorrow for a port visit and by the time we leave our deployment will be half over. You know I have been here before and I plan go back to that NATO Club, Flamingo, again but won't do any tours like I have in the past. Next time I see Rome and Pisa I hope to be a civilian.

Speaking of being a civilian. Chief Hill and I had a long discussion about my plans for when my enlistment is up. Yeah, getting close enough to think seriously about it. I told him I'd like to get out in January and start back up at the U where I left off. He made some good arguments for staying in but I'm definitely not a career man. I think the CO will approve my getting out early. Hopefully, this fall I can get home and check into early registration. Could you look into that for me, Mom?

Be Good and Take Care.

Love, Rich

⸺⊰◈⊱⸺

"This will make a great picture," Berglund said.

It was our last day of liberty in Naples before departing for the massive NATO at-sea exercise. A group of us had toured downtown and headed to the Flamingo Club for dinner. Along the way, we ran into Brewer and Hill, who joined in. We ended up eight strong at the table. "Give me your cameras. I'll take one on each, and we'll all have it as a souvenir," Berglund said.

Then the sea stories started, and each one called for a toast. The guys seemed to enjoy seeing Brewer and Hill loosening up a bit. "Before we go back," Hill said, standing. "One final toast to RM2 Herman. If we can get him back aboard tonight, quietly, it will be the first time he has ever gone this long on a Med cruise without causing an international incident."

"Hip, hip, hooray," they all started in. While everyone laughed and clinked glasses, I could do nothing but blush. Chief Hill was right.

June 3, 1969

Hi Folks,

Time to get a letter written and into the mail before we head out to sea again. We had our last day of liberty in Naples today and I enjoyed it with a group of us touring and then having dinner at that club I told you about, the Flamingo. Eight of us had our picture taken and I'm going to be sure to send you a couple copies. It has both RMC Hill and RMCS Brewer in it with me and Stark so it'll be one I'll want to keep as a souvenir. All we were missing was LT Vargas but officers usually don't hang out with enlisted.

Your place at the river sounds like it's really coming along. I wish I was there to help Dad. Is there any fish in the river? Just curious.

I need to tell you something too. Guess it's mainly for you, Mom. In Dianne's last letter, she talked about graduating, doing some teaching job interviews and then she mentioned how nice she thought it would be if I took some time off when I get out and just come spend it with her. She's getting way too serious for me, Mom. I just wanted you to know I am writing her to tell her that and I still plan on going to the U with no intention of settling down or living with anyone. Basically, I think this may be the end of our relationship and I figure she'll definitely come by to see you.

Well, as I said, we're leaving port tomorrow. It's going to be a large NATO exercise and then we'll be pulling into another port somewhere in Greece.

Be Good and Take Care.

Love, Rich

We had been in port, Thessalonica, Greece, for two days when Lt. Martin called me to his office. When I entered, I saw Chief Hill already there. Neither looked happy.

"Take a seat, Herman," Martin said. "I'm afraid you're not going to like what I'm about to tell you. We just learned that the Cambria will be deploying back to the Mediterranean in November for six months. I didn't realize until today, talking with Chief Hill, that you were going to request an early out and hoped to depart in January to go back to school. With all the good people we are losing before November like Stark, Reddy, Nash, and Hawkins, you get the picture, there is no way we will let you go. In fact, I hope you'll extend your enlistment and not get out in April and finish the whole cruise with us."

I sat stunned. Finally, I said, "Please tell me this is a joke."

"Wish it was," Hill said.

"I know this is a blow," Martin said. "Tell you what. Let's give it a rest for a few days and see if we get another modification to the ship's schedule. If not, we'll get together again and weigh options. I'll even talk to the XO to see if he has any ideas. Just hang in there, Herman. Chief Hill and I will do what we can, okay?"

"Yes, sir," I said weakly. "Appreciate it, but we all know the bottom line here, needs of the Navy. I won't hold my breath. Can I go now?"

When I returned to my rack, I wrote another letter home.

June 15, 1969

Hi Folks!

You may not appreciate this letter much and I hate to write it. I'm feeling about as low as one can get and that is unusual for me. I just need to tell you.

My ship is now going back to the Med in November. This means my plan to get out early and start school in January has blown up. My division officer and Chief Hill told me as much. We're losing too many trained guys and I've made myself too valuable to let go early. Sometimes it doesn't pay to be good. They'll even want me to extend my enlistment until May when the ship returns. Well, screw them. I'm going to make them fly me home in April.

I know I sound bitter. I think I have good reason. I've given this ship my all and done everything they've asked. Now, it's like a knife in the back. Bad enough I have to make another trip to the Med. My close friends like Stark, Hawkins and Reddy won't be with me. I'll be right back training new guys and busting my ass and for what? Plus, I'll miss two whole quarters at the U. The whole thing sucks!

That's what has happened. Sure, I'll be fine and do my job. Not sure if I can keep the good attitude though. All I can hope for now is there is another schedule change or the XO can help us think of something.

On the positive side, I did enjoy your recent letters. And I got a letter from a Mary Ehlert, Mom. She said she worked for you now and that you told her I like to get mail. Trying to set me up with someone else already? Anyway, she sounded like a nut and I did enjoy her letter. A Catholic girl?

Well, sorry for some of the language, Mom. I think I just needed a shoulder to cry on and hope for your support. We leave here and go to sea for a few more war game exercises and then things start to wind down. Not sure when I'll get a chance to write again but I'm sure I'll be more positive next time.

Be Good and Take Care.

Love, Rich

"Safe to sit down?" Chief Hill said, joining me on the fantail one evening when we were back at sea.

I looked up and smiled. "Of course, Chief." We'd left Greece several days ago and were well into our Marine war game exercise. There had been no further discussion of the change in schedule and our new deployment date of next March. "I'm fine and have accepted the position I'm in and the ship's too. You know I'll never let the division down."

"I know," he said. "Don't give up hope yet though. You know

the Navy; things can always change. After this exercise is over, we're pulling into Malta. Let's get together then and, like Lt. Martin said, look at all our options. Deal?" He put a new toothpick in his mouth and left.

The night before we pulled into Valletta, my good friend Stark couldn't help himself and told those who had never heard the story about how I ended up in jail here defending a shipmate, Cooper. I'm not sure if I was famous or infamous for that incident, but it was an excellent reminder to me to be on my best behavior here.

"RM2 Herman," Berglund said. "The XO wants to see you in the wardroom."

We'd been in port five days. I racked my brain on what I could have done. I'd been on liberty twice but didn't have any problems. None I could think of anyway. As I entered the wardroom, not only was the XO there, I also saw Vargas, Martin, and Hill sitting at the officers' dining room table.

"Sit down, Herman," Cmdr. Gordon said. "Up here, by me." I saw Chief Hill smile as I took a seat. "I understand you are aware of the change in our schedule, having us now deploy in November and returning next May. You may be faced with making a difficult choice as soon as we get back to Norfolk. One, you can extend your enlistment for a month and remain on Cambria for the whole deployment. Or, two, you can accept a transfer to another ship and get out on your scheduled date of April. The dilemma you face is, either stay in for another month and stick with us—or take your chance and transfer to another ship, which could deploy immediately for six months, but you would get out in April. You follow me so far?"

"Yes, sir," I said. "Lesser of two evils." I wished I hadn't said that.

"Well, maybe not," the XO continued. "Lt. Martin came to me this morning to discuss options. He told me about your plan to request a ninety-day early out to return to college. With the loss of qualified radiomen, I normally would have said absolutely not. Then, he and RMC Hill explained a possible compromise. I briefed Lt. Vargas to let squadron have a vote. The commodore relies on our communications, and, although it's our CO's ultimate decision, I felt we owed them that." The XO invited Vargas to speak.

"The commodore said to support RM2 Herman on any decision he makes," Vargas said. "He's done a superb job for us, and the commodore is pleased the ship has shown this effort to help him out with a difficult situation, not of his making."

"Thank you, Lieutenant," the XO said. "Here it is, Herman. You agree to remain on Cambria and deploy in November, and the CO will approve your request for a ninety-day early out. We expect you to train your relief and qualify as many personnel as possible before you depart. If you agree, you don't have to worry about turning right around and going back to sea, and we don't have to worry about losing you until January. We all think it's a win-win. Do you want some time to think about it?"

"No, sir," I said enthusiastically. "Where do I sign?"

July 5, 1969

Hi Folks,

Just a quick note. I know I was pretty down the last time I wrote. I hope I didn't upset you. Now, I have some great news. I consider it a late birthday, 23 now, present. My early out is going to get approved. The XO met with me and it turns out that LT Martin and RMC Hill came up with a plan so I could stay on the ship, and it's a scratch my back and I'll scratch yours. I promise to train my men especially hard and they will, in turn, let me go early. Anyway, I'll go with the ship to the Med in November and they'll let me out in January. I worried for nothing.

So, Mom, still plan for me to pre-register in fall and I can start the paperwork for the GI Bill. Not sure how it works but, we'll figure it out. I'm so excited again.

Enjoyed my visit here in Valletta, Malta. Did I tell you this is the most popular port to visit? And I behaved myself this time. Well, want to get this in mail.

Be Good and Take Care!

Love, Rich

CHAPTER 36

July 1969, Valletta, Malta

CAMBRIA DEPARTED VALLETTA, SCHEDULED TO MEET up with USS Shadwell (LSD-15) the evening of July 7, 1969. What occurred gave a whole new meaning to the word rendezvous.

Clang! Clang! Clang! It was 0300 when the ship's General Alarm sounded over the 1MC. A series of three strident beeps, repeated three times, followed by a blaring "Collision, collision, ship's bow imminent!"

I had been in my rack asleep, but before my feet hit the deck, I felt the ship shudder, and I was thrown forward about ten feet. We had collided with something. My immediate thought was, if I feel water on the deck, I'm as good as dead—our berthing compartment was well below the water line. It was dry. I heard a lot of yelling and saw some panic setting in, but for the most part, everyone's training kicked in and they made it toward the ladder to escape topside.

"Snap out of it!" Hawkins, in only his skivvies, yelled as he slapped a shipmate who stood shaking and frozen in place. "You're going to be okay, just nice and easy, step at a time." It worked, and the sailor started up the ladder.

Hawkins caught my eye and nodded; I watched him stand at the bottom of the ladder calmly directing traffic and helping those who appeared panic-stricken. When I approached, he winked. "See you in radio. I'll make sure everyone is out before I depart, just in case." I slapped him on the shoulder and headed up the ladder.

Emerging on the main deck, I looked to the port side and saw that Cambria's hull was embedded halfway through the starboard side of the Shadwell. We appeared to be stuck. I could see some of her crew, in what looked like the engine room, doing damage control. My eyes locked onto those of a chief; for a brief second, we shared something no sailor at sea ever wants to face, fear.

The force of our forward motion caused the Shadwell to swing around into our port side. As we hit side by side, an assault landing craft hanging over our port side was shattered into pieces like a little toy. I dodged debris and made my way to the starboard side up to radio as fast as I could.

"Collision procedures in effect," Lt. Martin was yelling. "Standing by for CO's orders." He saw me entering radio. "Herman, good, do you know how many are still in the compartment and if there are injuries?"

"No, sir. When I left, Hawkins was directing traffic and helping everyone get out. What's the status here?"

"I was preparing to relieve the watch on the bridge," he said. This explained why he was in full uniform while I was in only my skivvies. "RMC Hill is in the comm center with the emergency destruction team. RM1 Berglund is in the teletype shop with all the guys not on watch or involved in possible emergency destruction, awaiting instructions."

"Damage control center, contact the bridge," we heard over the 1MC. This wasn't good. The ship's interior communications must have some failures.

I got on the intercom. "RM1 Berglund, Herman here, have Reddy go tune WRT-1 number one to 500KHZ, full power, and patch it into CW position three. Place High Command Net to voice position three, and hang the Do Not Destroy tags on the transmitter." I looked at Martin. "We now have International Emergency Frequency, and voice net with chain of command, sir."

"All radiomen and signalmen personnel out of the compartment," Hawkins announced as he entered radio. "No reportable injuries."

I had to smile as he was now fully dressed and even had a toothbrush in his pocket. "I'll check in with Chief Hill." As he went by, he handed me my dungaree pants from my rack. Just another day at the office.

"Quarters for muster," came over the 1MC. "Quarters for muster."

Martin and all personnel, except the emergency destruction team and me at the emergency transmission post, left radio to join CR Division at the Emergency Quarters station. Once there, Martin would pass our muster count to the bridge to help in accounting for all crew members.

Capt. House entered radio, nodded toward me, and went straight to the intercom. "Bridge, CO here. I'm in radio. Pass the damage control status when ready."

"Bridge, aye."

"Communications status please, Herman," Capt. House said.

"Sir, RMC Hill is standing by to initiate emergency destruction of classified material if ordered. I have one voice circuit to reach our chain of command. If that fails, we have the International Emergency circuit to send the distress signal."

"Thank you, Herman." The CO closed his eyes, apparently doing some deep thinking. For several minutes, nothing was heard.

"Radio, bridge. Captain, XO here. All hands accounted for. At present no serious injuries reported. Minor damage to bow with several penetrations of the hull, all presently above the waterline. Damage to port side not considered significant and no hull penetration. Watertight integrity is being maintained and holding throughout the ship."

"Bridge, Captain, roger. Leaving radio and heading for bridge. Out." The CO saw Hill standing in the entryway. "Stand by for now, Chief." He looked at me. "Stand by and be ready to contact the chain of command. If that fails, then start sending the distress signal, and don't stop until I tell you." He started to leave.

I thought for a second, then said, "Captain, I thought the CO was the last one down with the ship."

Going out the hatch, he looked back. "CO and his radioman, Herman, CO and his radioman." He was gone.

Hill and I could see each other, but we remained silent. It seemed everyone onboard was in deep personal thoughts, waiting for the CO's decision on what would happen next. The answer came about fifteen minutes later.

"Secure from Emergency Quarters," came over the 1MC. "Set Condition Three."

"Radio, bridge. OOD here. CO says, stand down from emergency destruction and secure the emergency frequency network."

"Bridge, radio, roger," Hill said, putting a fresh toothpick in his mouth. He then broke into the biggest smile I had ever seen. "Damn, I'm getting too old for this shit!" I'd never heard him swear before and couldn't help but laugh. I knew it was a sign of relief, and it was better to laugh than to cry.

Still trying to comprehend what had just happened, our thoughts turned to the USS Shadwell and her crew. Also, with our damage, what was going to happen next? Lt. Martin entered radio.

"That has to be one of the strangest things I've ever seen," he said. "While we were mustering at quarters, the sea just went calm. I mean, we have damage to our bow, and the Shadwell has this enormous hole in her starboard midships, and all of a sudden, complete calm. No wind, no waves, and no threat at all. Like a miracle."

Within hours, rumors flew around the ship. It's amazing how many different stories there can be about the same incident. One thing became obvious—everyone would remember this collision differently, and we might never know the true story of exactly what happened. I tried not to let any hearsay affect my judgment and stayed with the facts. What I did know for a fact was everything that did, or didn't, take place in radio.

I also knew for fact, because I saw it in writing, that all personnel directly involved with the collision (CO, XO, OOD, navigator, and bridge watch, for sure) were ordered not to speak about it because of possible disciplinary action and upcoming official hearings held by an investigative board. That board embarked the same day of the collision, and shortly after their arrival, we and the Shadwell—which we were told had a new CO—headed for Valletta, Malta, for repairs.

"I can tell you only my thoughts on contributing factors to the collision," Martin told us. "We established communications with Shadwell and had them on radar when they were twenty miles from us. The OOD held periodic radio checks, and nothing seemed out of the ordinary. At about five miles out, we confirmed the rendezvous point, course, and speed both ships were to maintain. Everything was normal. At four miles out, Shadwell was to change course and didn't. Our OOD called the CO to the bridge. We contacted her, told her what course we expected her on, and she acknowledged but still didn't make any change in direction.

"At two miles, the CO took the con. When he contacted Shadwell to change course, he got an acknowledgement, but the Shadwell took no evasive action whatsoever. The collision was imminent, and at present course and speeds, our CO determined Shadwell would hit us amidships, where our berthing is. He ordered all back full and a rudder change, so that we would hit them in their engineering spaces, away from berthing compartments. The Shadwell never made one adjustment the whole time and just kept acknowledging our requests."

"Sounds like Capt. House made a great call and probably saved lives," Hill said. "Hope he doesn't take a fall for this."

"Like everything else, there'll be conflicting stories," Martin added. "Anyway, I don't think we'll get called to answer any questions, but you and Herman need to be ready in case they want to know about when the CO was in radio."

July 9, 1969

Hi Mom and Dad,

In case you read something about it in the newspaper, I need to tell you about an incident the other night. First of all, everyone is fine.

About 3 a.m. on July 8, I was asleep in my rack when the collision alarm went off. Where I sleep is below the waterline so my first thought was, I hope there is no water coming in. I don't mind telling you I was scared. When I got to our main deck, I saw that we had collided with the USS Shadwell. Our bow cut right through their starboard side and we were stuck for a while. It's amazing that the only injury was to one of their sailors who I think broke his back. I got up to radio and we soon learned that we were going to be okay. We have a huge hole in our bow but the ocean got real calm and we were able to get to port for repairs under our own power. Anyway, scary for a bit and just wanted you to hear from me that everything is okay. I know reporters may make it sound worse than it is to sell newspapers.

So, we are in Valletta, Malta, until repaired enough to be fit for sea. You know we love this port so it's a "throw me in that briar patch" time. Not sure how long we will be here but for now we are told we should still be going home in August. Will let you know.

Just when I didn't think it couldn't get any more exciting. At least this time I had nothing to do with it.

Be Good and Take Care.

Love, Rich

It was good to be safely docked in Malta. In my rack, I thought about how fortunate we were to have survived one of a sailor's greatest fears, collision at sea. I thought about how I and those around me performed during a crisis, something we trained for. I had learned that some people who usually come across as confident, appearing to be the ones you would rely on, didn't handle pressure well and were almost helpless. How I admired the confidence and leadership Capt. House showed. I was comfortable with my actions and proud of my overall performance as a leader. And then there were those who, out of nowhere, like Hawkins, rose to the occasion and became an instant leader, taking care of everyone around him before thinking of himself. I felt honored to know him.

"Let us pray," the chaplain said, and he delivered a moving blessing giving thanks where it belonged and asking forgiveness where needed. Amen. "Taps, Taps, lights out." The bugle played.

CHAPTER 37

July 1969, Valletta, Malta, and Taranto, Italy

AFTER TWO WEEKS, THE SHIP HAD RECEIVED THE necessary repairs to be certified safe for sea, and we departed to complete our Mediterranean deployment and satisfy our operational commitments, although now limited in their scope. The crew had enjoyed their extended stay in Malta, but it was time to go. Not directly involved with the repair effort, most of us were able to enjoy maximum liberty, and I didn't think I was the only one who was just about broke.

We definitely had one highlight while in port. With the CO's approval, on the evening of July 20, we tuned to and patched Armed Forces Radio into the ship's announcing system, broadcasting Apollo 11 and the first moon landing by American astronauts Armstrong, Aldrin, and Collins. When the lunar module touched down at 2117, and we heard the words, "The Eagle has landed," our crew joined that of mission control in celebration. Another cheer went up six and a half hours later when Neil Armstrong, the first human to walk on the moon, said, "One small step for man, one giant leap for mankind."

July 26, 1969

Hi Folks,

I know I haven't written for a while. No excuse, I just lost track of time enjoying our visit. One thing for sure, I love Valletta, Malta, and will probably return some day. More and more I am thankful I survived that unfortunate incident here with Cooper. We've been here since the collision and now have been repaired and back at sea.

Did you listen to the moon landing? We were able to get it on Armed Forces Radio and the crew listened to it over our entertainment system. All I can say is Wow! A lot of history there. I bet we hear that one small step for man comment for the rest of our lives.

We're on our way to Taranto, Italy, for a short port visit and then do a turnover in Rota, Spain, and head for home. Our schedule has changed as to what we will be doing but I'm still scheduled home around August 20.

I'll try and write one more time before we leave the Med. I don't expect much to happen but will keep in touch one more time anyway.

Be Good and Take Care.

Love, Rich

As we had a couple of years ago, we anchored in the harbor at Taranto. Immediately, memories flashed through my mind. Turning twenty-one, sleeping on the wrong ship. I didn't have a birthday or anything else to celebrate this visit so expected no problems.

"Hey, Herman," Stark said. We were in berthing getting ready to go on liberty. "Want to share with the new guys your past experiences being here?"

"Some things are best forgotten," I said. "Besides, I think everyone's heard enough of my sea stories and need to start some of their own." Stark, Reddy, Nash, and Hawkins would be getting out when we got back to the States, and we all decided to hit the beach together one last time. We figured we'd get off the ship for a couple of hours, have a few beers and a meal, and head back.

The liberty boat was on the same schedule of departing the ship on the hour and returning on the half-hour. We caught the 2000 boat and arrived ashore at 2020. It seemed nothing had changed, and we walked a few blocks to find an out-of-the-way café to order our first beers and some Italian pizza. We settled in and enjoyed our food and several more bottles of Peroni.

After dinner, we started back to the waterfront and were nearly there when I recognized the street and the café. "Guys, this is it. This is where I turned twenty-one." I went inside, and it felt like the clock turned back. Same tables, same décor, and, for all I knew, the same people.

Nash, Reddy, and Hawkins waved goodbye and left to catch the next boat. Stark joined me. "I'll have a beer with you," he said, and we walked up to the bar.

"*Ciao*," I said to the bartender. "*Due Peroni.*" He just looked at me.

"Why is he staring at you?" Stark said.

"*Piero, vieni qui.*" A man at a nearby table got up and came to the bar. The bartender reached in a drawer, pulled out a piece of paper and showed it to Piero, and they both looked at me and said, "*Si, si.*" They showed us what they were looking at—a picture from June 23, 1967. There I was, arm around Rosa and a shot in my hand. My class ring was on her finger. The word spread quickly in the café, and soon all the patrons were around us, wanting to see the picture and talking about that night.

"*Birra*," we heard, and the bartender started handing out beers. He then poured shots of Jack Daniels and handed them out. "*Bentornato*, Reech." Cheering, everyone downed their drinks.

"I think they just welcomed you back," Stark said. "No wonder you liked this place so much."

I laughed and then asked, "Rosa?"

"*Sposata*," Piero said. "*Bambino.*" He smiled.

"I'm pretty sure that means Rosa is married and has a baby," Stark said, grinning. "Sorry, Herman."

"No, that's a good thing. At least now I know I didn't get married that night. That calls for another drink."

We had another and then said our farewell. Piero handed me one for the road. "*Addio, amico,*" he said. Everyone came out on the street to wave, and Stark and I headed for the boat landing. Me, well, I had a beer in my hand.

I was standing, waiting for my ride back to the ship, when I heard, "You need to get rid of your beer, sailor." A master chief with a Shore Patrol insignia on his arm stood looking at me.

"Come on, Master Chief," I said. "This is our last night of liberty, and it's still half full." I was intoxicated but functional. "I'll finish it before the boat comes and put it in the trash can. Okay?"

"Just don't cause any trouble," he said. "Sit over here out of the way, and make sure you put it in the trash when you're done." He walked away.

Stark and I had been sitting for a few minutes on the side of the pier when a Marine officer stopped in front of me.

"Get rid of your beer, sailor," he said.

"I will, sir, just as soon as I finish it."

"I said *now*!"

"As soon as I finish, sir. See that master chief over there?" I pointed across the pier. "He said I could finish it, and I figure he's been around a lot longer than you, so I respect him more and will do what he says."

I was yanked to my feet, and that's all I remember, except for the look on the Marine's face as I saw him fall off the pier into the water. Oh, and the first club that hit me.

When I woke, I knew from the sounds around me I was on a ship and immediately hoped it was my own this time. I was disoriented, probably a combination of all that I drank the night before and whatever caused my head and body to be so sore. I found my glasses, both lenses cracked, in my shirt pocket, but they would be of little help anyway in this dark space I occupied. The brig? I sat for what seemed hours. I started to remember why I was here. Did I actually push an officer off a pier?

"Herman, stand back," someone said. I heard a key used, and then the hatch opened, and light entered, blinding me. "You need to use the head?" It was the CMAA. I held my hand over my eyes and nodded. I was escorted to use the urinal, under watchful eye, and was allowed to wash my hands.

"I know you're no threat," he continued. "This is standard procedure for someone who is facing charges as serious as you are. I'm taking you up to the legal office now, you'll be formally charged, and the JAG will take it from there."

"Drunk and disorderly. Resisting arrest. Disrespect and assault on a military officer. I think that about covers it," the JAG said. "I've read you your rights, and you waived your right to have another officer represent you. Now, let me tell you what your options are. *None*. I've already briefed the XO, and basically it's out of his control this time. He can't dismiss charges this serious. And he wouldn't want to if he wants to maintain order and discipline on this ship. Making it worse is you are charged with striking the Shore Patrol officer, Marine 2nd Lt. Stokes, which means another command is involved and the Marine commandant will be watching. With me so far?"

"Yes," I said weakly. "Do you think my career is over? Am I facing brig time?"

"Hard to say, and you could be. The XO will forward your case to Captain's Mast. The CO will conduct a review, probably with me, and decide whether he will dispose of the case with non-judicial punishment, NJP, or refer you directly to a court-martial. At this point, I would say the latter is quite possible. I've known you a long time, Herman, and you're not one to try and work or beat the system. Regardless of what the CO decides, I recommend you maintain your professional standards and take responsibility, line up as many favorable character witnesses you can, and then throw yourself on the mercy of the court."

The CO decided to hold Mast to determine whether NJP or court-martial would be appropriate. I was told to report, in dress blue uniform, to the CMAA at 1400, August 6. The ten days until then seemed like an eternity. I continued with my normal duties but was directed not to discuss my case, except in the preparation I thought necessary, and only then in the presence of Lt. Martin. I knew how serious my charges were and took the advice of the JAG to heart. The CO would automatically ask Martin and Hill about my character, so the only person outside my direct chain of command that I asked to say something on my behalf was Lt. Vargas.

July 30, 1969

Hi Folks,

Wanted to get one last letter mailed to you before we leave the Med. We do turnover tomorrow in Rota, Spain, with the USS Chilton and then will head for home.

About the only thing I have to tell you is I got into some trouble and will be going to captain's mast. Ironically, it came right after visiting the same café in Taranto, Italy, where I turned 21. I hope I never see that port again. Anyway, I celebrated too much and disrespected an officer. My only excuse, which isn't one really, is I was drunk. I will probably face a fine and maybe a loss of paygrade but I'm hoping my record helps. I'm hoping it won't affect my early out. Will let you know when I get home.

Expect a call around Aug 20.

Be Good and Take Care.

Love, Rich

"Captain's Mast is very formal," the CMAA said. "You and I will stand outside the wardroom until called. When I enter, you will follow. Place your feet in and follow the yellow footprints on the floor leading to the podium. When you get there, stand at attention, salute the CO; state your rate and name and that you are reporting as ordered. Follow the directions of the CO, and speak only when asked. When Mast concludes, about face, and follow the yellow footprints out the hatch."

At 1350, the CMAA escorted me to the wardroom; my knees were knocking. The wardroom door opened, exactly 1400, and the XO took one step out. "CMAA, carry out your orders."

The CMAA entered, and I followed, stepping on about a dozen yellow footprints to the podium. Along with the XO and JAG, I saw Martin, Hill, and the Marine I was charged with assaulting, 2nd Lt.

Stokes. I gave my best salute. "RM2 Richard Herman, reporting as ordered, sir."

"At ease, Petty Officer Herman," Capt. House said. "I want you to know that it pains me to see you standing there, and the only reason I didn't forward this matter directly to court-martial is your past record. I want to afford you the opportunity to explain yourself. First, do you dispute any of the charges?"

"No, sir," I said, hoping my voice didn't sound too shaky. "I take full responsibility and offer no excuses. I am ashamed of my behavior and for bringing discredit to the uniform. I can only hope that my past performance is taken into consideration and that I can be given an opportunity to recover from this unfortunate incident and still be of value to your ship and the Navy."

"Do you have anyone you would like to speak on your behalf before I make my decision?"

"I was going to ask Lt. Vargas from squadron to come forward, Captain, but I've decided to just let my record speak for itself." While I was talking, the door had opened, and I saw movement to my right. When I finished, I saw that not only had Vargas entered, he was accompanied by his chief of staff, three squadron watch officers, the Marine communications officer, the chaplain, and the ship's doctor.

"You want to rethink that, Petty Officer Herman?" the captain asked.

"If I may, Captain," the chief of staff said. Capt. House nodded. "I'll go ahead and speak for all of us here. RM2 Herman is the mainstay of your ship's, our squadron's, and the Marine command communications. We are all aware of the seriousness of the charges against him and agree he needs to be held accountable, but we also ask that, along with his performance, you factor in his character, leadership, and sacrifices he has made the past almost three years. Punish, yes; destroy, no. Thank you for allowing us to speak."

"No, thank you, Chief of Staff," Capt. House said. "Let me ask something, Herman, and I want an honest answer. Why did you push 2nd Lt. Stokes?"

"Sir, when I was yanked off the ground, I just gave him a push back. He happened to be on the edge of the seawall. I certainly didn't mean any harm."

"Mister Stokes," the CO said. I could tell the Marine was getting nervous and felt outnumbered. "Did you yank RM2 Herman to his feet? Did you actually initiate contact?"

"Yes, Captain," he answered. "I let his moment of disrespect get to me, and I also just reacted. Poor judgment maybe, but he was disrespectful."

Capt. House took the JAG aside, and, after a brief discussion, returned to the podium. He nodded to the CMAA, who called everyone to attention. "It is my finding that Petty Officer Herman is guilty as charged, with extenuating circumstances. I render the following punishment. Petty Officer Herman, you will report to 2nd Lt. Stokes within the next twenty-four hours and officially apologize. Upon completion of this apology, the JAG is to be informed, and all charges will be stricken from your record. Failure to apologize, or have your apology accepted, will leave me no recourse but to refer this matter to court-martial." Capt. House signed several papers and departed.

"RM2 Herman," the CMAA said, "post." I followed the yellow footprints out. I couldn't remember ever being so relieved or so emotionally exhausted.

The next day, I went to apologize as ordered. When I got to the door where junior Marines were berthed, I found this was going to be a lot harder than I ever imagined. I finally worked up the courage and knocked.

"Enter."

Stokes was sitting at a desk near the rear of the compartment. I proceeded back and stood at attention. "Sir, I sincerely apologize for striking you and causing you to fall off the pier into the harbor. I am relieved to know that you received no serious injury. I hope you accept my apology."

"Sit down, Herman," he said. "Apology accepted. I still can't believe you pushed me off the pier. And what I'm most upset about is, do you realize how embarrassing it is as a Naval Academy graduate to have an enlisted person get the upper hand on me? And all the ribbing I am taking?" Then he laughed. "Guess we'll both have a story to tell our grandkids about, huh? I have to think of a better ending though."

I grinned, finding I liked this guy. We talked for a few more minutes, then he shook my hand and wished me well. I did the same and meant it. He would be going to Vietnam soon and leading many of these Marines onboard into war. I hoped to see him someday as a senior officer and that we could look back and laugh about this day.

The night before our return to Norfolk, my mind replayed some moments from my third Mediterranean deployment. I'd made a significant contribution to saving a Marine with a life-threatening medical emergency, and I'd survived a collision at sea. Later, I'd escaped a possible court-martial, and my record had been cleared of all charges. Finally, Lt. Martin told me that the XO and CO still approved of my early out and the deal we had made. I could go home, pre-register for winter quarter, and make plans for my future after all. Bad news, I might never see my class ring again, but, good news, I definitely wasn't married. Life was good.

CHAPTER 38

August 1969, Norfolk

I'D ALWAYS HEARD THAT SAYING "THIRD TIME IS THE charm." As we docked in Norfolk, Mark and Patti were waving to me from the pier. My first time being met upon return from deployment—my third deployment. I never expected this and hoped they weren't here bringing bad news.

"Wow, guys," I said, hugging Patti and shaking Mark's hand. "A welcoming committee. Is everything all right?"

"More than all right," Patti said. "Come on, we have something to show you." When we were in the car, she was bouncing in her seat. "The kids are going to be so happy to see you," she said. "Oh, Mark, can I tell him one surprise? Please?"

"Go ahead," he said. "He's probably noticed anyway."

"We got married!" she burst out, showing me her ring. "And Harry and Gladys came and gave their blessing. We worried about nothing."

"Congratulations. I don't know what can top that."

"Can I, Mark, can I, please?" she begged. He smiled and nodded.

"Mark made chief. He'll put it on September 16. We got his khaki uniforms and all that good stuff ready to go. I'm going to pin one of chief anchors on his collar, and his commanding officer, the other."

"Now, that is fantastic, and I know what making chief means," I said. "Wow, you guys are full of good news." While we talked, Mark had driven us from the base to a residential neighborhood. He pulled into the driveway of a two-story wooden frame home with large fenced-in yard. "Home sweet home!" Mark said. "Bought, not paid for. Moved in last week."

"It's gorgeous," I said. "You guys are full of surprises. That's three, any more? Are you pregnant?"

"Not yet." Patti laughed and hugged Mark. "Working on it."

"Welcome back," Daro said, coming out onto the front porch with Betty. Patti's kids came running out, greeting me with hugs and questions.

"Kids," Mark said, "give Rich some breathing space." We went in and he showed me around the four-bedroom house.

"This place is fantastic," I said. "Good thing you made chief."

"Got that right," Mark agreed. "But there's a good chance I can be stationed right here in Norfolk my whole career. It's a great home for Patti and the kids, especially if I deploy. Another positive?" He opened a door and added, "It has a spare bedroom for you." He showed me a room that was furnished. On the pillow was a small American flag and a note: "Hope you like it, Love, the Newsoms."

Speechless, I gave him a hug. Downstairs, I told Patti and the kids, "You guys are too much." I had tears in my eyes when Daro handed me a beer and changed the subject. I told them a little about my deployment and heard about all the happenings here. Mark said I was welcome to use the phone in their bedroom to call home with some privacy. The call was on them as a welcome-home gift.

"Hey, Mom. I'm back safe and sound."

"Clayton, Rich is on the phone," I heard her yell to my dad. "Are you at Mark's new house? Harry and Gladys went down to visit and told us about their getting married. I told them before they left that everything would be fine and stop worrying what the Pope is going to say. Why can't parents just be happy for their children and not worry about what others think? Speaking about worrying. How did you make out at the mast or whatever that thing is you had to go through? You were disrespectful? We taught you better than that."

"Everything is fine, Mom. I apologized to the officer, and charges were dropped. Also, my early out is still approved. Now, before I plan to come home, what did you find out about pre-registration at the U?"

"There is a slight glitch." She told me about her discussion with the admission office. I could enroll early, but the earliest registration would be in December. Mom had a plan and explained it to me. She never ceased to amaze me.

"Sounds good, Mom. Let's make sure I have it straight. They have accepted me back as a student and certified my college transcripts on file; I'm officially enrolled. Being on active duty, the school will waive full tuition payment until my GI Bill kicks in. That sure helps. You can pre-register for me in December. You'll send me a listing of courses available, and I'll tell you the ones to sign me up for. And, until I'm back, Darrell will attend my classes and take notes. Boy, I owe him big time for volunteering to do that."

Mom said, "Now, I think you may not hear from Dianne again. You were right, she didn't like what you wrote her. She came to see me and asked if I would help change your mind. When I told her I don't interfere in my children's lives, she stormed off. Hate to say it, but good riddance. You hear any more from Mary Ehlert? Don't you remember her? You met her the last time you were home and stopped in to see me at work. She was the young blond assistant I have now. She's a nice girl. Here's Dad now. Love you, son."

"Love you too, Mom, and thanks for everything."

"Hi, son," Dad said. "Your mom is writing away, so I guess you've covered all the business, and she'll tell me about it. You coming home?"

"I don't think so, Dad. Turns out I can't accomplish anything with the U, and I'll be home in January so think I'll save my money."

"Sounds like a good idea, son, and, oh my, Darrell has been over a couple times. He's quite the character. We got out fishing one weekend. Well, son, your mother can fill me in on the rest. Say hi to Mark for us." When Dad was done, he was done. He hung up.

Our deployment came upon us in no time. We were as prepared as we could be with the short turnaround. The three weeklong underway periods we had went well, and Chief Hill's training plan resulted in record qualifications. After our first week underway, I felt confident that RM3 Payne and RM2 Larson were capable of stepping into leadership roles quickly. I asked Berglund to make out the watch bill supporting both to be put on the fast track, which would give me the ability to spend dedicated time to their training. It had paid off.

"Attention to quarters," Hill called out. "We leave in a week. Today is supply loadout with all E-5 and below on deck. Tomorrow, all hands who have not deployed to the Med on Cambria will muster at 1000 on the mess decks for a mission briefing by the CO. Trust me, you do not want to miss this. Commander Amphibious Squadron and his staff will start to embark today. As always, RM2 Herman will supervise getting them settled." The hatch opened and Lt. Martin, RMCS Brewer, and an unfamiliar lieutenant came out.

"At ease," Martin said. "Many of you will remember Senior Chief Brewer, and I would like to introduce the new squadron communications officer, Lt. Harold."

"I would just like to say hello to everyone," Lt. Harold said, "and hope that you will provide me the same support you did my predecessor, Lt. Vargas. I expect to make no big changes. We have a busy week ahead, so let's get to it." He smiled, waved, and walked off with Brewer.

"RM2 Herman, report to squadron; CR Division, dismissed," Martin said.

"Well, Petty Officer Herman," Brewer said when I caught up to him and Harold. "I'm glad to see you're still deploying with us." I shook his hand. "Lieutenant," Brewer continued, "RM2 Herman is the one Lt. Vargas and I were telling you about."

"Nice to meet you, Herman," Harold said. "Lt. Vargas spoke highly of you. He also said you could give me gray hairs and I could expect the unexpected from you. I'll just leave it at that." With a big smile, he shook my hand. "So, Senior Chief said you would only be with us a short while?"

"Yes, sir," I said. "It's kind of a deal I made with my CO, and Lt. Vargas got the commodore to support me." Brewer and I gave him the short version of my early-out situation. He didn't seem too concerned one way or the other, and we got to work getting them settled. Like Vargas, Lt. Harold carried boxes and worked as hard as everyone else.

If everything went as planned, I would be away at sea for two months. After making sure I had my uniforms in place and enough personal supplies to last, I went to spend my last day with the Newsoms.

We cooked steaks on the grill and enjoyed being family. The kids and Mark went to bed early, as he would take me to the ship in the morning. "Do you promise that you'll still come to visit after you get out?" Patti said that evening. I knew she was stalling to keep from saying goodbye. "We are going to miss you so much." She started to cry, gave me a hug, kissed my cheek, and ran off to bed.

"I won't get all emotional," Mark said when he dropped me off the next day. "We've been here before and both know what to expect. Write to Patti and the kids, okay?"

"Thanks, Chief," I said. He told me I could call him Mark, but it didn't feel right when he was in uniform. "I can't thank you guys for all you've done for me over the years. You take care of that great family you have now. And work on your bowling game." I got out of the car and walked over to his side. I reached in, shook his hand, and stepped away, giving him a salute and adding, "I love you guys."

Nov 12, 1969

Hey folks,

You know I always like to write the night before I deploy to or from the Mediterranean. Mail will go out before we leave in the morning.

As always, we will be going to Cherry Point, North Carolina, first and picking up about 900 Marines. Then we'll meet up with the other five ships that make up our squadron and start our transit across the Atlantic.

I know I covered this on the phone, Mom, but here are the courses I'd like you to try and get for me when you go to register in December: Calculus 202, Physics 201, Psych 201, Sociology 101 and any other course on list of mandatory. I trust you to choose if something I need isn't available. You did get Sherm through his PHD, right?

I had a great last day with Mark and Patti. I promised Patti I would be back to visit and I aim to make good on that. I'm sure I will because I've always been good at keeping my word. Reminds me, Mom, I got another letter from Mary Ehlert, and she said she'd write to me while I was gone if I'd promise to call her when I get home. Tell her I will, okay?

Well, I know it's short. Not sure when I'll write again so Happy Holidays in advance. If nothing changes, you should expect me home the middle of January. Keep your fingers crossed nothing goes wrong.

Be Good and Take Care.

Love, Rich

That evening, I finished my letter home and climbed into my rack. Two months, I thought, around sixty days, and I'd be heading home, out of the Navy. What could possibly go wrong?

"Taps, Taps, lights out." The bugle played.

CHAPTER 39

November 1969, Mediterranean Sea

ONE THING I'D LEARNED ABOUT MILITARY LIFE IS there is always constant change in personnel. Some people leave large holes to fill when they depart, but there will always be someone ready to take their place. I'd made a commitment to my commanding officer that I would qualify as many radiomen as needed to fill these holes. I would also train my relief. What I didn't tell the CO was, I felt obligated to fulfill a promise I made to my mentor years ago. I would select and teach my relief everything I knew, which, when added to what he already knew, would make him better than me. During this transit over, I had pushed the men, and myself, hard. I thought I knew who my relief should be.

"You're deep in thought," Chief Hill said, coming up behind me. "Figured you'd be here."

"Hi, Chief," I said. "Yeah, I won't have many more opportunities to enjoy being out here like this. *Deja vu* for us, on the fantail after midnight enjoying the moonlight. Tonight may be the last time I see the Rock of Gibraltar when we pass through the strait. I won't see it when I fly home. I will miss this."

"I'll come out here every now and then for both of us when you're gone," he said. "Hey, you've been busting butt these last two weeks. You getting any sleep at all?" He flipped his toothpick over the side and took out a new one.

"I've got a promise to keep, Chief, got to stay focused. I think we're doing pretty good on quals. After turnover in Rota tomorrow,

I'd like to talk to you and Berglund about where we are with that and discuss some ideas."

"Sounds good," he said. "One piece of advice; training can take a short break, get some sleep. You look like hell." He patted my shoulder and left.

The next day, I had RM2 Larson join me, and we met with Chief Hill and Berglund. "I have picked RM2 Larson to be my relief," I announced. "He will be the next RM3 Damon / RM2 Herman. I need him off the watch bill and assigned permanently to me."

"RM1 Berglund," Chief Hill said, "can you support the change to the underway watch bill?"

"No problem," he said. "During the transit over, I noticed how things were going and kind of thought Herman might propose this. Give me the word, Chief, I'll make it happen. And, if anyone wants my vote, I like it."

"Do it," Hill said. Berglund took the cue and left. "RM2 Larson, you now know why you were invited to the briefing. You look in shock—you okay?"

"Yes, Chief," he said. "Just don't know what it all means."

"RM2 Herman will explain it to you. Consider yourself his shadow from now until he leaves. And good luck. He's going to ask a lot from you." The chief put a new toothpick in his mouth and walked out.

"Let's get chow, and I'll introduce you to my favorite place on the ship," I said. Following dinner, I took Larson to the fantail, and we found it unoccupied. The sun was setting, and we leaned on the railing looking at the ship's wake. "Let me tell you about a man named Damon—RM3 David Damon." I told how I was trained to take his place as the training guru and earn the title "Top Radioman." I told him about the concept of passing on everything so that, as my relief, he would be better than me. I told him about getting my ass kicked so hard I saw stars, but not to expect that from me—not my style. I told him Damon's philosophy on leadership and how it affected me.

When I finished, I let what I had said sink in, then added, "I have chosen you to be the next Damon." I left the fantail. I'd given RM2 Larson a lot to think about.

My instincts were proven correct; Larson not only met but surpassed my expectations. He had gained the respect of Hill, Brewer, Martin, and Harold. Yes, Petty Officer Damon, mission accomplished.

"All I know is," Martin said to Hill and me, "the XO said the CO wanted to see the three of us in his cabin at 1000."

When we entered, Capt. House told us to sit down at the table, then he walked over and sat at the head of the table. We all sat. "Don't look so worried. After all, you're not standing on yellow footprints this time." He laughed. "Go ahead, XO."

"RM2 Herman," the XO said, "you have an approved early out, having you leave us around January 14." I nodded. "The CO doesn't want to honor that agreement."

My heart sank. "Captain."

"I won't leave you hanging," the CO said. "CR Division has performed well in recent operations. Your division officer and chief inform us you have kept your end of the deal. I talked to the commodore, and we can't see any reason to hold you if you've already met your goals. Unfortunately, our schedule won't get you home in time for Christmas. However, I've told the XO to add a holiday early out to your school early out and get you off the ship to be home for New Year's. Unless you have changed your mind and would like to reenlist."

"I don't know what to say, Captain."

"You've been a CO's dream, Herman," the CO said. "You work hard, and you play hard. We all hate to see you go, but you deserve it. Best of luck to you. son." He stood and shook my hand..

"Paperwork is already being processed," the XO said. "We're pulling into Marseilles, France, for the holidays. You'll get off when we arrive and catch a hop to Rota, Spain. I think you can get a

Navy flight there to Philadelphia around December 28. The ship can't discharge you; it has to be done at a Personnel Support Activity stateside. Hopefully, they will have you out in time to celebrate New Year's with your family and be there for the first day of school."

Suddenly time flew by, and before I knew it, I was spending the day getting my discharge physical and checking out. By early evening, I had my orders and headed for berthing to finish packing.

"For he's a jolly good fellow, for he's a jolly good fellow," I heard the guys chanting.

"Always, guys," I said, smiling. Now that the time had come, I was finding it hard to say goodbye to everyone.

"All packed?" Larson said. "Want to go up to the teletype shop for a while?"

"Thanks for the invite, but I already have a date." I was glad to see the fantail was empty and sat to enjoy the evening one more time. I'd been onboard almost three years and had a lot of memories formed on this old gray lady.

I certainly had changed since that day I reported aboard and was greeted with a knife thrown at me. Young and naïve in so many ways with no set direction or path to follow. Perhaps the single most significant thing that changed my life since then was Damon sharing his philosophy of what a leader should be. I'd never forgotten that conversation and tried to live up to it every day. I still had a lot to think about before getting home. I decided to find Chief Hill and say goodbye.

CHAPTER 4

December 28, 1969, Philadelphia, Pennsylvania

I WAS FORTUNATE AND MADE GOOD CONNECTIONS with Navy flights in Marseilles and Rota. Landing in Dover, Delaware, I caught the bus to the naval station in Philadelphia and reported to the Naval Personnel Activity quarterdeck about 2130.

"Orders?" the OOD said. He took my orders and stamped them as arriving. "Here to process out, I see. Nothing will happen until morning, so I'll send you to central berthing, across the street. Welcome home."

"Thanks," I said, happy to be back on American soil.

At central berthing, the POOW said, "Grab a pillow, couple sheets, and a blanket. Take any empty rack. It's already after taps, so hold it down. Come back in the morning, dress blues, and they'll get you processed."

I was beat and felt it was too late to try and find a phone to call home. At 0800 the next morning, I arrived at the personnel office, following directions from the POOW.

"What you need, sailor?" a guy in working blues behind the desk asked me.

"Here to process out." I handed him my orders.

He went through all my paperwork, and suddenly he stopped. "You on an early out for school?" He looked at me, and I nodded yes. He stood up and went across the passageway to another office. When he came back, there was a chief with him. His name tag read PNC Shaw - PSA Personnel Officer.

"RM2 Richard W. Herman," the chief said, "here on an early

school out. Well, Herman, early school outs are for up to ninety days before the end of your enlistment. Your enlistment is up April 14, 1970. Now, I'm no rocket scientist, but even I know that means the earliest you can get out is January 14, 1970. You aren't going anywhere until then."

My heart dropped. "But, Chief," I said, "my CO added days for an early holiday out so I could get home for New Year's and be there to start school January 6."

"I don't care what your old CO tried to do. Navy policy is you can't combine early-out programs, and no one is allowed out any earlier than ninety days before the end of their enlistment. You belong to this command now." He walked over, wrote something on my orders, and gave them to the sailor at the desk.

"Have him report to the CMAA for duty until January 12." He looked at me. "Maybe we'll process you then and send you home to mommy. Maybe not. Remember, needs of the Navy, Herman. If we're short-handed next month, we'll keep you as long as we want, up to April 14. Don't piss me off." He walked off.

In shock, I couldn't think straight. Could this be happening? I decided I needed to do what I was told and reported to the CMAA office.

"Welcome, Herman," the CMAA said. "I'm Chief Crandall. I told Chief Shaw I needed a second-class petty officer to run my brig details, so I guess I owe him one." He explained that I would be escorting prisoners from the brig to their daily work details and back. He went on to explain some other things, but my mind was elsewhere. "Anyway, I'll give you the day to get settled into the barracks. Be back here at 0730 tomorrow."

"Of course, I'll accept charges," Mom told the operator. "Rich, is that you? Where are you? Are you okay?"

"Slow down, Mom. Yes, I'm fine, and I have some good news and some bad news. The good news is I'm in Philadelphia; bad news is I'm stuck here."

"What do you mean stuck? They won't let you out?" I could tell in Mom's voice she did not like what she heard.

"They won't honor my early-out request that was approved by my CO on the Cambria. Said they need me for the good of the Navy. I think they are keeping me because two chiefs worked a deal. Anyway, they won't let me out until January 14 and only then if they feel like it. They may keep me until April 14. Really sucks. Sorry for language, Mom."

"Honey, talk to your dad a minute, and I'll be back."

"Hi, son," Dad said. "Back in the U.S., are you? What did you tell your mother? She handed me the phone and stormed off. Oh, wait, she's back."

"Rich," Mom said, "I'm going to ask you to trust me. I know you're upset, but don't do anything stupid. Just hang in there and do what you have to. I may not be military, but I know when something doesn't smell right, and I don't like how they are treating my son. I don't think your commanding officer on the Cambria would either. Tell me the details and base you're at. It's the holidays, so be patient. Deal?"

I talked a few more minutes, and they told me that the family was gearing up for New Year's Day festivities at Margy and Irv's. I felt much better when I got off the phone. What could Mom be up to?

Tuesday morning, I reported to the CMAA and, after about fifteen minutes of training, started performing duties as a brig chaser. I couldn't believe I might be doing this for the next four months. If I was back on the ship, at least I'd be performing a job the Navy needed and trained me for.

Wednesday, I celebrated New Year's Eve and welcomed in 1970 early at the enlisted club. I was in my rack by 2200. Even the prisoners were given New Year's Day off, and I watched the Rose Bowl Parade and ball games in the barracks recreation room.

I picked up my group of prisoners Friday morning and escorted them to the base laundry, where I would watch them fold sheets and pillowcases all day. That was until about 1300, when a black sedan pulled up and Chief Crandall got out.

"RM2 Herman," he said, running up. "PNC Shaw was called into the CO's office this morning, and you could hear the ass-chewing for a block. Something about who did he think he was, overstepping his authority by disregarding the orders of a commanding officer of a U.S. Navy ship. The car is for you. Go, I relieve you."

I had no idea what was happening but didn't argue. I was taken back to the office, and a commander opened my car door. "RM2 Herman, I'm Commander Phillips, Personnel Support Activity CO." We walked to his office, past a very red-faced Chief Shaw.

"Apparently, there has been some confusion on the interpretation of Navy policy, and you have been detained longer than need be. I received a call this morning from the Chief of Naval Personnel himself, and he asked that you be processed out by close of business today. I assured him this would be carried out, and my staff is preparing your orders for discharge as we speak. I have been told you are booked on a flight to Minneapolis tomorrow morning. My duty driver will take you to the airport. I hope this is satisfactory and that you'll accept my personal apology."

Mom, what did you do? I thought to myself. What would she want me to say right now? "Thank you, Commander, mistakes can happen. And on the bright side, I can now put prison guard experience on future resumes." Shaking his hand, I could tell he was very relieved. The look I gave Shaw on the way out wasn't as forgiving.

I walked off the plane January 3, 1970, and was met by only my mother. After a big hug and the shedding of a few tears, she said she told my dad that she wanted a few minutes alone time before I started seeing family and getting busy with school. As we approached the car, she asked me to drive, so she was free to talk.

"I'm sure you're a little curious about what took place the last couple of days," Mom said, "and I wanted to share with you some things I've only shared with one other person, your Uncle Sherm. Rich, I didn't get to be the executive assistant to the director of social services for Minneapolis because I can type and take dictation. And I didn't start at the top either.

"When I was younger," she went on, "to make extra money, I used to type legal documents for up-and-coming lawyers. Over the years, these young men came to rely on me to also provide input to their work. The nature of their work was often sensitive, and I never once compromised their trust. Some of them branched into politics and through the years have gotten quite powerful. More than once, I was asked to go to Washington, DC, as an executive secretary."

"Why didn't you?" I remembered Sherm telling me she was the smartest one in the family.

"Don't interrupt me. As tempting and flattering as the offers were, I did what I thought was best for our family. I love your father, and there is no way he would survive living in DC. Also, your brother needed medical care that I thought only the University Medical Center could handle, and I wanted to remain close to Mayo Clinic. Finally, Minneapolis is a great city to raise a family. So that's why we stayed. I got to be known as a top executive assistant who, most importantly, could be trusted. I was introduced to Camillo DeSantis, and we've been together ever since."

"Ever look back and wish you had done it differently?"

"I said, don't interrupt me. Anyway, over the years, more times than I can count, I was told, 'I owe you one, Angie—if there is ever anything you need, just call.' Well, I decided to take one of them up on it. Remember I told you about the young, up-and-coming? Well, Hubert Humphrey may have lost his bid for the presidency, but he's still pretty powerful."

I almost drove off the road. I looked at Mom and saw a beaming smile. "You called Hubert Humphrey?"

"Not directly, but he has a young man following in his footsteps, and that young fellow and I go way back. I told him what was happening to you, and he said he would look into it. We exchanged holiday greetings, he said he would let Hubert know, and that was it. You need to pick your battles, son, like I picked this one, and make use of your assets. Guess what? We won!"

"You're amazing, Mom. Thanks for sharing."

"I wanted you to know this about your ol' Mom because I think you take after me. You're smart, and you deal well with people, never looking down on anyone. I'm sure you know I could never talk about this with your father. He's a good man and has a lot of pride in being the head of the family. I let him think he is." She reached over and squeezed my hand. "He doesn't truly understand how you are getting to come home. He's just glad you are, and that's good enough for me."

"Absolutely," I said, pulling into the driveway.

It was great getting home and putting my things in my bedroom. Now that Louie was married, I felt comfortable about living here. When I joined my parents in the kitchen, Mom showed me my schedule for the courses I'd requested.

"I have one last thing, son," she said. "I hope you know how proud we are of you and how much we love you. I don't think we tell each other that enough. These are for you." She pushed a cardboard box toward me.

I opened the box, which was filled with letters. I pulled one out; it had been written while I was in boot camp. "My letters?"

"Yes. I kept every one you wrote since the day you left for boot camp. I want you to know that we have them and will keep them safe until the day you settle. You are a great letter writer, and every time we received one, it was like getting a gift. Maybe one day, you'll use them to write a book, and the entire family and your heirs can live your experiences through them. Make it a gift to them all."

I hugged Mom and kissed her forehead. "You know, Mom, I might just do that someday. After all, this whole chapter of my life did start with 'The Letter'!"

EPILOGUE

Present day, Fernandina Beach, Florida

ONE THING I LEARNED FROM WRITING THIS BOOK IS that "The Letter" was more of a factor in determining what direction my life would take and what kind of man I would become than I ever realized. I was one of the 27 million young men who faced a turning point in their lives, as we went from being innocent bystanders in our own little environment to active participants in world events.

When I shared this story with a good friend, he said, "This explains a lot, Rich, but I have one question for you. Why do they now call you the Commander?"

I had to laugh. The truth is, that unopened letter continued to play a role in my future after I reentered civilian life in 1970 and returned to the University of Minnesota. But that is another story.

ACKNOWLEDGMENTS

First, thanks to all the men and women who have worn a military uniform and served this great country. A special place in my heart is reserved for those who served during the Vietnam Era (1964-1975).

Great appreciation goes to Jessie Lee Jr., USS Cambria shipmate, boss, mentor, retired naval officer, and a man I have tremendous respect for—and most importantly, my friend for over fifty years.

Many thanks to my daughter-in-law, Hannah Lee, my confidant when I began writing. I will never forget the day when I was discouraged with my efforts, and she told me, "Don't give up!"

I am deeply grateful for Emmett Henderson, Lieutenant Commander (USN-ret), a valued friend who was the first person to read my original manuscript. It was his unabashed "the good, the bad, and the ugly" review that gave me the confidence to seek publication.

I could not dream of being successful without my family and friends who unselfishly volunteered their time to review my manuscript and be advocates for promoting my work. I owe a special debt of gratitude to Keith Post, Executive Director, St. Mary's Submarine Museum, for his passionate review and offer to host my book launch. To Vice Admiral Albert H. Konetzni, Jr. (USN-Ret.), Dr. Thomas C. Whitesell Jr., Gina Engh, Bruce Cosby (Lt. USN-Ret.), Jennifer Helgeson, Mary Carroll, Donald Wilder, Laura Williams, Frederick "Rick" Smith, my sister, Marlys Foster, cousins Jackie Irene and Sonya Sanders, stepson Jeff Williams, and sons Chris and Scott Herman, I say thank you for your patience, insight, and encouragement.

When I finished writing, I asked, "Now what?" My answer came when Emily Carmain, my editor, returned my phone call, listened, then introduced me to Marie and Mark Fenn of Giro di Mondo Publishing. These three guided me with their expertise and wisdom, not to mention tremendous patience, to make this book a reality. They were truly a godsend to this indie author.

A special nod to Roseanna White Designs. One comment that I've heard many times over is how fantastic the book's cover and design are.

Finally, thanks to my wife, Kathy, who came into my life when I needed someone most. My biggest "champion," she turned a spare bedroom into my office. On top of a newly assembled desk, she placed the box containing my old letters, along with a book for beginning authors—and her note: "When you are ready, you will know." Yes, she knows me well.

THE AUTHOR

Commander R.W. Herman (USN-Ret.) was born in Minneapolis, Minnesota. While attending the University of Minnesota in 1965, he received his draft notice and chose to enter the United States Navy for four years, three of which were spent on the USS Cambria (APA-36). Two years after his return, he reentered the service and continued a career spanning over thirty years.

Following ten years of enlisted service, he was commissioned through the Limited Duty Officer Program in 1979. At retirement, he was the senior submarine communications officer in the Navy, having led the silent service into the twenty-first century maintaining connectivity superiority. He and his wife now reside in Fernandina Beach, Florida.

Visit the author at www.rwherman.com.